Guilt

Guilt is an original, closely argued examination of the opposition between guilty man and tragic man. Starting from the scientific and speculative writings of Freud and the major pioneers of psychoanalysis to whom we owe the first studies of this complex question, Roberto Speziale-Bagliacca goes on to focus on the debate between Klein and Winnicott in an enlightened attempt to remove blame and the sense of guilt from religion, morality and law.

Drawing on an impressive range of sources – literary, historical and philosophical – and illustrated by studies of composers, thinkers and writers as diverse as Mozart and Chuang Tzu, Shakespeare and Woody Allen, *Guilt* covers a range of topics including the concept of guilt used within the law, and the analyst's contribution to the client's sense of guilt.

Previously unavailable in English, this book deserves to be read not only by psychoanalysts, philosophers, scholars and forensic psychiatrists interested in the theory of justice, but also by the ordinary educated reader.

Roberto Speziale-Bagliacca is a professor of psychiatry at the Medical School of the University of Genoa, a Training Analyst of the Italian Psychoanalytic Society and a full member of the IPA. He has written widely on the interface between clinical psychoanalysis and psychological and sociological manifestations of power. His works, published in different languages, include *On the Shoulders of Freud* (Transaction) and *The King and the Adulteress* (Duke University Press), a reinterpretation of *Madame Bovary* and *King Lear*. His latest critical biography, *Freud messo a fuoco*, includes an account of the impact of Freud's "mother complex" on his theory and on the psychoanalytic movement.

Colpa

Considerazioni su rimorso, vendetta e responsabilità

Roberto Speziale-Bagliacca

Guilt

Revenge, remorse and responsibility
after Freud

Roberto Speziale-Bagliacca

Foreword by Frank Kermode

Edited by Susan Budd

Translated by Ian Harvey

The translation of this work has been funded by SEPS
SEGRETARIATO EUROPEO PER LE PUBBLICAZIONI SCIENTIFICHE

Via Val d'Aposa 7 - 40123 Bologna - Italy
tel +39 051 271992 - fax +39 051 265983
seps@alma.unibo.it - www.seps.it

Brunner-Routledge
Taylor & Francis Group
HOVE AND NEW YORK

First published 2004
by Brunner-Routledge
27 Church Road, Hove, East Sussex BN3 2FA

Simultaneously published in the USA and Canada
by Brunner-Routledge
29 West 35th Street, New York NY 10001

Brunner-Routledge is an imprint of the Taylor & Francis Group

Originally published in Italian as *Colpa: Considerazioni su rimorso,
vendetta e responsabilità*

Copyright © 2004, 1997, Casa Editrice Astrolabio – Ubaldini Editore,
Roma

Typeset in Times by Mayhew Typesetting, Rhayader, Powys
Printed and bound in Great Britain by TJ International Ltd, Padstow,
Cornwall
Paperback cover design by Hybert Design

This publication has been produced with paper manufactured to strict
environmental standards and with pulp derived from sustainable
forests.

British Library Cataloguing in Publication Data
A catalogue record for this book is available from the British Library

Library of Congress Cataloging-in-Publication Data
Speziale-Bagliacca, Roberto.
   [Colpa. English]
   Guilt : revenge, remorse, and responsibility after Freud /
Roberto Speziale-Bagliacca ; foreword by Frank Kermode ; edited by
Susan Budd ; translated by Ian Harvey.
        p. cm.
Includes bibliographical references and index.
   ISBN 1-58391-963-5 – ISBN 1-58391-964-3 (pbk.)
   1. Guilt. 2. Psychology, Pathological. 3. Psychoanalysis. I. Budd,
Susan, 1941– II. Title.
 RC569.5.G84S749 2004
   152.4'4–dc22

                                                    2003023171

ISBN 1-58391-963-5 (hbk)
ISBN 1-58391-964-3 (pbk)

To Karmentxo

"Passionate and absorbing, at times moving and amusing, this book marks a breakthrough in a vast area of human behaviour, forcing us to face up to some age-old secrets of guilt without recourse to any form of hypocrisy. *Guilt* deserves to be read not only by psychotherapists, philosophers, scholars interested in the theory of justice, but also by the ordinary educated reader and, possibly, ethically-minded politicians."

Jan de Viller, Historian

"Guilt is not only a legal and moral concept, as well as a state of mind, but it is also an omnipotent way of thinking. Speziale-Bagliacca's intriguing book leads us to such a conclusion and indeed obliges us to recognise its truth."

Joyce McDougall, author of *Theatres of the Mind*

". . . a unique book, at once obvious and revealing, which conveys all the nuances of guilt, as subtly and vividly as Holman-Hunt's famous pre-Raphaelite picture *The Awakening Conscience*. It is itself a picture, instantly recognisable but with details so finely shaded that they only appear on a second or third reading, each itself a new revelation."

Nicolas Barker, Chairman of the London Library

Contents

Foreword

I cannot speak as a psychoanalyst, but an interest in guilt is not confined to that profession. Immediately after I had finished reading Speziale-Bagliacca's book I opened the *Times Literary Supplement* (28 March 2003) and found a review of a book on *Hamlet* by Alexander Welsh, a scholar I greatly admire. Speaking of Hamlet's guilt, Welsh observes that "the very word *guilt*, in twentieth-century parlance, has come to stand first for guilt feelings and only secondarily for criminal accountability". Apparently he regards this as a reversal of the original meaning, in part attributable to Hamlet. His reviewer is more forthright than Welsh, affirming that "'guilt' is a cant-word, in its secondary, non-judicial sense. The feeling of culpability, of mere mental discomfort, cannot displace the legal necessities of guilt that are embedded in language and culture." And he appears to think we should abandon the non-legal use of the word altogether.

As I had just read Speziale-Bagliacca on this very subject I was equipped to see that this apparently firm discrimination is in fact trivial. When Hamlet sets out to prove his uncle's guilt he may hesitate but he cannot be said to have doubts about the nature of guilt in the legal sense; and when Claudius prays to be absolved he is aware that he is legally guilty and at the same time is feeling guilty. Prospero in *The Tempest* says of his enemies that their "great guilt" (criminality) is working in them like a poison (3.3.104); they are feeling their guilt. And Shakespeare quite often uses the word "guiltiness" to mean both the state of being guilty and the state of feeling guilt. In *Othello* Iago says that Cassio steals away "guilty-like" (3.3.39), meaning "like one conscious of his guilt". In *Hamlet*, "It started like a guilty thing" (1.1.148) obviously means "like a thing that was guilty and aware of it". And so on. Shakespeare could confute Welsh's reviewer on his own.

Of course it is possible to be guilty and not feel guilty (for instance, if you are the survivor of a duel) but it must be obvious that to ban the use of the word except in a judicial context is to say of language something that is not true. One must, as Wittgenstein liked to say, go back to the rough ground. We have to consider use, not apply some rule.

The present book is so far from making this mistake that it offers fascinating discussions of particular cases, and thoroughly surveys the theoretical structures that have been developed by those specialists in guilt, the psychoanalysts – for whom, as the author remarks, "the sense of guilt is always lying in ambush". These considerations require expositions of Freud but also of admired later practitioners, notably Melanie Klein and her admirer (though not her disciple) Donald Winnicott, who could not quite accept the tragic severity of the Kleinian doctrines. Above all it deals with the analyst herself or himself, and is richly informative on the counter-transference, a phenomenon of particular interest to the layperson because it seems to have declared its presence quite late in the history and theory of the discipline yet involves a personal relationship apparently not difficult to understand, at any rate in some degree, by analogy with other forms of mutual interaction in more familiar circumstances, as, for instance, between teacher and pupil.

These reflections on guilt are indeed highly relevant to that relationship. The author illustrates his argument from a wide range of literature and of music, and what is most striking is his sympathy with oriental philosophies and techniques: witness, for example, his recommendations as to posture and breathing. It turns out that a full study of guilt (guiltiness) in all its senses requires this very original kind of intellectual enquiry; yet for all its technical and professional interest it is throughout informed by care for the analysand, and by extension for the general condition – or plight – of humanity. That is why it will be an absorbing study not only for professionals, but for a much larger – and no less guilty – lay audience.

Frank Kermode

After re-reading: a preface

> A clash of doctrines is not a disaster, it's an opportunity.
> (Alfred Whitehead)

Taking up this book again some time after its original publication – in order to check through the English translation word by word – has given me the opportunity to rediscover it in the light of two intervening phenomena: the various opinions that people have expressed about the book and the fact that I myself have grown older. I think I now understand why, for example, Jan de Viller has written that I tend to expose myself in my books and therefore run the risk of being misunderstood. Probably this is because the themes I address relate to theoretical clashes which historically have opened up rifts and left wounds that have not yet healed. One such rift is the division between determinists and champions of free will.

According to André Gide, Montaigne maintained that there was nothing outside himself that he could ever *really* know: "knowing oneself seemed to him to be the essence of all knowledge". I have been wondering whether there might not be a contradiction between "learning to *really* know oneself", which many would dismiss as illusory, and the importance of the maxim "know thyself". Expressing myself with due caution (to avoid being misunderstood or being accused of ingenuousness and presumption), I would say that it is vain to think that one can *really* know oneself. But, in my heart of hearts, that is not what I really think. Indeed, I believe that as the years go by (and the idea of imminent death hangs over the chapter by Montaigne that Gide refers to) one can become, as Philip Larkin might have said, "less deceived".

I remember one significant occasion as a young analyst when I was undergoing supervision: I was defensively "rationalising" and shying clear of some of my more authentic reactions and my wise supervisor at the time, Tommaso Senise, who is no longer with us and of whom I still have very fond memories, said to me in his broad Neapolitan accent: "Roberto, mi fa che ti stai facendo fesso", which could be translated something like, "Roberto, I've got the feeling you're having yourself on". This pronouncement was clearly not made in a spirit of accusation and indeed its importance lay elsewhere. The expression, hardly typical for a supervision, was predicated on a high degree of freedom. He was not presenting me with a conclusive interpretation or judgement. After all, he left it up to me to decide whether his comment was fair or not. What he was doing was stimulating me, setting up an opposition between the two parts of my self that were in contention with each other: the part that did not want to recognise the truth and the other part that did, that wanted to get to grips with it. I owe much to the spirit reflected in this remark – a combination of playing things down and shrewdness which has helped me ever since in my lifelong attempt to avoid deceiving myself. Not "having yourself on" does not mean knowing the final truth about yourself. For me it is simply another way of saying that the need to deceive oneself dissolves, as it were, in the presence of the deeper pleasure of discovering that the many contorted problems and conflicts which cause suffering have become simplified. Montaigne in this context makes the following point: "Children are even afraid of their friends when they see them wearing a mask, and we are the same. We need to tear the mask off things as well as off people."

If we are to take off both our own masks and those of other people, we need to appreciate what my Neapolitan friend had understood, namely that we should not blame people – either ourselves or others. This does not mean justifying and accepting everything passively. The point I shall be making in the book is that this way of thinking is very different from thinking based on guilt. The key to understanding this point is to be found in Chapter 3, where I try to demonstrate the distinction which I think to some degree constitutes the book's originality – or at least the idea around which it was constructed. Just to anticipate this point briefly: guilt is not merely a particular form of anxiety known to us all (if we think that we have never experienced it, then we really are in trouble), nor is it simply an objective event caused by people (breaking a rule): guilt is a way of living and thinking. To translate this idea into English, some have suggested that I use the word "ethos", but I think that "logic" (both terms appear in the book) is also appropriate: there is a logic of guilt and a logic that I have called "tragic responsibility" which transcends the logic of guilt (this is not the same as Winnicott's "responsibility").

I think there will always be a danger of misunderstanding what I shall be describing unless this distinction is fully understood and constantly borne in mind. It should be remembered, however, that it is not a distinction I have discovered myself. It is one that goes back several centuries, although it has never been popular (allow me to warn the reader of the danger of skipping chapters in the book: they have been ordered and dovetailed into each other with some thought).

The tragic events of 11 September 2001, the wars in Afghanistan and Iraq, as well as the continuing violence of the Israeli–Palestinian conflict have all highlighted how pervasive the logic of guilt is, and how it tends, at moments of extreme collective anxiety, to spread and gain the upper hand, appearing as the only approach capable of mobilising a crusade (or anti-crusade) to cope with crises and avert dangers. The logic of guilt looks for the culprit, not the causes. It is on the side of separation and war; and it does not seek understanding – whether in historical, sociological, scientific or simply therapeutic terms. Or to put it another way: the logic of guilt does find causes, but they are not the *real* causes and certainly not the only ones, as it would have us believe. In other words, it simplifies reality, and does so brutally. In the last analysis it is an ideology which does not tear the mask off anyone, and, in fact, if it can, it adds further masks. As a matter of fact, during recent conflicts other radically different discourses have been voiced, albeit in a very disjointed way. They correspond to another logic, one that transcends the logic of guilt. I would also add that, in my view, this is the logic (or ethos) that scientists and therapists should embrace. It is, of course, a logic which is based on a certain kind of determinism. Psychoanalysis, believing as it does in the existence of the unconscious, is deterministic, although Freud's determinism is rather singular, because, under certain conditions, it also allows margins of freedom.

This second way of thinking goes in search of motives and causes but does so without passing judgement. It investigates in order to understand causes, to discover their underlying make-up. As a rule it considers human acts as the result of both manifest and hidden forces, whether they be biological, economic, psychological or other. Within this logic people are not accused or forgiven, for the simple reason that accusation and forgiveness are in contradiction with its basic premises and are therefore meaningless.

Nevertheless, it is not an easy distinction to digest, even for a lay person. Also, as we shall see, it does not revolve around a stable point of view. What is certain is that those who think solely within the logic of guilt cannot understand those who make an effort to adopt a different perspective. It is beyond them. This book could also be read as an account of the difficulties that people experience when they find themselves face to face with these two types of logic. Agreeing with the logic of guilt provides us with external enemies whom we can demonise, but it also unites the "good" and the "victims" within a single fraternity. It makes us feel safe, like "brothers" and "sisters" bound together in a sort of religious faith. To espouse the logic which transcends guilt also means accepting that one will be misunderstood and even isolated.

I believe that the credit for being the first thinkers to engage in the scientific study of the sense of guilt (and indirectly of guilt itself) within the perspective of psychic determinism goes to Sigmund Freud, Melanie Klein, W.R.D. Fairbairn, D.W. Winnicott, John Bowlby (and only a few others). In some other respects, Sandor Ferenczi also made an important contribution. My approach has been to investigate their way of thinking (their theoretical positions) as well as their conduct as human beings in an attempt to understand their merits and limitations without giving in to the temptation to idealise them, which again would be tantamount to entering into a religious kind of logic.

Recently, in my critical biography of Freud, I referred to his height, pointing out that he was apparently about five foot five inches tall. Despite this physical attribute, the first metaphor that I used twenty years ago to characterise Freud (not original, I should add) was that he was a "giant". Indeed I have written a book entitled *On the Shoulders of Freud*, a title based on the famous saying that "even dwarfs can see a long way on the shoulders of giants". The expression has been in use for some centuries, among others by Bernard of Chartres. And yet its obvious meaning has continued to offend the sensibilities of those who need to mythicise their masters in an attempt to shore up their own uncertainties and ambivalences towards them. Personally I have always been on the side of those who think that defending the work of Freud and of pioneers in general (even when the criticism is fair) is a sign of lack of trust in his (or their) ability to stand up to the verdict of history. Only by subverting the idealised image constructed by their followers can we allow true masters to emerge as figures that still have a relevant role to play in the ongoing debate that is essential to the history of ideas.

The ideas I put forward in this book were received in various ways. The book focuses largely on Melanie Klein; some have written that I attacked her, while others have maintained that the portrait I painted of her rendered her tender and more human. Some authoritative voices on the subject have argued that my position is closer to that of Winnicott. And re-reading this book, I think I understand why. My sharing of Winnicott's interests is visible in most chapters, but the amount of space I have devoted to Klein's discoveries (and their consequences) ought to have served as a warning. I do not believe I am "having myself on" when I say that I do not feel that I have sided with either Klein or Winnicott, or for that matter with any other "masters" or pioneers. Leaving aside her theoretical ideas, I would argue that Klein is much more "inter-subjective" than some believe her to be, although she did tend, as I point out in Chapter 5, to put a great deal of emphasis on innate factors and did not work out a detailed theory or phenomenology of interaction. She does not describe how the actions of the external object affected the Self, other than in the general statement that bad experiences exacerbate anxiety and good experiences alleviate it.

I have never held the view that Winnicott and Melanie Klein have uttered the last word on child development. The reason I chose their dispute as an example was that I wanted to show the reader the way in which these "ancestors" of ours strove to help us along the path to *real* self-knowledge. At the same time I also wanted to emphasise both the level of commitment and endeavour and the conflicts and mistakes that accompanied their efforts.

The apparatus of endnotes in the English edition has been very much scaled down compared to the original edition. After decades of teaching as a university professor, I had conceived the first version of this book primarily with researchers and scholars in mind. The idea of reducing the number and size of the endnotes in the English edition grew from my realisation that the book could reach a broader readership. Any interested scholar can always consult the Italian (or indeed the Spanish) edition.

While working on this edition I have come to realise that my style is by no means easy to translate into English, and so I am grateful for the care with which the translator, Ian Harvey, has tried to achieve the difficult balancing act of reconciling my style with the often divergent demands of the English language.

I am grateful to a number of friends and colleagues who agreed to look at the manuscript and gave it back to me with glosses and suggestions that have led me to rethink some of the points I make: Simona Argentieri, Franco Borgogno, Carmelo Conforto, Federico Flegenheimer, Francesco Gana, Gabriele Pasquali, Laura Tognoli, Almatea Usuelli, Dina Vallino. To this list I would add Andrea D'Angelo, George Downing, Giampaolo Sasso, Giuseppe Sertoli and Parthenope Bion, a young friend now tragically deceased, who have all given me ideas. Others have very kindly supported my work: Antony Alexander, M. Giovanna Parodi da Passano, Mario Vegetti and particularly Cesare Sacerdoti, whose help has been invaluable. Last but not least I would like to mention my daughter Dianella and my son Andrea. As always, Aldo Canevari was an untiring, sensitive and generous source of stimulating ideas. I would also not like to forget my dear friend León Grinberg, whose work formed the starting point for my research. My thanks go to the staff of the Warburg Institute in London, the board of the Musée des Beaux-Arts in Strasbourg, Andrea Chandler, head of the British Psychoanalytical Society Library, Jen Lindsay and Sarah Shababi, who helped in compiling the scholarly apparatus. In conclusion, I would like to express my gratitude to Paola Mariotti Tuckett, who has worked so hard to have this book published in Great Britain, and to Susan Budd, who through the miracle of e-mail has been constantly by my side at my desk, generously giving of her unrivalled editorial expertise. I sincerely hope, however, that none of these people will be deemed "guilty" of anything about this book that might be considered debatable or worthy of criticism.

Bogliasco, 15 February 2004

Guilt:

My conscience hath a thousand several tongues,
And every tongue brings in a several tale,
and every tale condemns me for a villain
                        . . . "Guilty, guilty!"
                              Shakespeare, *Richard III*

Containment

And I would hurt you,
Lord, but my soul is weak: if I
offer you my torment,
it falls at once to the ground,
mild and cold like snow.
                    R.M. Rilke, *The Monk's Lament*

Chapter 1

A view from the past

Young criminals are often extremely loath to admit that their parents might be bad or guilty and yet are only normally reluctant to acknowledge that they themselves are bad or guilty. This book offers a series of reflections that may allow us to formulate some hypotheses capable of explaining apparently paradoxical phenomena such as this.

Sigmund Freud never actually wrote a book dedicated entirely to guilt, but the various comments he made on the subject throughout his work make him the true initiator of the study of the sense of guilt and certainly the first person to approach the question systematically. Moreover, Freud the thinker shed much light on the logic upon which guilt is based. We shall be looking at the meaning of the term "logic" (or ethos) at greater length later, so readers who find themselves unable to grasp its meaning immediately should bear with me. Freud was gifted with deep insight into certain aspects of the world of guilt, and this enabled him to embark on a difficult enterprise whose conclusion, however, he did not live to see: the construction, piece by piece, of the _psychological_ as opposed to the moral or legal category of guilt. There were at least two sides to Freud's project: one was to look at the multiple aspects of the sense of guilt, the other to examine the responsibility human beings bear for all forms of objective guilt, that is to say, guilt that is felt as a result of causing harm to another person.

In order to give an idea of the break with tradition brought about by psychoanalysis in its early stages, it is perhaps worth describing the cultural climate that still prevailed at the time when Freud, who had already made significant advances in his understanding of the sense of guilt, was writing _The Ego and the Id_ or _The Economic Problem of Masochism_, in other words around 1923 or 1924. To this end we need only read, for example, the entry under "guilt" in the famous _Dictionary of Philosophy and Psychology_, edited by James M. Baldwin (at the time a professor at Princeton University) and published in 1925. Leading contemporary scholars and thinkers from America and Europe were invited to contribute to this work: Pierre Janet, for example, the great psychologist from the Sorbonne, a protégé of

Charcot, the man who was to contend with Freud the credit for being the first person to introduce the concept of the unconscious; John Dewey, William James and C.S. Pierce, the acknowledged fathers of American pragmatism, as well as the Italian anthropologist, neurologist and psychiatrist Enrico Morselli (whom Freud a year later in a letter to Weiss called "an absolute jackass").

The entry reads as follows:

> [Guilt is] the state of having committed a crime, or consciously offended against moral law. The absence of guilt is innocence. The view of guilt differs according as the standpoint is that of law or that of morality. From the former point of view guilt means a transgression of a positive law, though this view is often modified in the judgement passed upon the act by taking into account the transgressor's knowledge or ignorance of the law, and even his temptations to transgress. From this point of view it has been regarded as the contrary of merit.

The conclusion to this article by Professor W.R. Sorley of the University of Cambridge suggests that he was writing without any significant psychological sources to draw on:

> Merit is only present when the moral action is performed in opposition to a psychically present immoral tendency; guilt is present only when the immoral action is performed in spite of a psychically present moral consciousness.

Although meant for a dictionary of psychology, Sorley's article concentrates solely on objective guilt and makes no reference to personal experience, to "sense of guilt" or remorse. He mentions the fact that a person has to be conscious of having caused offence, he talks about a *psychically present immoral tendency* and refers to other phenomena relating to moral conscience, but goes no further than that. The impression is that he had absolutely no conception of "sense of guilt". One would have thought that inadequate definitions such as this would find no place in a post-Freud dictionary of psychology, but the reality was different.

Freud's insights were also to affect our understanding of the terms Sorley was looking at: responsibility, crime and wrong-doing. Freud was a champion of psychic determinism, which has had many eminent advocates since ancient times. One such was the second-century AD figure of Galen of Pergamon, the leading exponent of Greco-Roman medicine before its decline. Galen asked himself the question: how can one praise or reprimand, hate or love (and thus also blame) a person who is not good or bad as such but only because of his or her disposition, which is clearly the result of other factors? If one pursues this line of reasoning, a person need not feel any sense of guilt; but equally the question has to be asked whether it is possible to talk of authentic voluntary participation in a guilty act.

For Galen, the causes that have a determining effect on people's freedom are the processes that form the embryo and the climatic, food and environmental factors that influence the state of the body. Accordingly, in his view, the clinician should not judge the patient. Judgement and criticism are incompatible with the desire to understand and to heal. But, as will become clearer in the chapters to come, it is not only the physician who should not judge.

Freud's discovery of the dynamic unconscious, which enabled him to argue that our Ego is not as free as we would all like it to be and that no-one is responsible for his unconscious, seems to belong to a very similar perspective. That guilt should not be a question of judgement is also suggested by the fact that one synonym of guilt is "error". The idea that guilt is linked to error has survived across the ages, from Homer to the present day, in the word *fault* or the French *faute*, Italian *fallo*, Spanish *falta*, which can all refer to both "blame" and "error".

What do we really mean when we talk about guilt as a psychological category? Several emotional as well as theoretical obstacles stand in the way of a simple answer to this question. We can begin by saying that guilt and sense of guilt have entered the common vocabulary we all use and have become part of the language itself. For many guilt has replaced the idea of "sin" and, paradoxically, even the idea of "cause"; we can see this when, in an example of the survival of animistic thinking, we say that an overflowing river is to blame if someone drowns.

Since time immemorial, the idea of relinquishing the perspective that looks at things in terms of guilt (based on the need to find a culprit, to punish and be punished) and giving up the hope of redemption has always seemed to provoke panic and anxiety. The Galen perspective unleashes fears of anarchy, ungovernability, destructive impulses and nihilism.

Often, though not always, people are unable even to conceive of a way of thinking about guilt which departs from this traditional approach. The reasons for these fears, this difficulty, are deeply rooted: our entire civilisation has indeed been built on the ethos of guilt and responsibility.

The function of the analyst

> Our analyses teach us that there are people in whom self-criticism and moral conscience – in other words, highly valued achievements of the psyche – are unconscious, and, as such, their most relevant effects . . . not only the deepest things but also what are for the Ego the highest things can be unconscious.
>
> (Freud, *The Ego and the Id*)

On the subject of guilt, the science founded by Freud has always found itself in an impasse. This contradiction has been described by the French researcher Jacques Goldberg, who has made an effort to understand the fundamental importance of guilt in psychoanalytical theory and practice. Expecting the psychoanalytical approach to this subject to offer a morality that would be expressed in terms of the imaginary, or even in terms of ideology, he was disappointed that this was not the case. "Instead of freeing us from guilt, psychoanalysis has no difficulty in saying that we are all guilty and more 'immoral' than we think. But our guilt is often unconnected with any motivations we might adduce". However, he asks: "can we do without this idea? Indeed, what, according to Freud, constitutes the universe of mental illness if not the painful feelings connected to guilt and the expectation of punishment? And did not Freud even go so far as to compare psychoanalysis to a legal hearing during which the culprit has to be discovered and, in some way, forced to confess?"[1] In his very direct way Goldberg points to a series of problems, including the judgemental moralism that seems to underlie Freud's metaphor. Is this analysis accurate or is it unfair? This book is an attempt to examine these questions.

Later Freud was to look more closely at the complications of guilt/sin, but initially his interest was attracted by something much more limited, something which caused his patients particular suffering. As he studied the crazy, cruel and punitive way obsessives constantly reproached themselves, he discovered that self-accusation came back "unchanged but rarely in a way to draw attention to itself, thus remaining for some time as a pure sense of guilt without content".[2] Since nowadays we are accustomed to the idea that there is a vast unconscious world inside us all, it is perhaps difficult to appreciate the brilliance of this observation and the originality of the model Freud was working out. He was immediately aware of the complexity of the subject. His metaphors almost seemed to turn emotion into a person, an interlocutor: "The conscious Ego stands in the presence of obsessive representation as if facing something extraneous that it does not trust". He also talks about the appearance of depression: the Ego can be "affected by a form of episodic melancholy".[3]

More than ten years later, his thinking became more precise and concrete; he talked of a "sense of guilt about which we know nothing . . . an awareness of guilt . . . which we must define as unconscious, although this is an apparent contradiction in terms. It has its source in certain remote psychic processes, but is constantly revived in the temptation that is renewed at every relevant occasion, and on the other hand gives rise to a lurking, waiting anxiety, an expectation of disaster, connected through the idea of punishment to the internal perception of temptation".[4] Not only is the Ego not master in its own house, to use his famous metaphor, but it would not even recognise all the drives that make it act. These drives are also to be found in the moral and religious sphere.

If accepted completely, these ideas call into question traditional ethics as well as our everyday sense of morality. Freud moves into a bewildering area that defies easy understanding: "the obscurity that still envelops unconscious senses of guilt has not been illuminated by any discussions about it. All that has happened is that the complications have multiplied", he sums up.[5]

It was at this point that Freud started to become interested in the origins of the sense of guilt. He wavered between two explanations which both ultimately proved to be of little use in dealing with patients. On the one hand, in *Totem and Taboo*, one of his most daring and controversial works, he posited a connection between the sense of guilt and a primitive situation that had obtained at the dawn of time, a situation in which the father was domineering and jealous, kept all the women for himself and drove away his children as they grew up. Guilt results from the murder of this father (a "criminal act", thus objective guilt) committed jointly by his children, but it is also generated by the ambivalence felt by the children: "they hated the father, a powerful obstacle to their need for power and their sexual claims, but they also loved and admired him". After committing patricide the sons consumed the totemic meal which allowed them to internalise the father: this was the beginning of a process of identification with the hated and beloved father–enemy.

In *Totem and Taboo* Freud does not say which of these elements is to be considered the primary source of guilt. The situation is complex, the result of a combination of determining factors: "it is probable that . . . the moral conscience is born, on the basis of an emotional ambivalence, out of specific human relations which create this ambivalence", as well as out of certain "*conditions*".[6] However, it is not easy to discard the hypothesis that, although the story has the truth-content of an allegory, Freud the writer (if not exactly Freud the theoretician) sees the hate of the sons as originating in the violence of the father. This question was later to give rise to much discussion. This sense of guilt led to the two principal taboos of totemism: the bans on patricide and on incest.

However, as we said, Freud's thinking was also moving in another direction. In *Beyond the Pleasure Principle* (1920) he sought to explain the roots of the sense of guilt by referring to the death wish; in other words, the tendency of the psychic apparatus to try to reduce tensions completely and to restore all living things to the inorganic state ("every living being necessarily dies by natural causes"). This idea of a "death instinct/wish" is a hypothesis which Freud himself called "speculative" but which he used to explain various phenomena observable in the relationship with the patient. The antagonist of the death wish is the life instinct, whose task is to tame and free the death instinct, turning it to the outside through the use of the muscles. This is at the origin of the concepts of the destructive drive, the drive to possess and the will to power.

This concept of Freud's provoked several radical reactions: Ernest Jones was one of the many who criticised him, arguing that the idea ran counter to all biological principles. And even today the most reliable theories seem to prove Jones right: for biologists death remains a mystery.[7]

One of the many possible explanations for this change in direction is that Freud probably realised that he lacked an adequate theory or strategy for dealing therapeutically with the "complicated", disturbing and previously unsuspected experience of guilt and consequently felt forced to step outside psychology. He did not turn to theology, moral philosophy or law, but nonetheless had to move away from too close a relationship with the patient. In this sense we can say that Freud at this point had yet to fully explore the psychological dimension of guilt.

Freud thought he could deal with guilt by shifting it (into biology) or by condensing it (for example, in the myth of Oedipus).[8] By doing so, however, all he was doing was following his customary approach of moving between myth and biology. However strange it may seem now, he was unable to imagine that, in the psychoanalytic relationship, much happens and is resolved (when it is resolved) through the rapport that becomes established between the patient and the therapist, between the emotions and the thoughts of the latter (countertransference). It is also partly a sense of guilt that makes this relationship so terribly engrossing. Even assuming that biology and myth can help us to understand this guilt-ridden relationship, they certainly cannot resolve it. Or at least, not for the time being. A clear idea of the importance of the relationship between analyst and patient in understanding the onset of a sense of guilt can perhaps provide us with a model that is valid for human relations in general.

A coherent theory capable of explaining what are called "object relations" (that is, significant relationships between individuals) was not available during the early stages of psychoanalysis. This was true even though the relations between human beings, real and imagined, in the external world or in the psychic world, were a constant focus of Freud's interest.

Freud wrote *Mourning and Melancholia* (1915) under the influence of the events of the First World War, which forced him to think of man's recurrent destructive capacity. Here he set out his first theory about sense of guilt. The context was depression (for which "melancholy" was virtually a synonym). Freud noted that melancholy was characterised psychically by a deep and painful dejection, a reduced interest in the outside world, a loss of the capacity to love, an unwillingness to engage in almost any activity and "by a feeling of despondency about self which expressed itself in self-reproach and self-berating, culminating in the delusional expectation of punishment":[9] *delusional* because it can go as far as suicide. The self-reproaches that the melancholic directs against himself "are really reproaches directed against a love object which are then diverted away from the object itself and aimed at the patient's Ego".

In his attempt to explain the mechanism that makes us feel guilty, Freud thought of a split in the Ego between accuser (Super-Ego) and accused (Ego).[10] The self-reproaches which the depressed person directs against himself are accusations and complaints which were originally aimed at someone else, the love object. Only later are they directed against the Self. Implicit in this model is a line of therapeutic investigation. Once the accused has been tracked down, it is time to discover the real culprit. As we have just seen, the wrong committed by the other comes first, according to this early Freudian insight.

Though later superseded, this hypothesis remained historically important because it introduced the new idea that the sense of guilt might have its origin in the relationship between the Ego and the parts and objects of the Self which inhabit our interior world (which in fact amounts to a more modern definition of the Super-Ego). These systems are connected to reality, to the external world, but in a complex, intricate fashion. According to Freud, guilt has the effect of making the Ego submit to the urgings of the Super-Ego out of fear of losing its love and protection.

At the risk of interrupting the thread of my argument, I would like to make a short digression starting from this last statement. Much psychoanalytic literature is characterised by indiscriminate abuse of the term "love". The impression one gets is that there is no space for nuance nor even for some fairly important distinctions between different feelings; it is as if in-between feelings did not count. Perhaps the creative energy which led psychoanalysis to seek new theories to fill the gap left by its abandonment of old paradigms made it feel the need for grandiose abstractions. Thus "love" and "hate" become categories rather than terms, containers for diverse feelings. Ultimately this phenomenon had an effect on future psychoanalytic theories. Freud himself probably contributed to this abuse, although in *Civilization and Its Discontents* (Freud, 1929) we find this passage: "The problem we face is how to free ourselves from the greatest impediment to civilization, that is, men's constitutional inclination to be aggressive towards each other . . . It is impossible to obey the command 'Love thy neighbour as thyself'; such an enormously inflated view of love can only reduce its value, not free us from difficulty." Often what is meant is not love but diverse phenomena which may even be components of love, such as thoughtfulness, concern or something we could call "narcissistic nourishment"; in other words, kindness, admiration, "warmth", which all give Self the sense of worth it needs.

To come back to the fascinating relationship between patient and analyst: psychoanalytic strategies start from the remarks by Freud we referred to earlier. In the period immediately after these first attempts to provide a scientific explanation for the phenomenon of the sense of guilt, the analyst introduced himself into this distinctly internal relationship inside the patient (the relationship between Ego and Super-Ego) in order to take the place of one or more of the parties in the conflict tormenting him. The intention was clear: when it remains inside the suffering person, the conflict occurs between unknown entities, whereas when one of the two people involved is the analyst it comes out into the open and is cleared up in detailed and dramatic fashion. When guilt appears, then the analyst sometimes plays the role of the accused, sometimes that of the accuser. However, this "performance" is not "theatrical" in the true sense of the word: one of the characters (the patient) *is* himself, whereas the other (the analyst) knows he is an actor, or in the most extreme cases (in other words, when he acts under the effect of projective identification), a puppet manipulated for a short time by the patient.

The result of an analysis depends largely on the psychoanalyst's ability to recognise that he is a simple actor and on the ability (an ability which at times verges on an art) with which he manages to escape from the intractable relationship that the patient has created. When the analyst finds himself without this ability, or perhaps not fully equipped to come on stage, what is established is not an emancipatory relationship but a sado-masochistic one in which guilt may contribute to destroying or paralysing hope.

In some ways the relationship established between patient and analyst resembles the relationships that characterise religions. The comparison is legitimate because in fact the two phenomena are very similar. When therapy is successful, however, the results are very different: the relationship proves to be emancipatory, while emancipation and autonomy are phenomena which religions (and their surrogates, such as political ideologies) cannot afford to concede, as we shall see Schleiermacher arguing later.

However, the therapist can fail in the task of rendering the patient emancipated and autonomous. More frequently than one might think, this lack of success manifests itself in very subtle ways. For example, the patient feels to a certain extent "satisfied", "free", "independent", but fails to appreciate that his state of well-being is based precisely on this relationship of *unresolved* dependence on his analyst. In these circumstances we find ourselves faced with a relationship in which the person who represents the authority of the parents is idealised in an uncritical way. And this idealisation, accompanied by the impossibility of entering into an authentic relationship based on mutual exchange, is typical of religious dependence. This we have known at least since Spinoza described religion as a system for exacting obedience.

As we shall show later (the phenomena in question are complex), the sense of guilt is a means whereby an individual's obedience or disobedience is obtained. Bound, at least in part, to remain unconscious, it is responsible for much suffering and – among other things – leads to an idealisation of the persecutor, as well as to imitative behaviour (by imitating him the victim becomes his persecutor and in this way deludes himself that he has him under control). The core of these processes can be found in Abraham and, to a certain extent, Job, but we could go even further and also find uncritical idealisation in the submissiveness shown by Socrates' disciples.

Guilt and sin

In *Totem and Taboo* Freud began to penetrate some of the conflictual dilemmas of guilt that he and later generations of psychoanalysts were to revisit on numerous occasions. It is my intention here to follow some of the paths laid down by Freud and others as I make some opening remarks and introduce the thinking of the authors I shall be discussing in later chapters.

In all religions the sense of guilt – sin – results from disobeying commandments (although paganism does not seem to contain any idea of moral rules laid down by a just god). In the experience of neurotics and psychotics the two terms – guilt and sin – seem to merge. It is not easy to say to what extent the two terms are experienced as similarly constituted phenomena. For example, is it possible to sin unconsciously? Freud argued that there was such a thing as a sense of guilt that operates out of the unconscious. This hypothesis still stands. In the *Vulgate*, Psalm L is dedicated to conscious sins, but Psalm XVIII appears to refer to unconscious sins: "Ab occultis meis mundame", asks the psalmist. Lewes and Short in their *Latin Dictionary* (Oxford, 1980), translate *ab occultis* as *from my sins*: "purify me from my hidden sins".

Various attempts have been made to clarify the distinction between guilt and sin, but from the psychoanalytical point of view, the core of the two phenomena seems to be the same. There may indeed be significant differences between the religious approach to sin and the moralistic approach to guilt, but the most radical difference is that which exists between these two approaches to guilt on the one hand (which both judge) and the clinical approach on the other, which, as we shall explain better later, must understand and not judge.

The distinction between the clinical and the religious perspective is fairly easy to make: they are two mutually incompatible systems. One need only think of the seven deadly sins: avarice, wrath, envy, pride, gluttony, sloth and lust. Each corresponds to a symptom of one or more psycho-pathological syndromes. Wrath and sloth are typical of depression. Gluttony can be found in bulimia. Avarice can take on paranoiac form, and so on.

The sacred is marked by the conflict between purity and impurity and by contamination. The person who commits "impure acts" offends the gods and therefore he or she sins. But this connection between impure acts and sin does not hold up from a clinical point of view, where the terms acquire different meanings. One can think, for example, of a mysophobe, a person with an apparently unjustified excessive fear or anxiety about dirt, the impurities that gather, say, in drawers, between the pages of a book or in pockets. His greatest fear is of being contaminated and he develops paranoiac rituals so as to avoid this contamination. Psychoanalysis has discovered that in this way the person is trying – among other things – to keep at bay senses of guilt and bitter persecutions.

It may also be useful to look at what the two systems we are comparing – the moralistic system of guilt and the religious system of sin – have in common. Both, in a way, "legitimise" many people's reactions towards others who, depending on the individual circumstances, can be considered "immoral", "guilty" or "sinful". When we judge that someone is a sinner or is guilty, our judgement contains a rejection. This rejection can take the form of simple annoyance or even disgust and revulsion. The religious approach, but also any approach based on a common notion of "good manners", can help overcome and control these reactions but, at least in most people, they cannot eliminate them completely.

In most individuals psychic disturbance, in many of its various forms, also elicits variably intense negative feelings. If we try to recall the behaviour of a strongly narcissistic person, we think of his disagreeable lack of authentic interest in the things we tell him, his habit of waiting (at best) for us to finish talking but only so that he can then expound his own ideas – for him the only ones that count. If he has maniacal traits – this is one example among many – we will probably want to reject his attempt to win us over to his cynical ideas. The ambivalence of neurotics can be very annoying, in the same way as the rituals of obsessives can be exasperating for those forced to observe them when they are carried out in public. The psychotic can be violent in many different ways. Attacks of envy hurt. With this in mind, one can put forward a hypothesis which would explain why many diagnostic terms, such as "hysterical", "maniacal", "obsessive" and others, have become derogatory terms or even insults in everyday language. Another good example is the etymologically neutral adjective "perverted" (*pervetere* in erudite Latin meant to disconcert, to disrupt) whose use was later banned for the politically correct reason that it was considered pejorative and degrading.

If we accept that common reactions are "naturally" reactions of rejection, it will be easier to trace possible reasons why also wrath, envy, pride, as well as gluttony and avarice (one could even include lust and sloth) were at one time commonly accepted as mortal sins, in other words, sins that deserved to be severely punished.

There are various facets to the relationship between guilt and sin. In primitive cultures we encounter not so much an interior sense of guilt as "objective wrongs", defined externally and socially (like breaking a taboo), and these misdeeds correspond to a conception of sin as a demonic reality which operates without man really being responsible for it. With regard to the restrictions laid down by taboos (which always involved *forgoing* or *abstaining* from something), it is well known that primitive peoples subjected themselves to these taboos – which represent the oldest unwritten laws – without knowing the reason why. All they knew was that any possible violation would bring down punishment upon them. Sin and guilt thus seem to be linked to a more general concept of evil to which, in some religions, even the gods were subjected.

For Freud, guilt/sin, with its prohibitions, taboos and conflicts, runs right through the development of mankind, but also that of the individual. Psychoanalysis made an effort to understand the vicissitudes of the relationship between guilt/sin on the one hand, and God or the gods and equally omnipotent evil spirits on the other. These beings were sources of guilt and instigators of sin, and psychoanalysis saw them mostly as figures whom we had in the past introjected into our interior world and whom later we projected into some usually ill-defined external space: up in the sky, in the underworld or at the centre of the earth. In the pagan religions, however, they were also seen as inhabiting parts of the globe, such as Mount Olympus, the home of the gods and the dwelling-place of Zeus.

Understandably, the claim made by psychoanalysis to interpret sin mortally offends the sensitivity of the believer, who cannot accept any position he sees as inadmissibly reductive.

In *Moses and Monotheism* Freud expressed himself radically about religious beliefs and spoke of a distortion which "may be described as a *delusion*".[11] In his 1937 *Constructions in Analysis* he came back to this subject, saying that if we consider humanity as if it were an individual human being, we find that mankind too "has developed delusions which are inaccessible to logical criticism and which contradict reality".[12] If we ask why these formations nevertheless manage to exert such extraordinary power over men, the conclusion suggested by research is, Freud argues, the same as the one we reach in the case of the single individual: "they owe their power to the content of historical truth which they have drawn from the repression of ancient, forgotten ages". This is the same argument he put forward in *Totem and Taboo* for sense of guilt.

As we have seen, Freud traces the origins of the sense of guilt to a distant event akin to a myth, a "primordial experience of family". Today this way of thinking can be seen as a kind of defence. By his own admission, Freud had to bear the cross of depression, and all depressives are acquainted with the burden of guilt. It is therefore probable that he himself was uncomfortable with the sense of guilt and tried to keep it at a safe distance.

But let us leave aside this hypothesis. Once we have accepted that an excessive sense of irrational and infantile guilt (whose effects are almost always unhealthy) can be preserved in the unconscious, we must also recognise that there is another side to the question, one which Grinberg has pointed to. The high spiritual value attributed to religious feelings and beliefs seems to owe much to the fact that "it satisfies deep longings of the human psyche and in some way appeases unconscious moral guilt"

(Grinberg, 1963–1971). For this reason it should come as no surprise that for many people it comes to represent the most precious thing in their lives. Indeed, underlying every religion is the need to "allay the sense of guilt and to appease a paternal substitute implicit in the image of God, endowed with super-egoistic characteristics and towards which people have deeply ambivalent feelings" (ibid.).[13]

In the monotheistic religions this reconciliation with the father is obtained through two means, and these have given rise to two widely differing types of religion. Jewish monotheism (the religion of the Father) has only one divine representative, and all relations must be maintained directly with the father-figure. Echoes of this exclusive relationship can be found in the Protestant version of Christianity.

The second means is that which is typical of Christianity, the religion of the Son (in fact, the situation is much more complex because the Son acts in accord with the Father). Here we have a divine intermediary who is half-man, half omnipotent god, as well as other intermediaries such as the Virgin Mary and the saints. In this approach we find the Son of God who, despite being innocent, is killed and who takes upon himself the sins of all mankind.[14] This brings us to the fascinating subject of the scapegoat. Pardon and reconciliation, love and salvation are obtained on condition that the sinner identifies with all other believers, in "an identification aimed at re-establishing the harmony of the original family situation, overcoming the jealousy, rivalry and hostility latent within it".[15]

In 1957, Theodor Reik put forward the hypothesis that the Jewish sense of guilt towards God the Father was maintained with such intensity because this guilt concealed another much more persecutory sense of guilt that had its origin in destructive feelings towards the mother.[16] As we shall see in later chapters, Fornari was to call this shift of interest from the mother to the father "primary paranoia". He considered it a characteristic of the form of development of each individual which was capable of having an influence on the Oedipus conflict.

On the subject of delusion and madness, the eminently secular existentialist philosopher Jean-Paul Sartre argued no more than a few decades ago that there is no such thing as an innocent victim. From an exclusively psychological point of view, that is to say, from the point of view of the experience of each human being, statements like these – although probably in part dictated by the desire to *épater le bourgeois* – are probably partly true. In most of us, as Freud was first to point out, a sense of guilt can break out even when (from an objective point of view) we are completely innocent; otherwise Freud preferred to speak of remorse. Psychoanalysis has shown how in these cases the event in question becomes a pretext, a kind a catalyst which re-awakens old, assuaged senses of guilt.

However, this is probably not what Sartre was getting at. So the question becomes: how much unconscious residual moralism is contained in what

Sartre is saying? In other words, is Sartre suggesting that victims in a concrete sense always collude with their tormentors, perhaps because of the evil they have inside them? I do not believe that this idea corresponds to reality, and yet it has been enormously successful, even outside the ambit of what is now referred to as the *Stockholm syndrome*, where the victim actually sides with his torturer. We know how much the feminist movement has had to fight against the prejudice according to which *deep down* every woman wants to be raped. When people make casual comments about disputes along the lines of "the truth lies somewhere in the middle", this seems to reflect the idea that we are all of us liars to a certain degree, and thus guilty. It is difficult not to be a moralist.

The comment made by the existentialist philosopher Sartre was a pretext for re-examining the desperate moral dilemma which less than a hundred years earlier had tormented the soul of Søren Kierkegaard, considered by many the initiator of the existentialist vision of life. The son of elderly parents, the last of seven children – five of whom died before reaching the age of twenty-two – and brought up according to the highly rigorous moral code of pietism (the current of Protestant renewal to which Kant also belonged), he suffered under a father who at a certain point confessed to him an old wrong-doing. This was the "great earthquake" that was to upset his entire life. His father's misdeed was such as to make Kierkegaard think that a divine curse lay upon all his family.[17] Much of his work, from *The Concept of Anxiety* in 1844 to *The Sickness unto Death* five years later, is permeated by the despair that marks man's relationship with himself and his "paradoxical" relationship with God.

In Kierkegaard we find a way of thinking that is Jewish in origin: the possibility to sin generates guilt which leads to anxiety. For him, original sin is connected to sensuality and procreation. In order to pass from the state of innocence into concrete history, there has to be a leap into sin: Adam's original sin and the repetition of this first sin by each individual. We are still in the Judaic–Christian tradition (a similar model will be found in Freud). Freedom is founded on the possibility to sin.

But guilt and sin generate suffering and profound angst: this is the basis of Kierkegaard's philosophy, one which is also favoured by those who think that the only remedy is to learn how to *live with* psychic pain even without the support of religion. Psychoanalysis offers the secular project of learning how to overcome pain through change. It introduces a ray of hope at the same time as offering many illusions. The knowledge accumulated by Freud's disciples shed light on another aspect which Kierkegaard antici-pated lucidly: despair "unto death".

In *Fear and Trembling* (1843),[18] written after he had called off his brief engagement to Regine Olsen, Kierkegaard proposed the suspension of ethics in the face of religious need. To illustrate this point he referred to the story of the sacrifice of Isaac. The theme is that of the sacrificial lamb, which occupies such a cherished position in the pietistic tradition.[19] God forces Abraham to sacrifice Isaac, as He forced Søren to give up the prospect of marrying his beloved Regine (for fear of making her unhappy).

> There was many a father who lost his child; but then it was God, it was the unalterable, the unsearchable will of the Almighty, it was His hand took the child. Not so with Abraham. For him was reserved a harder trial, and Isaac's fate was laid along with the knife in Abraham's hand. And there he stood, the old man, with his only hope! But he did not doubt, he did not look anxiously to the right or to the left, he did not challenge heaven with his prayers. He knew that it was God the Almighty who was trying him, he knew that it was the hardest sacrifice that could be required of him; but he knew also that no sacrifice was too hard when God required it – and he drew the knife.

Although they too went through tormented and uncertain periods, psychoanalysis and the theory of the double-bind (which we shall be discussing at length later on) are probably the only theories that offer a key to understanding the psychosis which underlies stories such as this. Kierkegaard himself realised this: "If God does not exist, it is impossible to demonstrate it, but if he does exist, it is absolute madness". It must be remembered that Kierkegaard died in 1855 at the age of 42, little more than 20 years after the death of Friedrich Schleiermacher, the tormented German philosopher and theologian who, in a moment of enlightened lucidity, defined religious experience as absolute dependence. But absolute dependence brings with it certain consequences: rebellion but also ambivalence. The words sung by the choir at the crucifixion in the *St Matthew Passion* come to mind:

> *Wie wunderbarlich ist doch diese Strafe!/Der gute Hirte leidet für die Schafe.* (How wonderful is this punishment! The good shepherd suffers for his sheep.)

Bach's music for this chorale seems to act as a commentary on the word *wunderbarlich*: while the basses sing part of the ascending chromatic scale (going up in semitones) there is dissonance between the first note sung by the sopranos and that sung by the contraltos. Smirnovich talks here about ambiguity.[20]

Guilt and revenge

> The sense of guilt is the most important problem in the development of civilization . . . and the price we pay for progress is the loss of happiness due to the heightening of the sense of guilt.
>
> (Freud, *Civilization and its Discontents*)

Using guilt as a moral or legal category is, when one thinks about it, a way of simplifying things enormously. "Fault" can, as we have already pointed out, become a simple synonym for "single and exclusive cause". In this way a complex phenomenon, which is the product of many interacting forces, becomes immediately comprehensible. The simplification offered by guilt is one possible reason why it has survived across the centuries.

At any rate, the existence of an unconscious sense of guilt complicates any simplified reading of the phenomena we are observing. On the one hand, we can include within the sense of guilt those emotional reactions which are triggered by a negative event for which the individual feels "responsible" for reasons which may or may not be realistic. In this category we could include the remorse of the criminal, the realisation of having harmed someone, but also self-reproach. We might also include the vague sense of personal unworthiness that an individual may feel but which is not prompted by any particular act. The feeling of guilt, if examined using advanced techniques of introspection, is sometimes experienced as a tense atmosphere, a kind of mental pall, which, given the right stimulus (everyday events, flashes of memory, and so on), provides the backdrop for dramatic representations that play out according to long-standing personal patterns that always involve a sense of guilt.

This book will look at guilt from various angles, although the prime perspective will be clinical in nature. Analytic treatment is not to be seen as a process of moving towards pure self-knowledge, a journey into hell or any of the other expressions people use to justify analysis; it is rather a process of *healing*, in other words, an attempt to bring about a definite and stable reduction in suffering, together with an increased capacity to contain it (without expelling it), with all that that implies in terms of loss of symptoms, control over the compulsion to act according to rigid, fixed patterns, but also the capacity to think and live better as well as other phenomena attendant on a relatively stable change. Healing is not always possible: anyone who has experienced the vehemence with which the Super-Ego besets certain psychotics knows very well the feeling of impotence and dejection felt by those who try to come closer to it.

The sense of guilt can be avoided by various defence mechanisms; it can be displaced from one object or topic to another. A mother who feels unconsciously guilty for having brought up a son or a daughter who has turned out to be a criminal or a drug addict can deny this experience and, as a way of remedying the damage which she unconsciously thinks she has inflicted, dedicate herself to voluntary work, helping the homeless or the sick. And she does this without the slightest suspicion that the two are connected.[21] Our sense of guilt is sometimes separated from us, split off and projected subtly or violently onto someone else. Guilt can be exploited to obtain masochistic pleasure, to attack other people by making them feel guilty or as a way of exercising real sadistic control.[22] But it can be directed towards one's own interior world (this is the hypothesis that, as we saw, interested Freud) in order to attack oneself.

Finally – but the list could go on – it can help keep alive sexual excitement in a forbidden relationship between lovers. This last situation is an example of the typically human behaviour pattern of deriving pleasure from infringing taboos and bans. In one of his *Chroniques italiennes*, the *Cenci*, Stendhal tells of a seventeenth-century princess who exclaims while licking an ice-cream on a hot summer's evening: "What a shame it's not a sin!". In his *Aphorisms*, Georg Christoph Lichtenberg, philosopher and scientist of the latter half of the eighteenth century, wrote: "An Italian once said: what a shame it's not a sin to drink water. That would make it taste so good!" It is probably no accident that he thought of Italy – the hallowed site for the administration of sin and forgiveness.

But the characteristics of guilt go much further: on the one hand, in the extreme situation of the most severe pathologies every act (the simple turning of a page, picking up a knife from a table, solving a mathematical problem) can be laden with guilt; on the other hand, real responsibility, as we shall explain in the note on terms at the end of this book, can easily be detached from all sense of guilt. This is true both because the individual – the hardened criminal, to take the obvious example – does not experience any remorse (although this is perhaps only apparently the case), and because the culture in which he lives or grew up exculpates him.

Guilt provokes two opposing responses in other people: revenge and forgiveness. We all know that, matching the maxim that says that "the best revenge is forgiveness", there is another based on an ancient, mythical morality which claims the right to revenge (*timorìa*). According to Theodor Reik, those psychologists who do not consider the unconscious find nothing strange in the fact that we forgive those who offend us or have done us harm: "But," he pointed out, "it is in fact a rather unnatural reaction".

The thinking that the best revenge is forgiveness would seem to be based on the (ambiguous) logic of Angelina, the Cinderella story set to music by Gioachino Rossini: "Sul trono io salgo, e voglio/starvi maggior del trono,/e sarà mia vendetta il lor perdono." (I ascend the throne and wish/to be greater than the throne,/and my revenge shall be their forgiveness).

We also know that the victim finds no peace beyond the grave until he has been avenged: "Which if not victory is yet revenge".[23] Amphiaraus was a soothsayer protected by Zeus and Apollo. He was forced by his wife Eriphyle to go off to war against Thebes although he knew he would perish, so he entrusted his sons with the mission of avenging him and killing their mother. Polymester killed Polydorus, Hector's brother. Polydorus's mother, Hecuba, avenged him by luring the murderer into a trap and tearing out his eyes after the Trojan prisoners had killed the two sons Polymester had brought with him before his very eyes.

In later periods, poets and philosophers expressed themselves on the subject of revenge in contrasting ways: while Dante in one of his songs writes, "Ché bell'onor s'acquista in far vendetta" ("Because one acquires great honour when one takes revenge"), and Francis Bacon insists that "Revenge is a kind of wild justice; which the more man's nature runs to, the more ought law to weed it out",[24] there are also those like Heinrich Heine who take a more ironic stance:

> My thoughts are very calm. And I have no other desires than this: a modest thatched hut, a good bed, good food, milk and butter, freshly cut flowers on the windowsill and trees outside my door; and if the Lord wants to make me completely happy, he will grant me the joy of seeing six or seven of my enemies hang from those trees. Before they die I will be moved to forgive them for all the harm they have done me during my life. Yes, one should forgive one's enemies, but only after one has seen them hanged.[25]

Theodor Reik calls Heine courageous and agrees with him. He quotes this passage, adding the comment that only a madman, a hypocrite or an ill person could deny the deep and voluptuous satisfaction that appropriate revenge can afford, or the extraordinary feeling of liberation, or rather "of deliverance from suffocating psychic oppression which follows from successful revenge". In his view the sentimentally female observation made by Mme de Staël – that understanding means forgiving – is profoundly false also when applied to analytic practice. An understanding of motives and instinctual forces in our peers can sometimes – and I emphasise sometimes – make us judge them with greater benevolence. But it needs to be pointed out that understanding is of no help when we are the wronged or offended party. He concludes that the wise are right to wonder at our strange and illogical attitude of forgiving more quickly and readily a wrong done to another.[26]

When one thinks of the nature of revenge, one might ask oneself whether it does not come into play after our biologically-rooted reflex defensive response has failed. Revenge could be this response deferred in time, a kind of "descendant" of a failed response or one made impossible by the circumstances. In Freud's *Studies on Hysteria*, there is a passage that seems to bear out this hypothesis: "The fading of a memory or of the emotion that accompanies it depends on several factors. First of all, what is relevant is whether one reacted energetically or not to the extraordinary event in the first place. By reaction we mean the whole range of voluntary or involuntary reflexes whereby, as experience shows, emotions are vented: from crying to the act of revenge" (Freud, 1895, p. 179).

From an ethological point of view, we would be in the presence of an obstacle to reactive discharge within the "attack–flight" system; hence the persistence of rancour and the desire for revenge. Revenge (which in the words of the Italian saying is "a dish to be savoured cold") derives considerable added pleasure from deferral in time, the relish of planning. It is a *pleasure reserved for the wise*, suggests Da Ponte (*The Marriage of Figaro*, I, III). The fact remains that this archaic response has been handed down intact both in the collective imagination and in social reality. It was the driving force behind the Lombard feuds in the Middle Ages, the blood feuds of the Mafia, and it persists in present-day Albanian law, not to mention the acts of revenge that are regularly carried out inside families and institutions.

It still has die-hard supporters who even today wish to see its direct application. One need only think of the success of westerns that have it as their main theme. Each time the guilty come to an ignominious end we experience undiluted pleasure. Revenge recurs constantly in opera but, as in ancient myths, it is never straightforward. Revenge in opera tends to misfire. When the duty to exact revenge has been inherited from others, as in the case of Azucena in Verdi's *Il Trovatore*, obliged to avenge her mother who had been burnt alive, or when it is planned, as in the case of Rigoletto, it never produces a natural result as it typically does, after many trials and tribulations, in westerns. Destiny comes along and throws a spanner in the works, as it were. The only opera in which the unconscious appears is Bellini's *La Somnabula*. Azucena sends her own son to the stake rather than the son of her hated enemy, and Rigoletto's hireling, Sparafucile, instead of killing the Duke of Mantua, kills Rigoletto's beloved daughter, who sacrifices herself in place of her loved one (II, XX). Iago's revenge, although it achieves its aim, recoils upon him. In Mozart's *La Clemenza di Tito*, the words spoken by Tito, someone who fails to take revenge, are interesting:

> If a severe heart
> is necessary to the empire,
> oh Gods, take the empire
> away from me
> or give me another heart.

But revenge, at the very beginning of tragedy, shows its extreme conflicts, its absolute folly, in Euripides' *Medea*, which had already been anticipated by Neophrone. Medea, the desperate and humiliated woman, the woman who "goes astray" because she "rejoices" when she ought to be "feeling terror", the wife who takes revenge on Jason, who has abandoned her, and kills their children. Medea, the most unnatural mother, the mother who, perhaps for this reason, has also tormented the minds of many great thinkers and poets from Aristotle onwards, who criticised the epilogue harshly (*Poetics*, 1454b, 1).

Medea: . . . and now you can call me
as you please, lioness or Scylla:
I have given you back your misdeeds!

Jason: You suffer, too, I think.

Medea: As long as you don't laugh, I enjoy suffering.

Jason: Children, what an unworthy mother has befallen you!

Medea: Children, to what death has your father condemned you![27]

Chapter 2

The use and abuse of theory

We all try to adopt internal strategies to allay our sense of guilt; the depressive who commits suicide represents the most spectacular failure of such attempts. As we have already mentioned, the strategies deployed by the therapist to avoid feeling guilty can also fail – either totally or in part. When an individual uses himself as an instrument to cure others (that is to say, when he comes into contact with the sense of guilt and with the real wrongs committed by his patient), he cannot avoid provoking counter-transference reactions which can be either conscious or unconscious. We shall be looking at the concept of counter-transference in more detail in Chapter 6. One of the duties of the various schools of psychotherapeutic training should be to provide guidelines on how to deal with the vast range of thoughts, emotions, conflicts and defences that make up the analyst's reaction. Each psycho-analytic or psychotherapeutic school – whether in the form of explicit theory or actual practice – should, as one of its basic tasks, propose a model for dealing with the sense of guilt both in the patient and in the analyst himself.

Freudian analysts should in general be agreed about the prime import-ance that the sense of guilt has in the origin of any type of psychic dis-turbance, just as they should also agree that the sense of guilt accompanies the individual throughout his development. However, although they may accept this truth rationally on a theoretical level, this does not mean that they have sufficient first-hand knowledge to enable them to master any situation that might be set off by the experience of guilt.

The list of mechanisms and tactics used to deal with the sense of guilt is a long one. Apart from the specific defences which we shall encounter at various points throughout this book, we could add some further examples. As we are all only human beings, when we want to tone down the harshness of internal accusations, we use our ability to create more or less realistic fantasies which turn us into objects of approval. In other cases we employ sophisticated techniques to provoke others into accusing us unjustly, solely in order to then be able to defend ourselves with ease. Intense sado-masochistic relationships demonstrate several of these techniques: the most frequent is constructing a situation where the *other* figure is the guilty party.

Finally, we can try to share with others the blame and responsibility for the misdeed or crime we ourselves have committed. Analysts are very familiar with the way patients create an external authority who, in league with the analyst, helps them to avoid feeling guilty.

Intellectual knowledge of the complex dynamics at work in the sense of guilt does not always coincide with their practical mastery. Intellectual knowledge and concrete mastery are not usually attained either simultaneously or in a linear progression. The integration of the intellectual with the emotional is for the most part achieved through a series of insights gained across a person's lifetime. It should come as no surprise to discover that such integration signals one of the highest levels of maturity that the individual is capable of attaining.

In the field of psychotherapy the scientific debates that most often end in deadlock, and the discussions where positions diverge most radically, frequently, if not always, have to do with the sense of guilt and the models used to explain it. As we shall see later, the discussions in psychoanalysis about the death instinct and the moment when guilt arises, as well as the debate about the notions of the depressive and paranoid–schizoid positions introduced by Melanie Klein, tie in closely with the question of guilt. The various hypotheses that have been put forward about the relationship between sense of guilt and reparation, or between sense of guilt and responsibility, are also relevant to this question. There is, in fact, no agreement even about the strategies for dealing with the sense of guilt.

The fundamental importance of the choice of one theory over another is explained by the fact that these theories exercise an influence – usually preconscious or unconscious – over our choice of a course of action.[1] Such decisions are normal and also purely functional, providing that we do not accept the theory dogmatically. Often, however, our dependence on a theory eludes our control. We make a choice that is not guided by prudence or watchfulness but rather by a vested interest. We may, for example, embrace a theoretical model because unconsciously we feel it chimes with the rationalisations we have constructed to justify our actions.

Let us imagine an analyst who is struggling with a depression which he has had no chance to explore (unconsciously he fears coming too close to his own repressed guilt) and which he deals with by using obsessive defences. We can be fairly certain that in his therapeutic practice he will be unwilling to embrace a theory which maintains that the sense of guilt should be brought out into the open and analysed. He will prefer not to interpret the patient's unconscious sense of guilt so as to be able to continue deluding himself.

Another case could be a chronically, though perhaps not openly, depressed analyst who fails to deal decisively and radically with his own core of guilt and ambivalence, preferring to let it lie dormant. For this type of "undecided" analyst, a theoretical model which offers no way out but which sees endless investigation of the sense of guilt and mature reparation as the ultimate aim of analysis could be very useful: "a trouble shared is a trouble halved". If we are all a bit depressed, there is no reason why I shouldn't be able to live with my depression.

To set the historical record straight, however, it should be added that controversies in psychoanalysis have been contained and mediated in ways which would be unthinkable in other fields where the sense of guilt plays a huge role. We need only think of the wars of religion and the insurmountable difficulties of communication which, despite official declarations to the contrary, exist between various forms of fundamentalism. Or we can think of politics and the clash between ideologies. Political ideas and projects, like religious aims, have always been connected to the sense of guilt. One policy can lead to an increase in unemployment; another, which protects employment, may provoke economic damage by encouraging the flight of productive investment. Other spheres include family law, the legislation governing divorce and abortion, restrictions with regard to adoptions, sexual discrimination and immigration control. The list could easily go on.

There are those who think that such questions fall outside the province of psychoanalysis. In my view this is not true because psychoanalysis and psychotherapy are more than methods of treatment: they are also organisations and means of transmitting knowledge through institutions. The two things are intimately connected; the sense of guilt must necessarily also play a part inside psychoanalytical institutions.

With regard to these "sociological" questions, León Grinberg has described what is probably the most important divergence between the various strategies adopted to interpret the sense of guilt. Some psychoanalysts see their interpretations as a way of freeing patients from guilt because for them guilt is a negative and pathological feeling to which patients subject themselves masochistically. In this internal conflict between Super-Ego and Ego, the Ego is forced to accept the unjust burden of guilt which a severe and terrifying Super-Ego threatens to impose upon it. In other words, the patient feels "obliged" to accept his sense of guilt under pressure from a Super-Ego that threatens punishment. Seen from this angle, the aim of analysis is "to show the patient that this sense of guilt leads only to the repression of his (erotic or aggressive) instinctive life and to the masochistic search for self-punishment and deprivation, and that ultimately it will maintain his difficulties".

Another group of psychoanalysts seems to embrace a diametrically opposed theoretical and technical principle. According to these analysts, the core of each neurotic conflict consists in the denial of the sense of guilt felt because of one's aggressive fantasies against objects.[2] The therapeutic aim of those who advocate this way of dealing with guilt is to make the patient aware of this denial and consequently conscious of his fantasies, his behaviour and the underlying sense of guilt. "The advocates of the first thesis," concludes Grinberg (1963–1971), "criticise the analysts of the second group because they believe that they identify with strict superego images, thus increasing the guilt of their patients and its pathological effects. The latter contest the operative validity of a theory which, in their opinion, leads to manic attitudes of denial and a flight towards healing instead of a profound and authentic solution."[3]

Here we run into one of many paradoxes: for either side to recognise the partial validity of the criticism levelled at them by their adversaries might mean, for example, feeling guilty towards their own patients who, if the others are right, are receiving bad treatment. Equally, it may also mean losing the protection that belonging to a "dogmatically" cohesive group usually provides. Surely the reason Abraham was prepared to sacrifice Isaac was so as not to lose the protection of his creator. The delicate balances that have been created often depend on well-structured defences that leave no room for dialogue. The sense of security provided by the group that we belong to encourages us to think that we possess the Truth, and this satisfies a deep longing for protection from guilt.

Besides, the sense of guilt is always lying in ambush, because the risks which each side warns the other about are real risks which very often are *not* avoided. A prisoner of orthodoxy will only be able to change if he is assailed by doubt, but equally doubt will only have an effect if it is given enough time. The time necessary varies from situation to situation. The process goes through various stages and takes place over many generations. It is this "time necessary" that makes possible a stage-by-stage working through and coming to awareness. The passing of time is a factor that often produces positive effects and is helpful in working through the sense of guilt. *Zeit bringt Rosen*, "time brings roses", in the words of the German saying, which is more optimistic than the Italian version – "If they are roses, they will bloom" (*"se son rose fioriranno"*) – or the English "We'll have to wait and see".

Lying hidden behind the theoretical oppositions is probably a defect in theory – the extremely ambitious theory of psychoanalysis. Its aim is to address the themes of love and human destructiveness, or rather, the terrible disturbances which love and destructiveness can cause. It seeks, beyond all empty rhetoric, to capture the deep meaning of love, and tries to make love flourish when it appears to be wilting or is even completely absent. And at the same time it wants to deliver people from their destructiveness.

If the love that exists between mother and child, and between father and mother-with-child forms the framework which fosters the harmonious growth of children, it is easier to understand why some people experience fear, or terror, at not being capable of providing this framework, of making a mistake, or of having made a mistake; or more simply the fear of not having known how to love sufficiently. It should not be forgotten in this context that the massive reaction against psychoanalysis and social psychiatry in 1970s America, and the move from psychiatry towards biology and new forms of nosography, came about under pressure from powerful parents' associations and as a response to parents feeling that they were being accused and blamed for the psychic and mental suffering of their children.[4]

The two types of guilt

In a series of short essays on characters from Shakespeare and Ibsen, as well as people he calls guilt-driven criminals, Freud tried to show that the sense of guilt can arise out of unconscious fantasies rather than real actions.[5] He even went so far as to say that guilt is not always the result of having committed a crime; frequently the crime is committed as a *consequence* of the sense of guilt. This phenomenon is particularly evident in clinical cases involving children. Little U.U. calls his mother and tells her: "Look what I've done! I've broken the Christmas tree decorations!" and starts to crush them before her very eyes. If the mother tells him off, he goes on to break even more of them. He is waiting for the figure of the witch to appear in his mother, the figure who gets angry and frightens him; he wants to hound her out from his unconscious and make her real. What later actually appears (the mother as witch) was already inside him.[6]

This is another of Freud's devastating observations. Talking about illegal acts, such as theft, small-scale fraud, even arson, committed by people "who later became highly respectable", Freud (1916: 3) adds:

> Analytical work has produced . . . the surprising result that such acts were committed mainly because they were forbidden and because carrying them out brought psychic relief to the person who committed them. The patient suffered from an oppressive sense of guilt of unknown origin and, after committing the wrong, he felt that the weight had been lifted. At least the sense of guilt was attributed to something.

Dostoyevsky had anticipated Freud when he wrote in *Crime and Punishment*: "As to the question whether it is the illness that generates the crime or whether the crime, by its very nature, was always accompanied by something like an illness, [Raskolnikov] still felt unable to resolve the issue". The moral masochist is in a very similar situation: he feels threatened by guilt in much the same way as Damocles must have felt as he stood under a sword suspended from a horsehair; the masochist prefers to cut the hair with his own hands rather than have that ever-threatening sword hanging over his head.[7]

Melanie Klein follows Freud in linking the sense of guilt to aggressive-ness: every time we feel guilt, in one way or another it is activated by our (real or only imagined) destructive aggressiveness. But Klein's investigation takes her along her own very personal path: for one thing, for her there is a connection between sadism and the epistemophilic impulse (in other words, the impulse to carry out research, to acquire knowledge), which is very important for the whole development of the child and the adult. This impulse first turns towards the body of the mother, seen as "the scene of all sexual processes and developments". The child is dominated by a force that makes it want to appropriate the contents of that body: "He thus begins to be curious about what it contains, what it is like, etc. So the epistemophile instinct and the desire to take possession come quite early to be most intimately connected with one another and at the same time with the sense of guilt aroused by the incipient Oedipus conflict".[8] For Klein the sense of guilt also arises out of the child's sadistic fantasies about devouring the mother, especially, as Abraham suggests, the mother's breast.

Freud, on the other hand, thought that the Super-Ego (the agency responsible for any sense of guilt) was structured at the time when the Oedipus complex was in decline, around the age of five. Melanie Klein places the birth of the Super-Ego in an earlier period, or rather she back-dates the entire Oedipus complex.[9] Furthermore, she also shifts the accent. Freud saw the conflict between love and hate as taking place within a three-party situation, whereas Klein develops the idea of conflict inside the two-person relationship of mother and child; it is here that the sense of guilt emerges. This is a very innovative insight that takes its cue from Freud's original and in itself revolutionary insight: after Klein no psychoanalyst would ever consider the Super-Ego in the same way as Freud.

Throughout her work Klein shows that she considers aggressiveness (together with the inhibition of aggressiveness) as the most important problematic impulse during the child's development.[10] Consequently the sense of guilt takes on a very special role. She also considers sadism as a manifestation of the death instinct.[11] In 1935 she makes her most important statement on the subject of guilt: she describes guilt as something that arises out of what she calls the depressive position and which she therefore terms depressive guilt. Klein thinks that only a sufficiently integrated personality can feel this kind of guilt. In other words, in order to experience depressive guilt, we must be capable of representing inside us a person who suffers because of what we have done. On this hypothesis, the sense of guilt is not a primitive human phenomenon: if the individual is to feel guilt, he needs to have reached a certain "maturity".

To illustrate what this depressive guilt is, it is necessary to step back a little and look at what Klein means by the depressive position and the paranoid–schizoid position, two concepts which have now become an integral part of the lexicon of many psychoanalysts, even of the non-

Kleinians. The discussion in the next two chapters should provide us with a fairly clear idea of these two positions; for the moment, however, we shall have to settle for an outline that allows us to continue our discussion of what it is about guilt that interests Melanie Klein.

To begin with, we need to explain that Melanie Klein chooses the term "position" because she wants to mark herself off from Freud, who talked about "phases" or "stages" to define the important moments in the development of the individual, moments which for him occur in sequence. First comes the oral phase, followed by the anal phase, then the urethral, the phallic and finally the genital. These past moments influence a person's behaviour in adult life. In reality, Klein points out, these moments of development follow each other only at the beginning. Subsequently they overlap and, more importantly, a certain adult behaviour pattern can be influenced by more than one phase from the past. For this reason she thinks that the term "position" (which indicates a cluster of anxieties, impulses and defences) is clearer and more useful.[12] It is important to emphasise this choice because it shows that Klein's theory about human behaviour saw it as a complex system. It is almost as if she were implying that in this respect Freud had tended to simplify things. Our internal world, which is after all the territory where the sense of guilt exerts its power, has to be observed from different angles of vision if we are to grasp its varying and contrasting features.

The paranoid–schizoid position that Melanie Klein describes as part of the development of each individual is the one that comes first and is defined by a situation where the small child fights against its innate destructive impulses (death instinct) by using particular defence mechanisms. These mechanisms are: splitting (a concept that Melanie Klein took from Fairbairn more than from Freud), projection, and projective identification (which she was the first to elaborate), as well as the tendency to stifle emotion. Added to these are the idealisation and the denial of both internal and external reality.

In splitting, the other is experienced as an object divided into two: good on the one hand and bad on the other. Essentially this is an expedient for ordering one's emotions when ambivalence (in other words the coexistence of hate and love, attraction and repulsion) is felt to be unbearable. The split that occurs in what Klein calls the paranoid–schizoid position thus has a "physiological" function which endows the maturing individual with the ability to distinguish between good and evil.

It is important to make this point about the role of splitting because it has an effect on a large part of the human imaginary. Let us leave aside the clinical aspect for a moment. *Maria lactans*, the Mary who breastfeeds Baby Jesus, is a cherished figure in Medieval Christian art. She represents the reassuring side of the same woman whose wicked side has been split off, the mother who embodies the thousand witches that throng our fantasies, from Lady Macbeth to Snow White's stepmother. The breast itself, to use

Klein's terms, is divided into good and bad. Splitting can divide up each of the important figures of childhood. Ingmar Bergman, in his film version of Mozart's *The Magic Flute*, was following an obvious psychoanalytic agenda by suggesting that the figure of the father can be split into two characters: Sarastro and Monostrato (the trusted father and the tempter). Many have seen Leporello as a part split off from Don Giovanni and Sancho Panza as a part split off from Don Quixote.

Through projection (the other concept inherited from Freud and psychiatry) the individual brings internal conflicts to the outside or projects impulses or parts of himself or herself. Or again, he projects previously introjected objects which have now become parts of his internal world (but Klein does not seem to emphasise this).[13] Among the prime tasks of these defences is to exclude or keep at bay the sense of guilt.

The depressive position, on the other hand, comes about when the child's developing cognitive faculties make him aware that the "fairy godmother" (the idealised good mother) and the witch (the completely wicked mother), whom he previously had had to keep apart, are in fact two sides of the same person.[14]

The process that leads from one position to the other is neither simple nor straightforward.[15] Even in the depressive position we experience various anxieties which are persecutory in nature; however, the child who enters this position makes an important step forward from the paranoid–schizoid defences which characterised the first six months of its existence.

For Klein the child's anxiety and sense of guilt (which persist in the immature adult) stand in direct proportion to the aggressiveness it feels. According to her, early infantile sadism is expressed in fantasies of damaging or destroying, cutting up or devouring the other who is consequently experienced as damaged or destroyed. This makes it into a source of worry and of *pining* (a term to which we shall return later).

In summing up, I would like to point to what I consider the real turning-point. One could say that in the first position – the paranoid–schizoid position – the individual is concerned exclusively about himself, about what is happening or what could happen to him. In the depressive position, on the other hand, attention is no longer focused on the self and concern shifts to the object, to others (as well as focusing on the self in a different spirit).

We made the point earlier that the process of transition is laborious. This experience gives rise not only to suffering, feelings of loss and the sense of guilt. For Klein the individual starts to feel guilt when he comes to understand that the suffering he has caused his loved one is the – real or imagined – result of his own aggressive impulses. The desire to repair this damage grows out of this realisation. For this reason depressive guilt, as it is called, has come to be identified as the driving force behind reparation.

To understand depressive guilt better it might be useful to start from this concept of reparation. Although today all schools that deal with the psychology of guilt see reparative behaviour as a fundamental characteristic of that experience, the credit for being the first person to examine reparation extensively and for opening up the debate on this phenomenon must go to Melanie Klein.[16]

For Klein, reparation is indeed the strongest force among creative and constructive impulses.[17] There is a tendency in her writings to consider all creative activity, whether that of normal people or artists, as reparational and to view reparation as a normal process whereby the individual resolves his intimate ambivalence towards others. This point of view is not shared by all psychoanalysts: Charles Rycroft describes reparation simply as a defence mechanism put into operation in order to reduce guilt. He thus deprives it of the pre-eminent role which Klein had attributed to it within her concept of early infantile sadism.[18]

If we leave aside "false reparations" for the moment, we can go on to say that – staying within the Kleinian concept – reparation not only accompanies the need that one has to redress a wrong one has done to another, but also, more importantly, that being capable of reparation presupposes that a change has taken place in the subject. This corresponds to the task of reconstructing our internal as well as our external world. Observing her own child, Eric, Klein noted that "he showed occasionally both in phantasy as well as in games a shrinking from, an alarm at, his own aggressiveness . . . At that time, too, if he had knocked himself he would say, 'It's all right; that is the punishment because I was naughty'."[19] Klein says that she was struck by one thing in particular: "I must say that the impression I gain from the way in which even the small child fights against his anti-social tendencies is rather touching and moving". The reparative impulses also lead to another step in the integration of the subject: "Love is put in sharper conflict with hate and is active both in controlling destructiveness and in restoring and repairing the damage done".

But beside this type of the sense of guilt, which leads to reparation and which is a sign that the individual has reached an important stage of maturity, there is another, hidden in Klein's own theory. That is to say, there are really two types of guilt. The credit for having identified them in Klein's observations and for first having given them a broad phenomenological description goes to León Grinberg.

In *Envy and Gratitude*, Klein had written that one of the consequences of excessive envy "is an early onset of guilt. If premature guilt is experienced by an ego not yet capable of bearing it, guilt is felt as persecution and the object that arouses guilt is turned into a persecutor."[20] Surely this observation contradicts her previous remark that guilt arises during the depressive position as the result of a process of integration. Grinberg suggests that in these two cases Melanie Klein, without saying it explicitly, is referring to two different types of the sense of guilt.[21] This latter type, borrowing terminology introduced by Klein, is *persecutory guilt*. This has its origins in the first moments of life, its effect is very long-lasting and continues to haunt the individual even when he is grown up; as does the other guilt, which takes its name from the depressive position. In other words, the two types of guilt do not arise in sequence; they can coexist and interact.[22]

Let us think back to some of the main features of the two types of guilt. Among the indicators which signal the presence of persecutory guilt we can cite self-reproach, to which we can add "stray" reproaches, so to speak, uttered by the various characters we encounter in dreams or in the episodes of everyday life that are narrated in analytic sessions. Obviously the same could be said about the stray reproaches uttered in normal conversations. We are talking here about the experience of the patient in therapy, but it goes without saying that other considerations can be extrapolated from this context. Another sign that points to the presence of persecutory guilt is the fact that a person may feel inhibited. But equally, other symptoms associated with depression, such as insomnia, if investigated thoroughly enough, can also reveal the presence of attacks that are typical of persecutory guilt. Persecutory guilt can give rise to somatic reactions and obsessive rituals.

So persecutory guilt can be seen as being at the source of other apparently contrasting behaviour patterns, for example, excessive, reactive or manic lack of inhibition, or sadism which is the product of a desire to identify with the aggressor. In these cases someone (who has been unconsciously incorporated) attacks us, blames us and we then divert this attack onto others.

Again, another sign of the presence of persecutory guilt could be resentment (which can degenerate into rancour), despair, masochistic (or sadistic) behaviour and the tendency to enter into sado-masochistic relationships. In certain acute situations, people try by all possible means to establish intimate relationships and emotional ties by using the whole range of their seductive powers: they first bind the other to themselves and then offload onto the other the guilt that oppresses them. Sado-masochistic relationships – which are characterised by the mutual exchange of accusations – have this function. If both partners suffer unconsciously because of the presence of an excessive amount of guilt which is not used up in the need to expiate, the sado-masochistic relationship tends to be very tenacious because each party needs the other to discharge his or her own excessive sense of guilt. If the other distances himself and refuses to become embroiled, the sense of guilt becomes more acute and can set off a spiral of anxiety whose consequences can be either deleterious or beneficial.

Sado-masochistic relationships and seductiveness tend to elicit moralistic judgements. Seductiveness should not, however, be demonised, not even when its aims are vindictive. We know that there is a tradition of dangerous seduction which goes back to Homer's sirens. But even in festering sado-masochistic relationships we very often find authentic requests for and possibilities of affection and intimacy, the capacity to love, true and deep self-sacrifice, and generosity.

Typically, in terms of content, persecutory guilt sees us as unjustly or mysteriously accused by some indefinite and vague persecutor who may also bear some resemblance to certain characters in Kafka. Sometimes this persecution weighs on our lives without us knowing the reason why. On other occasions, however, the persecution is connected to the sins of others. When we live in the world of persecutory guilt, we are so to speak victims of guilt, a guilt that can be handed down from father to son, even down to the fifth generation, as the Bible has it. We mentioned earlier the divine curse which Kierkegaard imagined weighing down on his family as a result of his father's sin: this was persecutory guilt. Raskolnikov, the protagonist of Dostoyevsky's *Crime and Punishment*, is another exemplary case. We shall return to him in another context.

We can, however, also talk of the depressive sense of guilt when we are convinced that it is we, through our more or less blatant actions and intentions, who have caused damage and suffering to others and ourselves. In this case we believe that we are the evil ones, the tormentors, the torturers, the murderers. The damage suffered or apparently suffered by the other, the victim, results from what we have done, thought or desired. This type of the sense of guilt corresponds to what is generally understood by this term.

A criticism

At this point it is perhaps worth making a brief digression. The distinction between the persecutory sense of guilt and the depressive sense of guilt has been criticised by Goldberg.[23] It will be useful to look at this criticism because it will open up a general perspective from which to view our subject.

Goldberg argues that while distinguishing, as Grinberg does, between two forms of the sense of guilt may be valuable on a descriptive level, it does not affect the nature of guilt itself, "which is essentially persecutory in its origin, in its nature and in its means of functioning". He defines it as a traumatic internal attack which produces the affect of anxiety, an anxiety in search of a means of representation, as Freud put it. According to Goldberg, it is only possible to talk descriptively about two types of guilt: "if anything it would be better to talk of means of functioning and means of dealing with guilt. In so-called 'depressive' or 'normal' guilt we find ourselves in the presence of reparative activities".

My impression is that this comment of Goldberg's is a misleading simplification. For one thing, we might be led to disregard Grinberg's entire explanation. Grinberg's declared aim in separating the two types of guilt was to better understand their dynamics on the basis of a broader picture of the content and nature of the relationship with the object. The distinction was especially useful to him in his attempt to understand when grief was normal or when it ought to be considered pathological. Basically what he was trying to do was to "refine our knowledge", to use Goldberg's own words. However, by not distinguishing between the two types of guilt, Goldberg finds himself forced to leave aside all the problems that Grinberg examines in depth.

John Rickman, a celebrated English analyst active at the end of the Second World War, also distinguished between a persecutory and a depressive side to guilt, although in actual fact he continued to treat it as a single phenomenon.[24] But at the time Rickman was writing Grinberg had not yet drawn attention to all the consequences of this distinction.

We can discuss whether there is one sense of guilt or two, or whether we should talk only of two different modes of dealing with the phenomenon;[25] we can debate whether there are one, two or four types of guilt, as some have argued; we can discuss whether we should give terms like "melancholy" or "internal object" one meaning rather than another,[26] whether there are one or two instincts, or possibly dozens of instincts, as factor analysis claimed to have demonstrated in the 1960s. But in cases like this we can only say that no discussion makes any sense unless it starts from an explicit statement about which theoretical framework is being adopted and a definition of key terms.[27]

Further, we also need to formulate our objectives. Personally I am interested in "curing" the sense of guilt and believe that to this end it is necessary to think about guilt in the objective sense. I also accept Grinberg's distinction because it not only helps me to adopt what I think is the best therapeutic strategy but also allows me to monitor the progress that the patient makes towards the goal of reduced suffering and better understanding of the conflicts that produce that suffering.

Distinguishing between two types of guilt can prove very useful in several different circumstances. If persecutory guilt is not taken into consideration (the other form is accepted by everyone), we run the risk of not realising that it is at work; it can be mistaken for a form of anxiety, as Kierkegaard does in The Concept of Anxiety.[28]

Various situations have been identified as contributing to the creation of this primitive sense of guilt: the birth trauma, a bad relationship with the breast and with the mother, the predominance of frustration over gratification, and so on. Today we could sum up by saying that besides a series of conflicts one can also think of a series of affective deficits with traumatic effects. These deficits give rise to aggressiveness and can trigger senses of guilt, although frequently they remain unconscious. We have already mentioned that many analysts argue the case for the considerable effect that the incorporation of a truly wicked object may have, the incorporation of someone who has, with traumatic effect, attacked, raped or injured the body or soul in the many different sadistic ways of which human beings are capable.

There is no agreement about the moment in the development of the child in which nameless persecution morphs into persecutory guilt. The older the child becomes, the easier it is to isolate and describe this phenomenon.

I am now going to describe a brief scene taken from a psychoanalytic session that will perhaps recall other similar cases. P.P. is a middle-aged man with a divorce behind him, recently remarried but afraid that his present marriage will also fail for reasons he is unable to grasp. At one moment the idea of a spell intrudes into his thoughts. He does not consider himself superstitious and is therefore slightly embarrassed to tell me. He now realises that by leaving his first wife and children to marry another woman it was as if a nameless spell had taken hold of him: he will never be happy with another person; something will prevent it. Abandonment and a curse resulting from that abandonment: here we are in the sphere of persecution strongly tinged with guilt.

Every loss brings with it a certain amount of sense of guilt which comes from a sense of the deprivation and depletion of the Self.[29] Melanie Klein described a sense of guilt "connected to the fact of having neglected and abandoned the valuable content of one's own self".[30] Not only can being neglected or maltreated, or passively suffering traumas, generate the sense of guilt but the experience of guilt can also result from neglecting oneself. The poor individual seems to be surrounded.

G.G. is a woman who has "neglected" her profound need for love. She married an influential man whom she never loved (the only person she loved was a poor cousin), hoping to achieve fulfilment socially and in her career. At a certain point in her analysis, this produced in her an intense sense of guilt. For a long time she accused herself mercilessly of not having had, at the time, "the courage to risk things", the courage to "face loneliness", to "fulfil herself". These accusations paralysed her.

The Erinyes and Resentment

Among the prime emotions that come into play when guilt is experienced are resentment and rancour (resentment laden with hate). Resentment can be experienced towards someone who was previously loved and is now felt as responsible for our frustration, abandonment or aggression. The disappointment and betrayal caused by the loved or admired person can be seen as a kind of aggression. It needs perhaps to be remembered that the betrayal may only be imagined, a delusional construct, as in the case of Othello. But it can also be simply ideological: did Brutus betray Caesar? Perhaps according to Caesar he did, but not according to Brutus or Cassius (or for that matter Shakespeare).

But as in the case of G.G., resentment can be felt against oneself: "I'm angry at myself, I'm annoyed with myself!", she used to repeat at moments of acute crisis. And occasionally she would insult herself harshly. The accusation can be that one exposed oneself to the experience of abandonment, or narcissistic frustration (one thinks of the actor or writer who has experienced failure); but self-resentment can also result from the feeling that one has denied oneself sufficient instinctual gratification, say, a more intense and fulfilling sex life – now that it is too late. The refrain "now it's too late" is often part of the repertoire of resentful self-directed comments.

In extreme cases resentment can also be felt towards a dead person who has passed away and taken with them some parts of ourselves, consequently depriving us of the chance to give our life a certain kind of direction, a certain kind of satisfaction. The following case is not particularly serious but I think it aptly demonstrates the tortuous paths that resentment can take. A patient felt resentment towards his father who had died before he – the son – had become a father: "He didn't allow me the chance to give him the joy of having a granddaughter" is what he discovers himself thinking, much to his surprise and not without some emotion. Obviously such a thought is not so absurd if we explore a deeper and more complex level of thinking and desires: for example, if we discover the desire to allow ourselves a tender relationship with our father, to offer him our feminine parts (the daughter). In this particular case the patient reproached the father for leaving him forever precisely at the moment when, after long and difficult analysis, he was getting to the point where he could show tenderness towards his father. Behind this omnipotent reproach also lay the desire to annul the father's death.

These fantasies and emotions get in the way of working through grief, which then becomes pathological. The stronger the resentment, the stronger the persecution, according to the *lex talionis*. The use of the expression "an eye for an eye" is not precisely correct, even though it has entered common use as a way of referring to retaliation. The meaning of "an eye for eye" was originally restrictive and represented a less primitive stage than unlimited revenge – an eye for an eye, and nothing more. This does not apply to persecutory guilt, which returns in multiplied form. When we look at the unconscious self-punishing fantasies of neurotics or people with even more serious disturbances, we find strange and complicated means of punishment unknown to modern penal law (though not to pre-Enlightenment law): self-mutilation, letting oneself be chained up and whipped, allowing a sadistic partner to subject one to mental torture, even suicide or asking to be killed. The moral masochist knows no limits in his use of others or of the occasions life offers for courting defeat.

Signs of persecutory guilt can also be found in the body, not only in the form of hypochondriac or psychosomatic reactions,[31] but also "enclosed" within the contractions or hypertonic (or hypotonic) state of the muscles.

In many cases the persecutor is experienced unconsciously as a malign presence operating inside the diseased organ, or in the chronically contracted artery. People under attack from persecutory guilt tend to act compulsively and repetitively, showing masochistic or sadistic inclinations.

The Erinyes of classical mythology seem to be ideal symbols of the mythical portrayal of the persecutory sense of guilt. Similar to the Moirae (the Fates), they were primitive forces not subject to the authority of successive generations of gods. Even Zeus himself owed them obedience. Originally the Erinyes were indeterminate in number, but later the number was fixed and they took on specific names (which is also what happens with persecutory guilt). Three are known: Alecto, Tisiphone, and Megaera. Often they had leather or iron whips in their hands and, when they captured their victims, they tortured them and drove them crazy.

Often they were seen as bitches (dogs) who chased after men to sink their teeth into them. The references to whips, torture and biting are signs that we are dealing with the unconscious sense of guilt. Let me briefly cite the case of T.T.: at a party he meets his ex-wife, who asks him "Can I look after you today?", which she then proceeds to do, offering him food and drink, showing him the garden, following him around "like a little dog", in my patient's words. One of T.T.'s friends (for whom the situation must have raised his own very personal spectres) is drastic in his comment: "She was salving her conscience to ward off her pangs of guilt; I'd've given her a good whipping". Undoubtedly there are echoes of the Erinyes here: the pangs, the whip and even the "dog/bitch". It hardly needs pointing out that when the patient talks about his friend he is really talking about a part of himself.

From the time of Homer onwards the basic function of the Erinyes was to exact revenge for a crime, for an objective wrong. In particular they punished wrongs committed during family feuds, as in the case of Agamemnon and Clytemnestra, or indeed Oedipus. Meleager was killed by Althea under the influence of the Erinyes because Meleager had killed his uncles, Althea's brothers, during a hunting expedition. It is interesting to note that, although they represented primordial wrath, the Erinyes were protectors of the social order and performed what in psychoanalytic terms is the function of a group Super-Ego.[32] They punished crimes that disrupted the social order, and even persecuted arrogance or hubris, everything that tended to make man forget his mortality. They were older than the gods and superior to them, and yet were subjected (and thus allied) to the law of the community against the interests of the individual. The Erinyes dwelled in the nether regions.

There is one particular characteristic of the sense of persecutory guilt which it might be useful to focus on once again: usually (though not always) it leads to propitiation and to propitiatory reparation. Attempts are made to placate the persecutor. No real interest in or concern for the other is involved; the aim is purely to pacify him. Perhaps it was to flatter them that the Erinyes were called Eumenides (the "Kindly Ones").[33]

The unconscious reasons that generate persecutory guilt can be manipulated and made unrecognisable, or they can enter into other systems of thought. Shamans in the Andes, for example, fear the curse of Juanita, the mummy of a small girl who was apparently sacrificed to the gods some five hundred years ago. Juanita was found on Mount Ampato, perfectly preserved because she had lain inside a glacier. After the mummy came to the surface in October 1995 a series of disasters (a plane crash, people killed by falling high-tension wires) befell the area. According to the shamans this was Juanita's revenge; not, as our way of thinking might suggest, for having been a child sacrifice, at a young age, but for having been torn away from the cave where she was kept and watched over to keep the mountain gods happy. This kind of justification for a curse (the curse implies strong persecutory guilt) can also be found in the "personal religions" of some individuals.

Leaving aside such signs, how do we know that we are in the presence of a sense of persecutory guilt and not simple persecutory anxiety? Does it make sense to say that guilt is anxiety in search of a means of representation? Once again the question is not easy to answer because guilt itself and the processes that underlie guilt can remain unconscious and thus become visible only by reading clues and deciphering symbols. One could, for example, cite the French physician Lerminier, who at the beginning of the nineteenth century wrote:

> The effect of anxiety on the vital organs is at times so excruciating that sick people, in order to express such profound and unbearable pain, compare it to the effect of an iron or bronze hand which seizes and grips the organs of circulation and breathing.[34]

Is the metaphor of the "iron or bronze hand" sufficient evidence to prove that we are dealing here with unconscious guilt? Anyone trying to argue this point could base his argument on the fact that we typically talk about the weight or burden of guilt and that the idea of grappling or clenching can be related back to the stranglehold produced by remorse (which etymologically – re-morse – refers to "biting") that we clearly feel when guilt affects us. But for some people this might not be enough.

Perhaps the question needs to be asked within a more general framework. Arguably, we need to look beyond symbolic interpretation and deciphering to discover other clues and signs. The search for a kind of expiation or self-punishment (in which we can include masochistic setbacks in the face of the tasks and difficulties of life) can easily be traced back to guilt. But, as has already been pointed out, there are many situations which might suggest that felt anxiety is connected to persecutory guilt: dreams, fantasies or delusions involving judicial trials, judges, confessors, inquisitors, policemen, figures connected to crimes, wrongs, sins, punishments, as well as narratives taken from everyday life that centre on the state of being accused (where it is not important who is being accused).

It will be recalled that at a certain point in Shakespeare's tragedy, King Lear stages a kind of delusional trial full of rancour, a pantomime, against his ungrateful daughters Goneril and Regan, on whom he wants to take revenge:

> LEAR: Arraign her first; 'tis Goneril. I here take my oath before this honourable assembly, she kick'd the poor King her father . . . And here's another, whose warp'd looks proclaim what store her heart is made on. Stop her there! Arms, arms, sword, fire! Corruption in the place! False justicer, why hast thou let her 'scape?
>
> (Act III, Sc. VI, 46–55)

The trial is a figment of his imagination; the king is both author and director of the trial. And precisely for this reason we are justified in asking who is this *false justicer* who lets the accused go if not some unconscious part of Lear himself, which probably perceives him as a desperate, failed parent, a part of himself that accuses him of being a father who has wrongly charged his daughters with ingratitude. In one of my other books I sought to demonstrate that Lear fails to work through his persecutory guilt; he verges on depressive guilt in his relations with Cordelia, the youngest daughter, but not in his relations with his two elder daughters. He accuses them of ingratitude and feels intense rancour towards them. He does this because he projects onto them his own sense of guilt, which is based on his self-image as an egoistic father incapable of love. Persecution, in fundamentally "persecutory" fantasies such as this, is connected to early signs of depression. The judge releases the accused. Why should he do so unless his intention is in part to offer reparation?

This "false justicer" who lets his ungrateful daughter go rather than punishing her is a sign that there is a desire for change inside the old father. In cases such as this, if a patient with a Lear syndrome has sufficient resources at his disposal (which I do not think can be assumed in Lear's case) and moreover is fortunate enough to have by his side an analyst or at least someone able to help him and to identify this "false justicer", someone who can act with both sensitivity and firmness, tactfully, with the right timing and the right pauses, he might manage to overcome the difficulties involved in first transforming persecutory guilt into depressive guilt and then moving on beyond it.[35] Before the birth of an "ungrateful" daughter a parent was born who failed, but for reasons beyond his control. Anyone who has shared the real pain of someone suffering from Lear-like conflicts knows what indescribable, harrowing torment is involved.

Often one of the signs that a start has been made in the transformation of a sense of guilt that only affects ourselves into one that involves others is the return of emotionally-laden past memories. In general, memories re-emerge progressively and not sporadically. This is an indicator that most people disregard, perhaps because it is not easy to understand why the transformation and the re-emergence should occur at the same time. On close examination one notices a broadening and deepening of the narrow and obsessively single-track mental space typical of those who see them-selves as persecuted. The patient himself and the figures that people his internal world gradually acquire a past and thus a future. Often dreams occur in which appear broad meadows, open valleys, extensive views of the sea, prospects with wider horizons.

The reawakening of memories does not exclude the possibility of moments of persecutory guilt. In traumatic situations, in periods of mourning or at moments of depression, these fresh outbreaks of persecutory guilt normally intensify. In particular, it has been found that attacks of internal envy occur: one part of us attacks the efforts of the other. And the envy heightens the feeling of being persecuted.

Persecution and omnipotence

> Pues el delito mayor del hombre es haber nacido.
> [. . . since man's greatest crime is being born.]
> (Calderón de la Barca)

The sense of guilt we have called depressive and which springs from the wrong we have done to others can be imposed in a persecutory manner which is either blatant or subtle. This modality is given too little attention, but I believe it is important. Earlier I talked in this context of "persecutory guilt" *tout court*; now, however, I am saying that the content can be depressive in nature. Obviously it is not just a question of labels; what is important, it seems to me, is the description of the phenomenon and its place in the model we are constructing.

As we attempt to describe depressive guilt which is imposed in a perse-cutory manner it might be useful to refer to a dream of G.G.'s which she had on two occasions and which I have already mentioned. The dream consisted of brief flashes which appeared to her like scenes from the film *The Gospel According to St Matthew* by Pier Paolo Pasolini. In these flashes Christ points a finger at her, enjoining her harshly to "Repent! Repent!". The content of the message is depressive: think about the evil you have caused and repent. But the modality of the injunction is persecutory. Leaving aside the associations and meanings of the dream, what I would like to emphasise is the fact that this modality does not seem to be an appropriate means of facilitating access to a new way of living one's sense of guilt. The task is absurd and to a certain extent impossible.[36] It is impossible and absurd because no time is given to work through the task. It is precisely this lack of time that Don Giovanni fights against:

Statue of the
Commendatore: Repent, change your life:
                This is the last moment!
Don Giovanni: No, no, I will not repent.
                Get you hence.
Commendatore: Repent, villain!
Don Giovanni: No, old fool.
Commendatore: Ah! There is no more time . . .[37]

One problem is that the reasons behind such an injunction to repent (not infrequently it comes from a highly idealised figure, as in the Pasolini film) are often explained in a hasty and confused manner. Occasionally, however, the problem is even more serious: the reasons given are vague – you are a sinner! – or are taken for granted or as universally understood – we are all by our very nature sinners! – and this further heightens the confusion and the anxiety. This is obviously not the case with Don Giovanni, who killed the Commendatore. In these situations the vehemence of the injunction designed to make the other feel guilty and repent (the pointing finger) prevails over any clear idea about the reasons for doing so. It only becomes possible to think about and work through this guilt when the pressure imposed by the injunction to repent is alleviated.

In such cases some therapists are often in a hurry to furnish the patient with an unconscious motivation for these unclear motives. They would no doubt have found one even for Pasolini's Christ as he appeared to our patient. However, by doing so, they risk creating misunderstandings and speeding up the process in a way which is harmful and does not allow the patients themselves to contribute to the investigation.

In the case of the most primitive forms of persecutory guilt, as we pointed out, the hostile figure can at first be nameless but may later acquire a name. In the case of forcefully imposed depressive guilt, the initially obscure motive may later take shape, particularly if the therapist does not venture to identify it. In these cases the technique used to cure the patient resembles an art, the art of putting everything in its right place. It is important that the process of revelation is allowed to unfold progressively in response to subtle stimuli and without interference. Each insensitive error of judgement made by the analyst can heighten the sense of persecution in these situations.

At all events, even when the guilt we have called depressive arises as the result of an internal maturing process, we remain within the ethos of guilt, and a more or less intense residue of persecution survives. At best the pressure typical of persecution is transformed into a necessity that pushes the patient towards reparation. And this represents a way out. But reparational activity often obscures persecution. When depressive guilt is imposed forcefully, what we experience is very similar to what is provoked by real persecutory guilt.

A very elementary example taken from everyday life of the gap between guilt and the reasons behind it might help us to get a better grasp of our theme. Let us think of the experience of a child who receives a deferred punishment. He has done something he should not have done, but the mother leaves the telling off to the father who will come home later. The child thus learns that he has done something blameworthy but in the meantime he has lost any memory or concept of what happened. While the injunction may lead to repentance and reparation, we can be certain that they will not be authentic acts coming from the heart, but will be imposed, induced behaviour. This type of imposed reparation is after all propitiation and is not one of the forms of reparation – manic, obsessive and mature – described by Klein.[38] Although the child may not always feel anger and resentment in such situations, he is very likely to feel bewilderment, confusion, disorientation and even disappointment towards his parents.

The extreme product of depressive guilt imposed in a persecutory manner when no other outlets can be found is melancholy, understood as a more serious form of depression. The extreme product of persecutory guilt *tout court* (the Erinyes) is madness. The distinction between these two types of guilt is thus useful in formulating a prognosis as well as a diagnosis.[39] Pasolini's Christ stands somewhere between the two.

When it is not attended by impositions but is the result of an authentic internal working through, the outbreak of depressive guilt has its own characteristics and is accompanied by pain. This pain is coupled with an interest in the person one thinks one has hurt or caused to suffer. It is followed by a growing sense of respect for the other, as well as by other feelings such as nostalgia. All these nuances, the richness of these distinctions might not have emerged spontaneously if Melanie Klein had not paved the way. I emphasise this point also to make it clear that my criticisms of Melanie Klein are based on admiration.

There are different types of pain. One needs to be very careful about this point. There is a very thin dividing-line between the pain that accompanies the sense of guilt and the pain without guilt which follows a period of intense guilt. It is the line that separates two different logics: on the one hand, the logic of guilt and on the other, the logic that transcends guilt. We shall be looking at this theme in some detail in the next chapter.

From the phenomenological point of view we can note different intensities in these two types of guilt. We can think of a continuum that starts from normality (or the threshold of normality) and ends up in the most severe pathology. As has been noted by various writers, guilt has deep-seated connections with omnipotence. There are some who think that the birth trauma provokes not only persecutory anxieties, but also a kind of proto-guilt, a potential sense of guilt, if you like, which is highly persecutory in nature. There is little point in getting involved in this sort of conjectural discussion. It seems to me rather improbable, given the scientific instruments at present available to us, that we will ever be able to tell whether birth provokes simple anxiety or the first signs of persecutory guilt.[40]

From Freud onwards, many analysts have tried to look at the workings of omnipotence and so-called "narcissistic omnipotence".[41] This expression refers to the attempts that we all make to do something about our inability to dominate our unconscious, a failure which at best expresses itself as a decline in self-esteem, at worst in a sense of disintegration.

Let us think for a moment about the propitiatory behaviour of primitive peoples. What does the uncultivated peasant do when a volcano destroys his house and harvest, or even kills one of his family? He takes the few objects of value he possesses, the animals that remain to him, and as soon as the magma allows him to do so, he throws them into the crater to propitiate the god that has punished him for his misdeeds. This is paradigmatic behaviour which, in the form of more or less archaic expressions and rituals and through the mediation of magical–religious institutions, has continued across the centuries.

Even up to the time of the *Discours sur l'histoire universelle* by J.-B. Bossuet (1627–1704), a manual compiled for the Dauphin of France in 1679, the fall of an empire was seen as a divine punishment for men's sins. A famous French preacher and theologian, Bossuet talks about a "secret judgement by God on the Roman Empire and on Rome herself . . .: a mystery which the Holy Spirit revealed to Saint John and which that great man, evangelist and prophet explained in *Revelations*".[42] God uses history to punish the guilty in a chain of events: through the Romans he carries out his revenge on the Jews; with the unification of the Empire he prepares the world for the coming of Christ; by means of the Barbarians he avenges the blood of the martyrs and persuades the people to abandon paganism, and so on.

Guilt – whether unconscious, conscious, introjected masochistically or projected sadistically onto others – also has the property to transform the guilty person into an agent, someone responsible, who can be blamed for events he never wanted to happen and of which he was only a victim.

> Oh, wretched and unhappy am I!
> Oh heavens, I must know,
> Since you treat me this way,
> what crime I committed
> against you by being born;
> . . .

(leaving aside, oh heavens,
the crime of being born) . . .[43]

These are the words (reminiscent of Job) spoken by Sigismund in "Life is a Dream" by Calderón de la Barca. The point that I am making is that the sense of guilt, however unpleasant and painful it may be, makes us into *agents*, and so transforms us into much stronger people than we really are.[44] In a way it brings us closer to the gods and makes us akin to them. Indeed, if it is true that the gods are made angry and driven wild by our sins, this means that we are the ones that impel them to act. This transforms the situation: the defenceless victim becomes a force that stands in some ways above the gods, just as even Zeus had to obey the Erinyes. Freud was moving in this direction when he wrote that man "has assured himself a direct influence on the divine will and with it a share in the divine omni-potence".[45] Sin goes beyond this and seems to bring about – obviously in a secular sense – a real reversal; basically God's punishments result from the (free) acts of man. We can also speak of a reversal when we meet with an accident that turns into a spiritual medicine. In this case the more serious the accident, the more that just punishment becomes balm for our soul.

The Biblical myth of God's destruction of Sodom transfigures the cli-matic and geographical situation of that desolate, barren land: the inhos-pitable desert is seen as having been the result of divine punishment, which in turn was triggered by wickedness, by man's sins. This idea has important diagnostic consequences. Different degrees of omnipotence correspond to different degrees of intensity of guilt. People who feel responsible for major catastrophes are much more fragile (and therefore in need of omnipotence) than those who blame themselves for minor accidents.

The Child is Father of the Man

There is one discovery made by psychoanalysis that has had far-reaching repercussions on clinical practice and consequently on analysts' strategies and interpretations. It is sometimes termed the "genetic" factor and Wordsworth has a telling phrase that expresses it very well: "The Child is Father of the Man".[46] Behind this phenomenon (accepted also by paedi-atricians and, albeit imperfectly, even by public opinion) lies the fact that the very first moments of life inform the future of an individual. An obvious comparison can be made with embryo-genesis: the zygote already contains all the information necessary for our development into adult complexity; the environment can, however, have an effect on this information.

When we are involved in an emotionally fraught situation with those we love or those we depend on and this situation is so painful that it becomes unconscious, it does not for this reason stop influencing our lives, thoughts and actions. An impulse arises in us to resolve or bring to a conclusion old situations that have remained conflictual or incomplete, even though, thanks to our various defence mechanisms, we are no longer conscious of what we would like to resolve or conclude. At each stage of our life we insert the past into our present. Not only do we live in the present or for the present, but we are also driven to repeat unresolved or traumatic situations from the past – in particular, the enormous difficulties of our early childhood.

The tendency among many Freudian psychoanalysts today is to leave aside the genetic aspect and to concentrate on the relationship between analyst and patient, in the present, in the here and now. In my view, this approach is extremely limited. If analysis is to be liberating, the analyst should remain an instrument of knowledge through which – by means of transference – the patient can realise the extent to which the past continues to impinge on the present. If the analyst, in his attempt to eliminate his patient's conflicts (however "unreal" that situation may be), sets himself up as the sole privileged interlocutor and interprets everything by referring it to the current situation and the transference relationship, without reference to the past, I believe that there can be only two explanations for this: either the analyst is a genius and possesses superhuman wisdom, or he will unavoidably risk letting the therapeutic relationship degenerate at times into a *folie à deux*.

The process whereby the past is reproduced in the present is highly complex. First it needs to be said that if it has been misunderstood, this is partly due to a tendency already present in Freud himself. In linking adult behaviour patterns to a certain moment or an important relationship in childhood, I do not think that any particular moment (say, the period of breastfeeding) or relationship (the child at the mother's breast) should be seen as the only cause of certain adult pathologies. In my view, the point is rather that that moment and the vicissitudes of that early relationship have, together with other factors, created the premises for the manifestation of those undesired results. In this sense we could say that they are the necessary precondition and thus the possible "predominant" cause.[47] Unconsciously, however, the patient can experience that "concomitant cause" as the sole cause, and this point needs to be clarified. Here the two views of psychoanalysis – one which sees it as a kind of general psychology (attentive to concomitant causes) and the other which sees it as an instrument for making sense of patients' ghosts – diverge somewhat. I think there is a distinction here that has been ignored and this has given rise to a heated debate between supporters of psychoanalysis as a causal science and supporters of psychoanalysis as a form of hermeneutics. Indeed, the theoretical split between Klein and Winnicott, which we shall discuss later, is probably a reflection of this divergence.

The person who indirectly suggested posing the question about whether the sense of guilt can also be understood as a defence against the sense of impotence was the Scottish psychoanalyst Ronald Fairbairn. His work was appreciated by Ernest Jones, and at one point by Klein, but has subsequently been largely neglected despite periodic attempts to stress his importance.

What follows are some of the main points taken from his short section on "Guilt as a defence against the release of bad objects".[48] Shortly before this Fairbairn had asked himself from where bad objects drew the power they exert over the individual. If objects appear as bad to the child, why should he internalise them? "Why does he not simply reject them in the same way as he might reject a nasty pudding or cod liver oil?", he asks. In fact, he replies, it is not easy for a child to turn down cod liver oil, as we know from personal experience; he would if he could, but he is not allowed to. The same applies to bad objects: "However much he might want to reject them, he cannot remove them. They impose themselves on him; he can offer no resistance because they exercise power over him. So he is forced to internalise them in an attempt to control them."

But this is precisely where the snags come in. By attempting to control them he internalises objects which have power over him in the external world and which also keep their dominance over him in his internal world. In a word, the child finds himself "possessed" by these bad objects, as if they were malign spirits. But that is not all: "The child not only internalises his bad objects because they have power over him and he has to try to control them, but also, and above all, because he needs them".

If his parents are bad, the child cannot reject them, even if they do not impose themselves on him, because he cannot do without them. Even if they neglect or mistreat him, he cannot reject them, because this only heightens his need for them. But the internalised bad objects feed the Super-Ego which then mounts an attack and induces feelings of guilt. This amounts to saying that the need for bad parents is paid for in the coin of guilt. Analysts with experience of second analyses know that this phenomenon – through transference – often affects patients who have undergone analysis with bad analysts. In order to save the first analyst (and thus to avoid the feeling that they have been damaged by him, or that through him they have wasted a precious part of their life), patients prefer to feel guilty towards him.

As we can see, the external factors emphasised by Fairbairn are very different from those stressed by Melanie Klein. His hypotheses seem to provide us with an explanation of the paradoxical behaviour of young criminals mentioned in the opening lines of Chapter 1.

Fairbairn moves on from this point to reach the conclusion that the paradoxical need of the child (and also of the immature adult) obliges the analyst to take a particular problem into account. An analysis that aims only at relieving the sense of guilt can easily fail as therapy, because removing the patient's defence against the sense of guilt can be accompanied by an increase in the repression of persecutory objects. "I am fairly certain," concludes Fairbairn, "that . . . the deepest source of resistance is the fear that free rein is given to objects residing in the unconscious, because when these bad objects are released, the world around the patient will be peopled by demons too frightening to be faced."

Removing persecutory objects from the unconscious is one of the therapist's principal goals. Only when the internalised bad objects are, so to speak, brought out into the open can there be any hope that the patient will be able to free himself from that particular need for them which we have mentioned. Only in this way is it possible to bring sado-masochistic relationships to an end.

This in many ways remarkable line of thought points to what I personally consider the greatest tactical and strategic problem in the psychoanalytic treatment of the sense of guilt. According to Fairbairn, the best way to obtain a positive result is to use "prudence in interpretation at the level of guilt or the super-ego". Although on the one hand these interpretations may alleviate the sense of guilt, on the other "they can have the effect of intensifying the repression of internalised bad objects and thus leave unresolved the investment of these objects". But this line of strategy brings with it other consequences: for example, the analyst then needs to show the patient carefully and in detail how he himself is experienced by the patient as a persecutor. And this has to be done before he draws attention to the patient's childhood experiences that make him transform the analyst into a persecutor. In other words, he should not hesitate to become a persecutory object: if he does this with great simplicity and tact he will be able to take the drama out of the patient's persecutory experience.

Chapter 3

The "schizophrenic paradox": two types of logic

> . . . in the same way as cause attracts effect,
> so guilt, or rather the guilty
> person, attracts punishment.
> (Hans Kelsen, *Society and Nature*)

Perhaps the moment has come to discuss a state or condition in which we can all find ourselves. It is not easy to describe, and my first instinct is to exaggerate a little and call it a "schizophrenic paradox". Most ordinary mortals are forced to live with this paradox, at least all those who have not achieved – and probably never will achieve – the wisdom of the saint but who do not subscribe fully to the ethos of guilt.

The split that lies at the heart of this paradoxical state results from the fact that what I have called the two types of ethos – the ethos of guilt and the ethos that transcends guilt (which for the moment I shall call "tragic responsibility") – belong to two different systems.[1] If an individual is to move from one system to the other he needs to perform a kind of quantum leap that also involves accepting a degree of solitude – and probably much more besides.

What do we mean by the term "ethos of guilt"? Is it a purely clinical phenomenon – in other words, is it a disturbance that causes suffering in patients – or can it be found elsewhere? If we expand the notion to include collective phenomena such as ethics, laws, customs and even human thought as a whole, is this not likely simply to cause confusion? My view is that it is not limited to therapeutic practice. The ethos of guilt aims high; it seeks to explain everything in a reductive manner (and it is necessarily inadequate when dealing with reality in all its manifold aspects), and its main aim is to forestall the incursion of the tragic dimension. But let us take things one at a time.

We could initially define the ethos of guilt as an approach that underlies many human attitudes, thoughts and behaviours where not only a sense of guilt but also blame and responsibility are involved.

Its basic assumptions were "challenged" by certain deterministic theories which maintained that human beings are conditioned not only in the metaphysical sense but also in various other ways: physically, biologically, morally and psychologically. One such theory was Galen's complex determinism while another was the psychoanalysis of Freud, who maintained the principle of psychic determinism. Freud was a very special kind of determinist, but we shall look at this point later.[2]

The crux of Freudian determinism was its discovery of the dynamic unconscious. Of course, one can either believe or not believe in the existence of the unconscious; there are many well-known psychological theories and philosophies which deny that it exists. However, those who do believe that there is such a thing as the unconscious and that it exerts a strong influence on all of us ought then to face up to all the consequences. They cannot accept some and not others which might upset the geometry of their thoughts. If there is such a thing as the dynamic unconscious, its effect is to be felt not only in the analyst's room. In trying to explain what I mean I shall talk about the law (and in particular, penal law). I realise that this is a bold step because, however wide-ranging my example may be, it alone cannot do justice to the breadth of the subjects I shall be dealing with.

It is possible to define guilt as the violation of a norm. From this point of view guilt simply means that something "illicit" has been done, a person has broken the law. The German jurist and philosopher Rudolf von Jhering (1873) wrote that in ancient times there was a sense of justice that interpreted any violation of a right in terms of the wrong suffered by the subject "without taking into account the innocence or degree of guilt [*Verschuldung*] of the adverse party, and thus demanded expiation in equal measure from the innocent and the guilty". This view seems to exclude the subjective dimension of guilt.

However, even the Romans were interested in the personal aspect of guilt (culpability) and tried to distinguish between different subjective degrees of guilt. They talked about general guilt, slight guilt, etc.; distinctions which would later lead to endless discussions about the relevance of negligence, imprudence and inexperience when a law was broken. General guilt (*culpa lata*, which depends on *non intelligere id quod omnes intelligunt*, not knowing what everyone knows) is distinguished from slight guilt (*culpa levis*), etc. All this will lead to the important distinction between *malice*, which in penal law, for example, generally presupposes awareness that one is committing (or could commit) what the law defines as a crime, and *guilt*, which does not presuppose awareness. The fact is, however, that the legal situation is even more complicated.

The ethos, or logic, of guilt can perhaps be defined more precisely by means of contrast. We can better understand what it is if we accept the hypothesis that there are people capable of entering into an ethos which transcends it. This is an ethos that transcends the purely subjective dimension of guilt at the same time as recognising that a person has definitely broken a law (for example, he or she has committed a murder). It sees through and around this guilt and so is not interested in it according to the specific ethos of blame. This is not because, like the primitive law which von Jhering talked about, it embraces the idea of individual responsibility in all cases, but rather for the opposite reason: it accepts the idea that the Ego is subject to conditioning that can affect its responsibility.

The perspective that makes it possible to look beyond blame is interested in understanding and not judging. If you will, it is the observation point sought by the social scientist: the anthropologist, the sociologist, the historian. Why is it not possible to regard the psychoanalyst – the good clinician – as a social scientist? There is a reason for distinguishing between the two positions. The psychoanalyst is called upon to use this different ethos at the same time as being emotionally involved. By virtue of his function he is called upon to experience "compassion" in the etymological sense of sharing pain. Social scientists – anthropologists, historians – limit themselves to understanding human beings and the laws that govern their behaviour; their job is to observe and describe with detachment. Any psychoanalyst who was under the illusion that he could operate with detachment would soon be forced to realise how impossible this is. At best he might be able to adopt a position of involved detachment, but even this would take years to learn.

Moreover, the analyst is asked to facilitate a change in the patient, to free him or her from the pangs of guilt, precisely at the same time as he analyses his own emotional interaction with the patient. And he has to do this although the analysand encourages the analyst, in many different ways, to incriminate him/her and, in other ways, to feel guilty. Analysis faces us with extraordinary mental states and tasks.

Generally – and personally I agree with this position – the ethos which transcends guilt is considered inadequate to guarantee the rules governing human society, nor does it fulfil our innate need for justice. For these purposes the perspective of pure comprehension is of no use; what is needed is an ethos which is based on the assumption of individual guilt and responsibility. By way of expanding on this point, I would like to draw on the words of Albert Camus who, in his *Reflections on the Guillotine*, declared himself to be worlds away from the morbid complacency of humanitarians for whom "values and responsibilities become confused, all crimes become equal and innocence loses its rights".[3] Camus makes a noble and powerful case against the death penalty within the ethos of guilt: "The fact that Cain is not killed but bears a mark of reprobation in the eyes of men is the lesson we must draw from the Old Testament". If we are to transcend the ethos of guilt, however, and to face up to the very different laws of tragedy, we should not overlook another aspect of the story:

> In the course of time Cain brought some of the fruits of the soil as an offering to the Lord. But Abel brought fat portions from some of the firstborn of his flock. The Lord looked with favour on Abel and his offering, but on Cain and his offering he did not look with favour. So Cain was very angry, and his face was downcast.[4]

Here one has to ask oneself questions about the effects that unequal treatment by a father (or mother) can have on the psychic world of the child – not with the aim of absolving or condemning, but of understanding.

Staying within the context of the law, the ethos of guilt normally starts from the assumption that in the last analysis each individual acts freely, except in extreme cases as defined by the law (such as not being in possession – either fully or partially – of one's faculties), and that he or she is therefore responsible and punishable. The psychoanalyst, by focusing on the unconscious, enters into the logic of conditioning – psychic conditioning. I repeat: it is possible to disagree with Freud and psychoanalysis (even within psychoanalysis there are thinkers who have argued that the Ego retains a margin of relative freedom), but it still seems to me that psychoanalysis needs to be discussed as a discipline which calls free will into question and examines it on a new basis.

In my opinion, the corollary of this view is not as one might expect, namely that the therapeutic method of psychoanalysis robs the individual of responsibility. This is another of the paradoxes we shall observe together.

The expression I used above ("except in extreme cases") points to the Achilles' heel of the claim advanced by the ethos of guilt that it can guarantee that justice be fully done. Only a system of justice with high expectations of perfection can deny the possible practical effect produced by the will of human beings who may also act in response to unconscious forces.

Who decides what constitutes an extreme case? Who defines it? Why should a schizophrenic be considered as being not in full possession of his faculties as opposed to a criminal who has committed several murders for which he has been condemned to life imprisonment and who from a psychoanalytical point of view suffers from a congenital pathology of the Super-Ego?[5]

We might also add that simply by adopting a different theory the same individual changes from being "neurotic", in other words, someone suffering from a mild mental illness which would not exclude imputability, to becoming a serious case of a personality trying to defend himself against psychosis. When he was in the Sant'Anna hospital in Ferrara, the author of *Gerusalemme Liberata*, Torquato Tasso, was suspected of lying about his illness, but by the time we reach the age of positivism Cesare Lombroso judged him to be epileptic and paranoid.

The relationship between the individuals who are bound together in the state and the state itself can be conceived in different ways. The right to punish as it is at present understood in the west, in other words, as an exclusive prerogative of the sovereign state, is a relatively recent development.

The turning-point came towards the end of the French Revolution. Originally it was thought that the individual who suffered a wrong had right on his side. Violence authorised the aggrieved person or group to take personal revenge against the offender. Revenge does not, however, always presuppose the breaking of a law. It is possible to take revenge for a wrong that does not involve a crime as defined by the law: a critic reviews a book harshly and the author takes revenge by excluding him from a committee. And revenge did not have to stand in direct relation to the nature or seriousness of the offence. Later, the law of retaliation, *lex talionis*, introduced, as we have already noted, the idea of the proportionality of the response (from *talis*, meaning equal). Revenge is probably the response that comes closest to our instinctual, biological reaction when faced with a wrong, an aggression which in our inner world we experience subjectively as such, independently of what the legislator or even our community thinks about it.

Thanks to the supreme effort of morally upright men, Western civilisation went on to create modern law. The probable ultimate aim was to avoid confusion between guilt on the one hand and evil and immorality on the other, and to rid punishment of the elements of revenge and reprisal. Among those who paved the way for this development were thinkers such as Montesquieu and Kant. One of their precursors was Hobbes, who identified the origin of the state in a contract whereby individuals gave up rights based on force – including the right to exact revenge, which they enjoyed in the state of nature – in favour of a state which became the source of all right and the administrator of justice.[6]

The question is, however, whether this concentration of power really meant that justice ceased to be based on revenge or sadism. A positive reply to this question would only be possible once the Egos of men and women, the Egos first and foremost of legislators, but also of jurists, judges, lawyers and their experts, were endowed with full free will. In other words, when forming a judgment, these people would have to be able to leave aside – as extraneous to neutral judgment – primitive, unconscious emotions and pressures. The full free will I am referring to would imply the ability to set aside these distorting elements. The same would apply, obviously, to the work of the legislator.

Since this necessary psychological state (full free will) is not a realistic prospect, the social–juridical problem must be solved either by disregarding it altogether (with all the attendant risks that implies), or by seeking remedies in the use of formal legal and procedural instruments (strict categorisation of crimes and punishments, rigorous prescription of procedural guarantees, the obligation to justify verdicts using correct logic, a formal monitoring of the reasons for the verdict carried out by higher judges). These are remedies that are in fact adopted by the most advanced legal systems, although usually no appreciation is shown of the value of monitoring the risks of interference I have referred to. Otherwise one would have to conclude that the great construction of the law is a noble endeavour undermined by various types of interference, including the urges that come from the unconscious. If we think of how we really are as opposed to how we should be, we realise that it is not so easy to exclude the dark return of primitive conflicts.

All this is confirmed by the fact that in dispensing punishment the legislator provides for margins of judgment, setting down, for example, a minimum and a maximum term of imprisonment. The judge can, for example, fit the punishment to the seriousness of the crime committed. But then it cannot be excluded that his verdict expresses a subjective assessment of blame and punishment. There are crimes that are considered "abhorrent". Such particularly "brutal" or "repugnant" crimes deserve an "exemplary" punishment because the person who committed the crime is judged to be cruel or inhuman. He or she is not considered simply crazy or conditioned by various factors. Despite efforts to be objective, human beings think and judge on the basis of their ideologies, their conflicts and their drives. As proof of these statements one need only think of so-called "crimes against humanity". Here the tendency is to apply a modern *ius gentium*, suspending the statute of limitations and disregarding the precept of *nulla poena sine lege*, for such crimes might not have been deemed illegal by the legislation in force at the time and in the country where they were committed.

One society imposes punishment on the basis of guilt, another as a deterrent, and yet others for educational purposes or to placate the disturbed forces of the savannah. But can we really exclude the possibility that there is no spirit of vendetta underlying these different positions? In my opinion, the idea of a judge who is untouched by emotions, moral judgement or revenge is a further illustration of the notion of the neutrality of the observer typical of the positivism on which most modern thinking was based up to the time of Werner Heisenberg (and beyond). We shall return to this theme later. The basis of the modern concept of justice is neutrality, the independence of the judge's judgment. It is thus logical that the unconscious creates an enormous problem, a problem that can be denied (the unconscious does not exist), circumscribed (the whole thing is a clinical question), or accepted.

If we accept the existence of the unconscious – with all that that implies – it becomes easier to gain access to the tragic dimension. This is also true with regard to the judge who has to pass sentence and who is aware of the factors that condition human existence. It is "tragic" for a judge to have to condemn someone on the basis of arguments put forward by technical consultants when he is aware of their extreme limitations; it is tragic to convict someone in order to comply with the demand that justice create a deterrent, or for some other reason. The same judge, however, would not be conscious of any conflict if he were to think solely within the ethos of guilt. This precludes him from seeing how the defendant has been and continues to be subject to a series of pressures he is unable to cope with.[7]

Guilt follows convoluted paths both within the individual and within the social, juridical and religious framework. Humans are the only animals that are capable of creating symbols, but equally they are the only animals that can say that they feel guilty. The aspect of psychoanalysis that one is tempted to call "criminal" was that which broke established rules as it delved down into the complexity of our animal nature. This is where we encounter our drives, needs and desires, our impotence and basic fragility. And psychoanalysis explores all this in relation to the responses of the family, culture and society that we all experience from the very beginning of our lives – but also in terms of the individual's decision-making ability.

Anatomy of the ethos of guilt

The normal citizen – a category to which, failing proof to the contrary, even psychoanalysts and therapists belong – tends to accept, at least in some basic respects, the rules of the systems within which he lives (family, institutions, state, international community). If he suffers damage or harm, if someone causes him to suffer or hurts him, he can – or at least would like to – demand revenge, claim his rights, ask for justice. But then he must blame someone. Only within the ethos of blame can he hate the murderer who kills a loved one or accuse the lover who leaves him. Either that or, as we have said, he will forgive them. Blame is like a judge; it looks for a culprit. The ethos that transcends it, however, tries to understand without judging (in theory this ought to be the aim of all therapists: to seek to understand and to help others understand the source of their suffering).

Mary Douglas, the eminent contemporary anthropologist, doubted whether a community could be founded on the "categorical refusal" to apportion blame, no matter whether the person to be blamed was a persecutor, a rival or an enemy. When Michael Thompson presented her with "proof", she regarded it with suspicion, expecting to find it based on poor fieldwork and uninformed research about the conflicts under study. She was inclined to believe that, if at all, this could only happen in very small communities. She later changed her mind when she studied Thompson's research on Buddhist Sherpa communities in Nepal.[8] From a methodological point of view the psychoanalyst is in many ways perhaps more subtle and demanding than the anthropologist: in order to be convinced of the absence of guilt, he would need to know to what extent researchers had distinguished guilt from sense of guilt and whether they had considered, to take one example, the defences that can be used against the impulse to attribute blame or to feel guilty. In particular, he would want to know whether defence mechanisms such as denial and splitting or compensations such as reaction-formation had been taken into consideration.

Efforts have certainly been made, within the ethos of guilt, to restrict the interference of the most primitive and destructive impulses. Mankind has made concrete positive steps in the sphere of punishment, at least in some areas of civil life. There is perhaps no other field in which the human imagination has run riot to such an extent and given such evidence of sadism as in its choice of punishments. From the earliest times up to the period when the postulates of juridical enlightenment began to gain ground, punishments were aimed less at the juridical prerogatives of the condemned person (his personal and property rights) than at his body. Hence the term "corporal punishment", which is usually used to refer to certain punishments up to the end of the eighteenth century. In *ancien régime* France punishments were divided into "capital", "ignominious" and "non-ignominious". All these punishments presupposed different forms of the moral and physical degradation of the guilty person. The principal form of capital punishment was the death penalty, which not only took away life but did so in rituals involving sophisticated tortures that varied according to the social rank of the condemned person and the crime committed.

Already at the time of *The Odyssey* there had been an ignominious form of putting a person to death, or ending one's life, namely hanging. After the massacre of Penelope's suitors, Telemachus went against the orders of his father. Ulysses had wanted the maidservants to be put to the sword, but Telemachus decided to hang them instead:

> I swear I will not give a decent death to women who heaped insults on my head and on my mother's, and slept with the suitors.[9]

In pre-Enlightenment France, hanging was reserved for peasants, beheading for nobles, the wheel for the worst crimes, burning at the stake for crimes against religion and quartering for the most serious crimes against the state. Afflictive punishments – in other words those designed to cause torment and anguish – included the pillory, cutting out the tongue and cutting off the lips, branding, public flogging, hanging by the armpits or at the thighs or breasts. Punishments which today we would consider more "normal", such as forced labour for life or for a certain period, imprisonment, exile and fines, were less frequently inflicted.

Thanks especially to Cesare Beccaria (and to the influence Pietro Verri had on him) and to thinkers such as Jeremy Bentham, the process began which was to lead to a progressive reduction in the use of the death penalty and corporal punishment in favour of detention and monetary fines. The time must have been ripe if one considers that Beccaria's *Dei delitti e delle pene* (*Of Crimes and Punishments*) went through six editions in eighteen months. According to Foucault, "between the end of the eighteenth and the beginning of the nineteenth century the grim festival of punishment drew to a close". A period commenced in which the whole basis of punishment was reassessed in Europe and the United States. Modern theories emerged which emphasised the dignity of the individual. People started thinking of ways of improving the prison system and the first attempts were made to study the psychology of crime and to classify the various types of criminal, activities which were later to become the provinces of anthropology and criminal sociology.

The spectacle of public punishment disappeared, and "the ceremony of punishment tended to decline". Judgment was still passed on acts that were considered wrong under the law and labelled as crimes and felonies, but at the same time judgment was also passed on the "passions, instincts, anomalies, infirmities, maladjustments, effects of environment or heredity; acts of aggression [were] punished, so also, through them, [was] aggressivity; rape, but at the same time perversions; murders, but also drives and desires".

The final verdict has been pronounced also by drawing on all the notions that have been common among doctors and jurists since the nineteenth century and which, under the pretext of explaining an act to a judge, "are in fact a way of defining an individual", of using a theory to judge whether or not he was free to commit a certain offence.[10]

The schizophrenic paradox does not mean abandoning the necessary aspects of a system based on the logic of guilt (otherwise "all crimes become equal and innocence loses its rights", as Camus feared) but seeing things from a non-judgemental perspective, not condemning but understanding (comprehending and explaining). This paradox appears to be extremely hard to negotiate. Perhaps there are mystics capable of doing so. It is difficult to straddle the two "logics" or live only within the logic of tragic responsibility.

Or rather, it is difficult if we claim to be consistent, if we try to act without wavering or accepting compromises. In many institutional contexts people feel forced to observe the ethos of blame while at the same time realising – looking at things from the other perspective – that by doing so they are sacrificing something very important. As a member of a psychoanalytical association I have on occasions voted in favour of the expulsion of members I thought harmful to others (especially to patients), although personally I felt the people in question were in need of care and not punishment. But I had to accept the equally tragic fact that the people who had to be expelled did not want to be helped.

Proust – or at least the Proust that emerges from *La Recherche* – seems to have had a non-judgemental cast of mind and to have been able to observe things from a tragic perspective. But did this ability abandon him when he described the insensibility of the Duke of Guermantes? In the course of a conversation with Alberto Moravia, Jorge Luis Borges, who clearly liked to *épater le bourgeois*, made the comment that *Crime and Punishment* was primarily a story about a crime and not about remorse, also confessing that he preferred Conrad to Dostoyevsky. In *Lord Jim*, Borges felt, the central themes are courage and honour.

Is this in fact true? Did Borges really see the essential themes of Conrad's story? Or was he not rather denying the very existence of the laws that govern the sense of guilt? On the night the *Patna*, an old ship packed with pilgrims, is about to sink, its chief mate Jim, "in an act of cowardice", saves his own skin by jumping overboard onto the only lifeboat together with three other white men, thus abandoning the passengers to their fate. As it happens, the *Patna* manages to stay afloat and Jim is brought before a court of inquiry, from which he emerges bearing the stigma of disgrace. The question is: knowing that the inquest will condemn him to dishonour and conclude his tragic destiny, does Jim, unlike the other three who took to the lifeboat, decide to face the court of inquiry out of a sense of honour or out of a sense of (perhaps unconscious) guilt? Is it not the sense of guilt that leads the individual inexorably from unconsciousness to expiation? Does Conrad, all of whose novels reveal much about the complexity of the human soul, judge his characters? This is the impression we get. An author who does not judge, on the other hand, is Oscar Lewis in *The Children of Sanchez*. Flaubert, however, does, although he disguises it very cleverly and some readers don't even notice it.

The non-judgemental perspective can also be found in other art forms and is often shared by those who are able to empathise with the artist. Let us take an example from the cinema: Woody Allen's *Interiors*. The film examines, from the point of view of three sisters (a writer, an actress and a brilliant young woman without any particular talents), the effects on a wealthy bourgeois family of the father's unexpected decision to leave the cold relationship he has with his wife in order to marry a rather vulgar but vivacious woman. The man's first wife reacts by walking into the sea and committing suicide. Even among those who find themselves sharing Allen's point of view – which is *not* to express a judgement – there are probably very few who realise that the perspective they embrace in the darkness of the cinema stands in contrast with the ethos of the institutions within which they lead most of their daily lives.

Another example taken from the cinema is *Dead Man Walking*, directed by Tim Robbins and based on the book by Helen Prejean (the nun who was played in the film by Susan Sarandon). The framework within which the whole story of the man sentenced to death for rape and multiple killing is described is Catholic, but it also features many of the elements we are trying to illustrate: egoism, paranoia, inability to pardon, the need for revenge, the important cathartic function of confessing crime, the psycho-logical complex of the murderer in the light of socio-familial factors – all this is seen and presented without the slightest concession to sentimentality or moralism. Unlike Pasolini's Christ, as remembered by my patient G.G., the nun brings the murderer to confess because she is able to wait and not to force things. She achieves this result without judging too much, but basically by accepting the tragedy that surrounds her, a tragedy in which the murderer is not so much the protagonist as the victim.

When one identifies with the ethos that transcends guilt, one realises that it is essential not to demonise the sense of guilt. Later, when we go on to talk of guilt as a signal, we shall see that, while it is true that the sense of guilt is tied up with a feeling of omnipotence and thus readily becomes a cause of intense suffering, it is also true that it can play an important role in the development of the individual and his relations with the community. In moderate doses, a sense of guilt not only promotes common bonds (whether they be religious, ideological or social), but also – more import-antly – contributes towards creating our sense of identity and gives meaning to the lives of many people.

On the other hand, the perspective of tragic responsibility involves a non-moralistic vision not only of guilt and human destructiveness but also of other reprehensible feelings, such as envy. The German anthro-pologist H. Schoeck (1966) studied the subject of envy and writes about the *muru* attacks carried out by the aborigines of New Zealand. *Muru* in Maori means "to plunder". Such incursions are directed against members of the community accused of some crime against the community itself. But Schoeck shows that these crimes are in fact pretexts; anyone who owns something desirable can be subjected to a *muru*. Any deviation from the norm of daily life, any expression of individuality, even an accident that has left someone an invalid for a short time, offers a suitable excuse for the community to attack that unfortunate person and his personal goods.

A man whose wife has committed adultery, another whose child has died, a third who has set fire to grassland and let the blaze spread to a burial ground: all these represent cases in which a person might become the object of a foray, a *muru*. Those attacked do not defend themselves, because they know that any possible resistance would lead to injury and deprive them of the chance to take part in the next plundering raid. But in this way, comments Schoeck, "most movable goods passed from one person to another and gradually became public property".

The impression that emerges from Schoeck's research is that envy in communities such as this, or among the bushmen in the Kalahari desert in Africa, has a similar function to the control of hubris in Homer's society. Property owners must share their goods, and it is envy that forces them to do so. No one can put himself above the others.[11]

To return to the sense of guilt: the fact that there is probably no way of eliminating or avoiding it (except when we use defence mechanisms to give ourselves this illusion) does not mean that, at least in certain circumstances, it cannot be worked out in a more practical way, and thus somehow "negotiated". The psychoanalyst, whether or not someone has shown him how, is called upon by the very nature of his work to discover this more practical approach. On this point, I think, all schools will be in agreement. But any such theoretical agreement will once again prove to be worth very little in the face of the problems that remain to be solved.

The ethos of guilt and how to overcome it

> Full of doubt I stand,
> Whether I should repent me now of sin
> By me done and occasioned, or rejoice
> Much more, that much
> more good thereof shall spring
> (Milton, *Paradise Lost*)[12]

The ethos that distinguishes itself from the ethos of blame is founded on empathetic comprehension.[13] We come to understand that the events that give rise to guilt (the sense of guilt, the need to blame) are the result of a combination of hereditary, instinctual, familial, biological, social and other causes which we intuit rather than know. Freeing oneself from the ethos of guilt does not mean losing the ability to recognise what is good and what is evil. This is precisely the point that those who see every ethical issue in terms of blame and responsibility find most difficult to accept. We shall come back to this point later.

Comprehension is hardly ever our first reaction. The immediate response to something unpleasant, to a threat or to aggression, can often be violent and Manichaean. When a patient of mine was narrowly missed by a police patrol car that rode up onto the pavement as she was coming out of a shop, only avoiding crushing her to death by a split second, her reaction, with fear still in her bones, was not one of comprehension.

Today, some of the forces that affect people's behaviour appear at first sight to be clear – upbringing, for example. Of other causes, such as inherited personality factors, we can have only a vague and uncertain notion. Of yet others we may feel that most of them will forever remain unknown. What is absolutely clear, however, is the fact that the "moral" principles of the ethos of guilt lose their meaning and are replaced by different values. Once one has accepted the idea that there is such a thing as an unconscious upon which various pressures act and which can receive imprinting, the intentions of the individual must be re-examined and redefined.

Let us go back to *Crime and Punishment*, which Borges remarkably described as the story of a crime rather than a story of remorse (it is in fact the story of a crime *and* remorse). One can argue that this novel is an attempt to look at various forces acting on the human soul. There is a letter that Dostoyevsky wrote to Katkov, the editor of the periodical *The Russian Messenger*, in which he proposes the plot of a short story (originally this was the planned format):

> It is the psychological report of a crime . . . a young man is sent down from university. His origins are petty bourgeois; he is living in dire poverty. He decides to break out of his sad situation, acting out of a fragility of spirit and a lack of solid foundations and seduced by certain strange, "incomplete" ideas that are in the air today. He decides to kill an old woman, the widow of a councillor who lends money against security. She is stupid, deaf, sick, greedy – her interest rates are those of a usurer – a nasty old woman who bleeds people dry and torments her younger sister, who works in her house. "She is of no use to anyone", "Why should she live?", "If she were of any use, even to one single human being . . .", and so on.
>
> After brooding over such questions for some time he eventually decides to kill her and steal her money. His aim is to protect the well-being of his mother, who lives in the provinces, to free his sister, *dame de compagnie* in the house of a man of property, from her employer's licentious enticements – temptations that would ruin her – finish his studies, go abroad and later become an honest man forever. He is resolute and inflexible in doing "his duty towards mankind", who will, obviously, annul his crime, if killing a deaf, stupid, nasty and sick old woman who doesn't even know herself why she is alive can even be called a crime.
>
> Although normally such crimes are difficult to carry out – what I mean is that they are always committed carelessly, leaving behind obvious evidence and clues, and the guilty party is almost always caught – he manages by sheer chance to execute his plan swiftly and successfully.
>
> A full month passes before the final catastrophe. There are no reasons to suspect him, and during this month the psychological process of the crime unfolds. Insoluble questions assail the murderer; unexpected and unsuspected feelings torment his heart. The truth of God and the law of men achieve their due effect, and he ends up having to report himself, in order to enter human society again, albeit in a prison. His consciousness of isolation, his feeling of distance from humanity, which he felt immediately after committing the murder, cause him great suffering. The law of truth and human nature triumphs. The criminal – without even showing any resistance – decides

to accept punishment in order to redeem his act. (I find it difficult, however, to explain my thoughts fully.) In my story I advance the idea that the judicial punishment that is meant to punish the crime frightens the criminal much less than one thinks – at least less than legislators think – because he himself morally demands it.

One might suppose that the ethos of guilt owes its success partly to the fact that, as I have already briefly suggested, it appreciates some connections but is blind to others. It simplifies reality and is thus easier to transmit. The impression is that the problem exists on two levels: established stereotypes and prejudices can have a strong effect but even more powerful is the effect of ways of thinking which lack complexity and subtlety on uneducated, lazy, dogmatic minds, or simply on the less intelligent. On the level of personal experience, the ethos we have termed tragic responsibility always gives the impression of reflecting a more complete vision of the world. But the simplified thinking which characterises guilt is also the type of thought required by institutions, which try to cope with difficulties by following the line of least resistance. Ponderous institutions do not always give people the chance to work out intricate problems. And the result of this is often objectively cynical policies and strategies. However, none of this, it seems to me, suffices to explain the mysterious triumph of the ethos of guilt.

Anyone wishing to work in a scientific field has to accept that uncertainty is an integral part of what they do. The need to decide creates anxiety and feelings of guilt. Every step we take, especially when we have to make decisions that are important to us, we fear that our actions will bring down harm and punishment upon us; the envy of our rivals, for example, or the meanness of the revenue authorities (anxiety, persecutory sense of guilt), or we may fear that mistaken decisions we may have made because of our inability to cope with our problems will cause harm to ourselves and others (anxiety, depressive guilt, or rather, responsible guilt).[14]

But uncertainty comes in different forms which in turn depend on varying degrees of complexity. The uncertainty that is typical of the physical and mathematical sciences is almost always reducible to variables that can, at least approximately, be measured and compared. Perhaps this advantage characterises what is conventionally understood as science *tout court*. The human sciences, on the other hand, have to deal with a much more complicated structure. Within the general areas of sociology, psychology and biology there are various sub-areas: heredity, communication and language, ideology, and so on. And each of these sub-areas is in turn marked by a high degree of internal complexity. In other words, we are dealing with dimensions that make comparisons difficult and also make it difficult to move from one level to another. If we take the case of a depression accompanied by a feeling of guilt which is diagnosed on the biological level as being the result of a malfunctioning of the amine metabolism, how can this be translated into psychological terms?[15] We could also add that human scientists are often fiercely independent, discouraging the right approach to complexity and tending rather to remain entrenched in their own field and to idealise their own possibilities.

There have been occasions in the past few decades when both psycho-analytically-inspired psychiatry and biological psychiatry have been exposed to the temptations of hegemony. When a discipline starts to decline there is always a rival branch of science ready to take its place, often guided by an equally manic polemical spirit. At best, this complexity and the scarcity of means at his disposal forces the scientist working in that field to proceed empirically without a safety net and with the eyes of the official defenders of the scientific rule-books trained upon him.

We can now turn back to the "quantum leap" which changes our point of observation. Particularly dramatic moments can at times reawaken us from the everyday torpor which the schizophrenic paradox lulls us into. It is at such moments that we suddenly realise the difference between the two types of ethos. When faced, say, with the case of an uncle who rapes his young nieces although he knows he has AIDS (a detail considered by the press an aggravating circumstance and not a trigger), we may at first be disoriented, but after our initial "instinctive" reaction we then go on to reorganise our thoughts on a level where there is no room for responses such as the desire to inflict exemplary punishment or for feelings such as indignation, pity, pardon, compassion or other reactions that belong to the repertoire of guilt. Or rather, that margin remains, but these feelings fade, as it were, into the background and no longer take part in the debate.

What comes to take their place is sorrowful comprehension based on an acceptance of the inevitability of the tragic.[16] One can put forward hypotheses about the perverse behaviour of the uncle referred to above, behaviour which modern psychoanalysis would see as masking madness, but explicatory hypotheses are not essential to the tragic viewpoint, which is rather the result of an "insight" and a complex maturational process that personalities go through.

Psychoanalysts (and all those clinicians true to the spirit of Galen) are asked not to judge, not to respond according to the law of retaliation. The impression then is, however, that they are not always fully equipped to deal with guilt when it comes out in the therapeutic relationship. Here again it is worth distinguishing between different moments, different levels of complexity and different types of awareness. Usually a distinction is made between an "intellectual" and an "emotional" insight. For the purposes of formulating a diagnosis all one needs is the ability to produce the former. Although emotions do come into play in this case, they are usually few in number and limited in extent. If a psychoanalyst, or even a clinician trained in psychodynamics, is presented with a young man who experiences one failure after another in his studies and at work (presently I shall cite a case of this type and talk about the father's reactions), we can imagine a response that goes beyond moralising and passing judgement, which would consist of saying things like, "he is a good-for-nothing, a shirker" or making other comments taken from the lexicon of blame. So, for example, a nymphomaniac can be seen as the victim of a strong fear of being abandoned, and not, pejoratively, as a woman of easy virtue. In these cases, the ability to see the patient's conflicts from a viewpoint which transcends moralism (which would consider both the young man and the nympho-maniac as "guilty") can be acquired with training.

Usually the question becomes much more complicated if the young man who has a tendency to fail or the nymphomaniac enter into an absorbing relationship of transference–counter-transference with a therapist. In this situation it can prove much more arduous to maintain the same detached vantage-point adopted at the moment of diagnosis.

Guilt as signal

When the capacity to contain and work out the sense of guilt becomes such that it does not morph into persecution, or has become such that it leads to premature reparation, then probably something particularly useful is being expressed: guilt can manifest itself as a signal. Sometimes the guilt signal looks to the past: the individual feels a "pang" of regret for having done or not done something. In these cases – since the past obviously cannot be changed – the sense of guilt takes on omnipotent colouring. When, how-ever, it addresses the present or the future, the same "pang" acts as a signal that a more or less unconscious fantasy or drive, which could prove damaging or destructive, is about to come to the surface. In this case guilt sounds a timely warning.

All this is relevant to the perspective from which the analyst must deal with the sense of guilt; it has nothing to do with the existence of the sense of guilt itself, *which is a reality*, in the sense that the individual experiences it, which means that it produces an effect.

To return to the two strategies described by Grinberg that we mentioned at the beginning of the book: it may now be clearer why the sense of guilt needs to be brought out into the open, acknowledged and experienced by the patient. If guilt is not experienced with all its implications, it will continue to act in the unconscious and will never become a useful signal. Its influence will be only pathological and it will not be able to perform its function of helping the individual to mature. It is up to the analyst and the patient together to make this experience as easy as possible.

Earlier I suggested that there is a kind of leap between the sense of guilt we described as depressive and the vantage-point of tragic responsibility. However, from another perspective we could argue that the ancient adage *natura non facit saltus* (nature does not make leaps) also applies in this case and we could try to defend the statement – known since Aristotle – that nothing exists that is not the consequence of something that went before. The implication of this is that it is impossible to see the events of human life from the viewpoint of tragic responsibility without having first experienced moments of depressive guilt. But on this point it is probably better to leave the door open to doubt.

Whatever its origins, the depressive sense of guilt, as we said earlier, usually helps us to deny our limitations. It diverts our attention from them. But it also induces us to offer reparation to those whom we think we have harmed, and this suggests, at least initially, that reparation can put things right – which is hardly ever true. The task before us is not always reparation but can be both a much harder and subtler process. Or to put it more mildly: reparation can become realistic when there is no hurry (when the sense of guilt is not urgent), when it knows how to wait for the right moment, or when need is tempered by time. But then attention inevitably shifts on to the agent offering reparation.

The tragic sense of responsibility, to use a spatial metaphor, starts from a higher standpoint than that of guilt. Precisely for this reason, while it can better observe (or intuit) the complexity of things, it gains a sense of proportion and can understand how precarious our foothold is. It accepts the severe limits on our wishes and abilities, privileging knowledge and comprehension.[17]

We know that there are people who are all too willing to accept their limits because this allows them to indulge their laziness. But when analysed more closely this attitude proves to be conflictual. In order to reach the perspective of tragic responsibility we need to have worked through our grief at the loss of our "heroic" parts (whether victims or combatants), which are identified with Kafka's heroes, with Job or with Don Giovanni's rebellion. But this working out does not imply the renunciation or resignation that would mark the defeat of the heroic project. The hero needs to switch objectives, to choose some that are more realistic. Perhaps he can cling onto a few fragments of utopia, but he should concentrate on objectives more within his reach. All of us need to achieve the things we believe in, even if these goals can and must change over time. Those who operate from this perspective have given up accusing not only the gods, but also their parents, their neighbour and themselves. They have become reconciled, to use one of Freud's favourite words. And the next time they feel like blaming someone, they sense or know that they are exploiting their desire for omnipotence.

L.L. is a patient who has started to realise that his second analysis is coming to an end. He is a father forced to tell me about his only son's umpteenth academic failure. The son has been turned down for a Master's by one American university after another. From what I can gather, his son must be intelligent and well-qualified. At exams and interviews, however, he suffers from what René Laforgue calls "failure neurosis", a common inability to accomplish anything. He fails because he is unable to establish the right relationship with his examiners. At the beginning of the analysis the father spent a long time venting his resentment against his "soft and spineless" son. He saw him as a "thorn in his flesh" who prevented him from enjoying the affluent lifestyle he had worked so hard to achieve. Essentially, his was a narcissistic wound. His rancour was expressed in violent accusations directed at his son.

As time went on, he was helped to discover the role that his personality and his own personal conflicts had played in the formation of his son's character, and this led to his depression (which had always been latent beneath his over-confidence) coming out into the open. He had then gone through a long troubled period during which he came to understand the subtle, concrete ways in which he had negatively influenced his son's upbringing. While at first he had been sensitive only to the (all too probable) aggression against him contained in his son's failures, now his acute perception turned its focus on his own failures.

The particularly intense suffering he had experienced during his psychoanalysis, conducted with honesty and determination, led him to discover the "ingenious techniques" with which day after day he had passed on to his son, through projective identification, the immature and frightened parts of himself. On many occasions in the past these unacknowledged infantile parts had prevented him from exploiting his aggressiveness to achieve contractual power over others. During his son's upbringing, the father had progressively placed these parts of himself inside his son.

He went on making these discoveries with some insight, but also with a kind of lucid cruelty which at the beginning I had hardly noticed. A voice within me suggested that if I wanted to prevent him from constantly torturing himself I had to confront him with the "objective reality" of his psychological state. Later I realised that if I had listened to this inner voice, I would have been behaving like L.L.'s mother who, by protecting him excessively, had not given him enough time and space to learn how to cope with his suffering. So I was careful not to let him know that I thought that at that stage he was not even able to see the problems with which he was torturing himself. I could have tried to explain this shortcoming of his by referring to his parents' non-receptive attitude towards him during his childhood (his father had been distant and his mother over-protective). I could have made this and other connections. In other words, I could have pointed to something that "pre-dated" him as one of the main causes of his need to expel his immature parts.

In part this interpretation had in fact already been offered to him: in his analyses L.L. had come to learn the importance and usefulness of these connections. But in my experience this interpretative strategy would at best have placated L.L only briefly. Very probably the attacks mounted by his Super-Ego would have abated, but I knew that this would still not have alleviated his remorse or cut the Gordian knot of his guilt. What is more, I would have run the risk of impeding the laborious process of his self-analysis. I felt that authentic creativity (I am tempted to call it a desire for freedom) was at work; perhaps in a somewhat "mistaken" way, but at least there was some kind of movement.

I had noticed the cruelty of the words the patient used against himself. This cruelty was held in check, but nonetheless it was lucid and cutting. Interpreted wrongly it could have been offloaded on others. (Obviously, during analysis it had emerged that it was not only his relationship with his son, who was a kind of family scapegoat, which had been difficult.)

My instinct was to draw his attention to the rhythm of his thoughts, which at times could be feverishly fast. His sense of guilt at this stage in the analysis was depressive and his intent was clearly reparative towards his son, but the way in which he "threw it in his face" (this is the expression he used on one occasion when I pointed out to him his tone of "lucid cruelty") was clearly persecutory and this prevented authentic constructive thinking. He was lucid and perceptive, but, as Bion would have said, he was not yet thinking, not yet able to think in a productive way. I realised that solving this problem had to be the top priority.

Manichaean ethos and creativity

Guilt follows a Manichaean thought pattern: it's either you or me who's guilty, or again, either you're guilty or you're innocent. This ethos is clearly visible in a statement made by Publilio Siro, a mime at the time of Caesar whose fame endured among erudite misogynists right up to the nineteenth century: "women either love or hate; there is no third possibility".[18] This proves to be absolutely untrue when one recognises human ambivalence, which obviously affects women. The logic of guilt likewise offers no space for mediation and thus does not leave us free to think of new, creative solutions. It paves the way for stereotypes and prejudices.

When I finally managed to get L.L. to slow down the rhythm of his thoughts (which took some time), I drew his attention to some charac-teristics of his self-reproach. In particular, I pointed out a certain "fragility" in the "crystalline lucidity" which his ruthless investigation seemed to want to both reveal and conceal. When I made this point to him, L.L., without giving a logical explanation, associated it with the fact that he could never be moved by his own pain. In order to cry he had to use almost theatrical auto-suggested sobs. And he had to shift his attention – he could cry watching a second-rate melodrama but not at his own unhappiness. I asked him to talk freely about this unhappiness which he found so difficult to reach.

He started by talking about his previously unexpressed worries about what would happen to him if he opened that door. As in the myth of Pandora, what he feared more than anything else was the uncovering of his hidden pain. He was convinced – and in this both his parents provided him with a model – that he did not know how to contain or cope with pain. For this reason he separated it from himself and tended to locate it in others. Once this was clear he was able to move up to another level of thought. He got to the point where he understood that his intelligent reparations, his discreet helpfulness were not what his son needed: "He needs a completely different type of father . . . or perhaps not even so completely different, but simply different", he concluded.

This profound insight came to him "slowly but quite unexpectedly". At the next session, after a long silence, he said in a voice that now really was perfectly calm: "I woke up this morning with a very clear feeling which, though I wouldn't say it disturbed me, did surprise me. For the first time I saw in full detail certain problems of behaviour which in fact I've been aware of for some time, for years even." Then he went on to explain: "I think I understand now what guilt is. I've learned to recognise it. I am sure that I've caused my son and other people a lot of problems. I've also created problems for . . . [here he named a woman he had been deeply in love with and who had loved him too], for myself, my wife . . . for you, too, I'm afraid. What I realised this morning, as if a veil had been lifted, is that at the time I was unable do things any differently. I can still see myself confined in a cage. I'm not angry at myself but still I can feel a great pain . . . It's different from any pain I have ever felt before. It's very strong, much stronger than what I felt when I discovered my envy. Then I felt a kind of shame . . . But this is pain without shame. I am grateful to you for having let me come this far." And then he started sobbing.

I felt that this gratitude was genuine and free of ambivalence. And I thought that by losing certain illusions about himself he had managed to break away from the cruelty to which he had subjected himself for so long. Later, although he did not deny his role in his son's neurosis, L.L. managed to accept that other factors and other people may have contributed to creating it. It was a crucial moment, because it signified a further diminishing of the need for omnipotence which generally characterises guilt.

I have emphasised that I experienced his gratitude as genuine. I think it is important to highlight the fact that – contrary to what people generally think – one can feel gratitude even when one is manic, even towards a person who is idealised but who in other respects is deeply feared because he is seen (rightly or wrongly) as persecutory. This was not the case with L.L.

As far as I know, such clear insights are not very frequent (but at the same time they are not very rare). Most often they seem to me to occur once analysis has been completed. In the case of L.L., as I said, he was undergoing his second analysis. This goes to show that certain insights can only be gained once we have – however well or however badly – worked through serious losses such as separation from our analyst, or from a person who is very important to us.

Sometimes realisations like the one achieved by L.L. occur in a more progressive and less sudden manner. When this happens, perhaps the techniques used by the analyst and his personality are as much a factor as the patient's own personality.

Perhaps it is worth remembering in this context that in the Soto school of Zen, insight is seen as something that occurs gradually, and in this respect it differs from the Rinzai school of Zen. It is possible that the insight we have just been illustrating and the illumination referred to by the masters of Rinzai Zen have certain elements in common. Precisely how the result is achieved seems to be of secondary importance.

Insight of the type just described is in my opinion a sign that the logic of blame is being replaced or has been replaced by the logic of tragic responsibility. For L.L., who for a long time and with great suffering had worked towards achieving a change in perspective, it was then (relatively) easy to go back over it every time guilt imposed itself again. The new ethos had become a template he could always rely on.

The transition between these two types of logic (accompanied, as we have already pointed out, by inevitable oscillations) presupposes what Grinberg calls *reparations of the Self*, which are connected to *micromournings* or *microdepressions* for the Self. Melanie Klein, for example in *Mourning* (1940), says that the loss of a good external object brings with it an unconscious sense of having also lost a good internal object. Grinberg specifies, however, that there is also the loss of a part of the Self. Reparations of the Self can be manifested in ways that differ from person to person; they can be either more or less serious (the more moderate manifestations can be numbered among the phenomena that belong to the "psychopathology of everyday life"). An unrealised project, an unfulfilled aspiration (not of the intensity of those that tormented L.L.), an incomprehension, an unexpected snag, are examples of small frustrations which can involve "an aspect of self" and which can lead to small-scale depressive reactions, as well as to "fleeting threats to one's state of identity".

From a psychoanalytic point of view it is quite clear that whether they are positively resolved or become more serious, depressions will also depend on the way in which equivalent depressions were resolved in the early stages of life.

There is a passage in Grinberg's *Guilt and Depression* I would like to quote because, in my opinion, it marks what is probably a turning point:

> in order to achieve a successful working through of the depressive position or grief caused by the experience of damage or the loss of the

object, it is *essential* – in my opinion – *to have first satisfactorily worked through grief at* the loss or damage suffered by part of the Self.[19]

So the *successful* working through of grief – and the key word here is successful – depends on first repairing the Self.[20] Without indulging in any theorising, Grinberg confirms, with this detail, that he has placed himself outside the ethos of guilt.

In cases such as the one I have just cited, reparations – when they are not manic[21] – probably have a positive function. If nothing else, they pave the way for reparation of the Self. L.L. no longer feels that he is a bad father, or that he is the only cause of his son's neurosis. He is reconciled with himself. He has experienced reparative drives and this alone seems to have directed his attention towards his Self, his possibilities for love. It seems to me, however, that true reparation of the Self occurs when some kind of leap occurs, a change in one's point of view.

When one thinks about it, even the commandment "love thy neighbour as thyself" puts the emphasis on "thyself" – in other words, the term of the comparison. The Latin term "riparare" means not only removing damage or redressing a wrong, but also "re-gaining, recovering for oneself". It is very probable that it is the sense of guilt which makes people direct reparations first towards their neighbour. One needs to be careful not to confuse this type of interest in oneself with a narcissistic withdrawal, with what is called egoism or egocentricism. It is something different from the case of the depressive who buys herself a present, even though the present can be, as it were, a symbolic beginning.

Acceptance of the tragic dimension seems then to be connected to the process of reparation. One consequence is the downscaling of many projects. "Repairing" the Self is not a question of doing something extra-ordinary or "complete", as the demanding ideals of a still sadistic Super-Ego full of an infantile omnipotence would have it. On the contrary, first and foremost it means *accepting oneself*: accepting one's limitations, one's life story, one's traumas, one's irremediable shortcomings – a process that falls under what Grinberg calls mourning for the Self. Spending time over reparation of the Self also means putting oneself in a position where one can exploit one's talents to the full. My own personal experience as an analyst tells me that the patients who best manage to understand the importance of this phase are in general those who in the end are most satisfied with their analysis.

As I have already pointed out, reparation can in certain circumstances ultimately prove to be only a partial restoration, leaving certain areas still damaged. This can be a cause of suffering, although the suffering will diminish as the patient learns to use his or her resources better. Especially in seriously ill patients who are capable of a certain degree of adaptation (borderline cases, pre-psychotic structures), restoration takes the form of significant compromises. I am thinking of M.M., a top-flight company manager who, upon being offered a more responsible post as an international executive, entered an acute psychotic crisis – characterised by psychosomatic expressions of terror – which persuaded him to start analysis. He panicked every time he found himself having to take on tasks that his unconscious persecutory fantasies saw as beyond him. In the end he abandoned his career and changed his field of work. Despite the talent he had previously shown he settled for a much humbler job in terms of prestige and ambition. This position lowered his anxiety levels by wisely containing his psychotic parts. But even the project of carrying out reparatory actions towards people we love or to whom we are attached in some way, and for whom we would never want to be the cause of damage or pain, often has to be quite drastically scaled down. L.L. has to learn to live with the fact that his son will never achieve very much in life, at least judged according to his family's prevailing philosophy of life. He will probably always be neurotic. His father had wanted to put him into analysis with me, but soon realised how impracticable this idea was. He understood that now it was in his son's hands and that it was "just, even essential" that he should decide what to do: "He knows that I am undergoing analysis. If he finds that I have improved, he might ask for help himself."

When someone makes the painful discovery of his limitations, when he gives up his unrealistic view of himself (the big victim or the big culprit, as I said earlier), he realises that he has to also reconsider his own capacity to *give*. His whole self-importance is called into question. Often he realises – and this is sometimes even more dismaying – that he has never known how to love himself or others, at least in the way and to the extent that he wanted to. Likewise, he realises that he has deluded himself about this ability. It can then appear logical that "repairing" yourself is the first necessary step if you ever want to pass on something of value to others.

At another point in his analysis, L.L. went back to a different phase in his life and told me about a detail which might sow doubt in the minds of those who are convinced that only full-scale depressive guilt and completely resolved ambivalence are the true preconditions of full maturity. Recalling his relationship with the woman he loved dearly and with whom he had had a wild but also full and extremely gratifying relationship, he realised that one of his main reasons for breaking off the relationship had been the growing suffering he saw reflected in the woman's face and for which he felt responsible: "I couldn't cope with the sense of guilt that this caused in me. She got worse from day to day. She told me that I was the cause of all her suffering. And eventually I agreed with her."

In the end L.L. managed to make the following confession: "To be frank, I feel that, if I had to go back, I would make exactly the same decisions". He explained to me that his sense of guilt for the suffering he inflicted on his lover was outweighed by the importance their passionate relationship had for his entire life. "On that occasion I realised for the first time that a woman could love me completely and that she would fight to love me and to be loved. Only then did I realise that I was capable of love." I noticed a sad smile light up his face. I wonder if such an admission – which reflected his insecurity and pointed to wounds that had not yet healed but was also a particular way of expressing gratitude towards that woman – would come out in an analysis where the atmosphere was moralistic.

Several factors can create a moralistic – and thus schematic – atmosphere. I would include among them transference interpretations which are too mechanical or repetitive and which are applied to every single moment of the analysis. This approach seems to me to foreshorten perspective. Everything becomes equivalent to everything else. And this often leads analysis into a therapeutic impasse. If I had pointed out to L.L. that what he was saying had, or could have, implications which affected me as his analyst, this would in one sense simply have been a banal comment – made to a person who had reached a certain level of honesty and introspection – but in another more important sense, it would also have undermined the patient's hard-won capacity to make distinctions. Seen in perspective, his relationship with the woman and his present relationship with me the analyst were simply two different ways of relating to other people which belonged to periods marked by different conflicts. The fact that they existed side by side inside him did not mean that they were necessarily the same thing.

The statement "I would make exactly the same decisions" is very probably only a fantasy. L.L. is different now, and even if he wanted to, he would not be able to do the same things again. Nevertheless, the expression *excludes repentance*, at least in the sense in which it is traditionally understood. An ethos that transcends guilt can – in my opinion – accept guilt without causing too much turmoil.

The importance of reparation of parts of the Self can perhaps be understood more fully if one thinks that this is the way the individual spontaneously stops reproaching himself and others for his inadequacies, his emotional defects, for his unhappiness and instead, so to speak, "rolls up his sleeves". A clear sign of this taking on responsibility comes when a patient works hard to improve his situation and to change.

In these cases we have a new situation: the impulse no longer comes from outside, nor is it prompted by guilt. It seems rather to result from the overcoming of guilt. At the end of the nineteenth century, William James drew attention to the sense of "relief" we all feel when we give up pretensions, even simple ones such as the claim to possess musical sensibility when we know that we are basically unmusical.[22]

This impulse has to be spontaneous; otherwise it does not work or, if it does, it works only briefly and superficially. This is probably one of the reasons why the therapeutic process which started with Freud differs so radically from all other forms of teaching, pedagogical encouragement or philosophical or religious fascination. In fact Freud was responsible only for laying down the premises for this radical change, but that alone constituted a major achievement.[23]

When the perspective of tragic responsibility is consolidated, one realises that the pain that one feels at the loss of the idealised parts of the Self is replaced by that potential which we had somehow abandoned, and this brings us up to new levels of awareness and freedom. L.L., the father of the young man with failure neurosis, had overestimated his ability to help his son and did not realise that this was determined by an unconscious sense of guilt. Only by accepting the illusory nature of this ability did he discover that he possessed the necessary courage and real honesty. Did he embark on this journey into Hades primarily for himself or for his son? The question loses its meaning when the objectives merge into one another. Perhaps some will agree that the final stage of this process is responsible love. It is difficult to generalise about subjects of this complexity, but experience shows that the recovery of lost talents is common enough. Or at least it happens in those cases where the analyst does not intervene in such a clumsy way as to obstruct or derail the process.

The myth of Pandora confirms this. Upon reaching the earth, Pandora, the first woman, was so curious about the box containing all the evils of the earth that she opened it. Only Hope, which was at the bottom, did not escape; Pandora managed to close the lid in time. Now that the box is empty of pain, how does L.L. envisage his future relationship with his son? "He needs a father who is completely different . . . or rather not even completely different, but simply different." These few opening words – typical of the accusations made by a sadistic Super-Ego ("a father who is completely different") – are replaced by a much more moderate statement which suggests that hope still lies at the bottom of the box.

Approaches to guilt

One of the rarest codices that is still in perfect condition is the manuscript of the complete works of Virgil which Petrarch was given by his father and which is now preserved in the Biblioteca Ambrosiana in Milan. The manuscript not only contains the work of the poet, a commentary by Onorato Servio and hand-written annotations by Petrarch himself, but also opens with a stunning painting by Simone Martini. This illustration depicts Servio, the cultured *magister urbis* of the fourth to fifth century AD, who was famous as a commentator on ancient poets and in particular on Virgil, drawing aside a veil with one hand. Whoever is being unveiled – the gesture seems to be an attempt to show Virgil to Aeneas – it raises a question. Servio wrote some remarkable linguistic and grammatical observations, and his multiple interpretations of Virgil's poetry were rich on various levels:

mythological, religious and philosophical. It was Servio who was responsible for the image of Virgil which dominated the Middle Ages and fascinated Dante Aligheri. But the question we must ask ourselves is: can a
commentator, even an outstanding commentator such as Servio, reveal the
multiple aspects of poetry without sacrificing (re-veiling) others?

We can now come back to our commentary on L.L.'s densely significant
and telling words. At one point he said: "What I realised this morning, as if a
veil had been lifted, is that at the time I couldn't do things any differently. I
can still see myself confined in a cage." One notes that what in the past was a
cage, an object with great coercive power, has become a light veil. The
metaphor of the veil which is lifted is one which is frequently used in common
speech to refer to a moment of realisation or insight. We use expressions like
"unveiling" or "veiled hints". The expression "revealed truth" refers to an act
of faith, when one gives up autonomous thinking. But if we look closely, reveal (re-veil) means to cloud or shroud over again with a veil.

When he said, "I couldn't do anything else", that was precisely what the
voice of my counter-transference would have wanted me to say to him. If
my associations are correct (and I think they are), if I had spoken, I would
probably have "re-veiled" the mind of my patient; I would have deprived
him of the satisfaction of getting there on his own, albeit with my help.

He talked of surprise; his observing ego seemed to witness something
going on in his mind before his very eyes. The feeling is one of clarity,
another term that evokes the idea of light which is always present in the
metaphors that seek to describe this type of phenomenon. People commonly talk about "illuminating", or "shedding light" on, a problem. It
seems to me that all this has nothing to do with the imagery normally
associated with guilt. Guilt is akin to sin and sin in its turn evokes images of
darkness and shade.

Discovering the specific modalities with which he had projected parts of
himself onto others, and in particular onto his son, allowed this patient to
feel free all of a sudden. Giving up projection may produce an increase in
anxiety and guilt, but it also creates a feeling of enrichment which in turn
leads to a heightened sense of independence. This is quite logical: the more
tools one possesses (and the retrieved parts of our Self can become tools, if
nothing else then in the service of empathy), the fewer constraints and
obstacles one encounters. L.L. can now even feel gratitude towards his
analyst. But most importantly he seems to think on a broader scale and with
deeper perception. The impression is that the quality of his thoughts has
changed.

Achieving this kind of freedom is the result of recognising both one's
limitations and one's real abilities. The point I have just made can be linked
to one of Melanie Klein's most perceptive insights. It contains within it an
attitude which in concrete terms transcends that element of Manichaeaism
which guilt always brings with it. I am referring to Klein's idea that, though

complete and stable integration is not possible, the ability to retrieve the split parts is a prerequisite of normal development. In *On the Development of Mental Functioning*, she describes the advantages of the depressive position, adding:

> The more the ego can integrate its destructive impulses and synthesize the different aspects of its objects, the richer it becomes; for the split-off parts of the self and of impulses which are rejected because they arouse anxiety and give pain also contain valuable aspects of the personality and of the phantasy life which is impoverished by splitting them off.[24]

In summary, one could argue that the sense of guilt in its most terrifying form is reflected in the persecutory delusion of the paranoiac, or in its most decisive form in a depressive's suicide. Coming after it in terms of gravity of suffering is the unconscious persecutory guilt where no precise agent is responsible for the persecution. When persecutory guilt comes out into the open and the persecutor acquires a face, one can assume that the subject feels he has in some way enhanced his powers of containment. The persecutor has moved out of the shadows of the unconscious on to the stage of the conscious. Have the mechanisms of repression lost their former vigour? Although one could reply that in general persecutory guilt reflects a weak and incoherent Self, this personalisation of the persecutor seems to me to be a sign of progress; a sign that, for all this fragility, changes can occur that reinforce the containing capacities of the Self.

We know that when we are working with the psychotic parts of the personality we need to pay vigilant attention to even the slightest movements. And indeed, when dealing with a persecutory sense of guilt, attention to small steps and small details in the long run can not only be useful but may even prove to be the only possible path.

If at some point in the analysis the persecutor takes the form of the psychoanalyst, the situation may reveal itself to be pathological and burdensome. But the analyst should also bear in mind the positive side: when persecutory guilt is brought into the analytical relationship (with its implications of physical vicinity). This is a sign of greater trust towards the analyst and of a relative diminishment of persecution.

In G.G.'s dreams, Pasolini's Christ harshly accused her of an offence that demanded repentance. Now, if this Christ figure embodied a part of her or one of her internal objects, this would reveal a further step towards a more stable containment of her sense of guilt. Indeed, the situation the patient dramatises is one of urgency; she takes it to the analyst and suggests it as a point to be worked through. I underlined "if this Christ figure embodied a part of her" because we should never exclude the possibility that a dream like this contains a criticism of the analyst: "you're putting me under pressure". If this is true, the analyst must take it into account.

The strategies for coping with a sense of guilt belong to the main group of strategies that the analyst must possess (even though "forgotten" in the subconscious) if he is to conclude the process of individuation proper to every successful treatment. In other words, patients enter analysis with the identity their conflicts allow them to have; they turn to therapy to try to find, albeit ambivalently, a more reliable and genuine sense of identity.

The analyst must be able to contain or severely limit the projections of parts of the Self operated by the patient. This is why the external setting exists, a setting made up of concrete situations and rules backed up by experience. But what matters most is the setting provided by the analyst, whose most important feature is his ability to contain – psychologically and physically – what the patient projects inside him.[25]

If the analyst is free enough to express his own sensibility, then he should also be capable of realising that the patient provokes in him certain profound emotions (including hate, love and a sense of guilt) – which he experiences first and foremost in various parts of his body. The analyst's own "psychosomatic" self must be sufficiently coherent to hold up in the presence of intense emotions. Only then will he feel that he is sufficiently well equipped to accept within himself the violent emotions (which can also be expressed in subtle or masked ways) that otherwise the patient will try to hurl at him or to split off and live out dramatically elsewhere.

Regression leads us back to various moments in the past and is another factor that forms an integral part of the psychoanalytic process. If an individual is prevented from going back over the various stages of his life, then among the other problems which cannot be analysed are the roots of various kinds of guilt which he may have experienced (or continues to experience); these are ultimately neglected and thus remain unexplored.

Partly as a result of the regression facilitated by analysis, the patient often wants the analyst to be more active and, as it were, more "didactic". But by meeting this demand the analyst would not be helping the patient. The therapist must come to understand this rule fully; the analyst needs to have experienced at first hand that a certain amount of frustration is necessary and useful if a patient is to be able to direct his impulses "towards the search for the potential capacities of the Self".[26] The analyst administers a certain ideal dose of frustration to his patients when, for example, he does not gratify them but interprets. But this should not lead to the impression that in life (and thus also in analysis) frustration is always a strategy employed by someone else. That would suggest that the frustration might have been avoided; in reality it is impossible to avoid all frustration.

All this, as I said, requires time. But is it true that *Zeit bringt Rosen*? This German saying is misleading because it seems to suggest that all one needs to do is wait and sooner or later good old Mother Nature will cause the roses to bloom. But we know that nature at times plays tricks: she can also bring the frost that prevents the roses from blooming for ever.

Chapter 4

The search for a name

> Dogmatism deals in certainties but does not ensure them.
> (Andrea D'Angelo)

The "quantum leap" or radical change in perspective on the dynamics of guilt for which I am trying to find a name was anticipated by other similar shifts in the history of ideas at the beginning of the twentieth century. In the short space of a decade a group of scientists achieved what has rightly been termed the Nietzschean destruction of certainty: Sigmund Freud wrote *The Interpretation of Dreams* (1899); Max Planck formulated the basic hypothesis underlying quantum theory (1901–1902); the following year Bertrand Russell published *The Principles of Mathematics* (1903), and a little later Albert Einstein propounded the special theory of relativity; shortly after that Alfred Wegener published his first article about plate tectonics in which he put forward the hypothesis of continental drift, a theory which literally took the solid ground from under our feet.

In the space of a few years, then, the certainty and stability which had distinguished modern science from the sixteenth century onwards were shattered. Man's narcissism was dealt a severe blow. This disillusionment was among the factors that demolished the claims to omniscience which Enlightenment-based scientism seemed to have fixed for ever. These years saw the birth of the cinema, a medium which made it possible to lend form to all kinds of fantasies, and man's long-held dream of flying – a desire shared by Icarus and Leonardo da Vinci – became reality. These were monumental changes, and the twentieth century opened under the sign of tragedy and a manic trust in technology that is well reflected in the ephemeral music of *Ballo Excelsior*.

The twentieth century was to see numerous changes in perspective. The most important – our changed view of ecology – is perhaps the most recent, at least for the west. The old paradigm was anthropocentric, while the new paradigm looks at the earth as a whole and is eco-centric. This change restores values which had in the past been sacrificed and neglected.

The search for a name or a label to refer clearly and unambiguously to the logic (or ethos) which transcends the logic of guilt has turned out to be long and, above all, frustrating. At times one is tempted to think that perhaps the solution does not exist because there is no word in the language. Not even recourse to mythology – with its ability to accommodate contradictions – can guarantee the right direction. And in fact, the expression that I eventually decided on – tragic responsibility – is still not absolutely convincing.

The word *responsibility*, for a series of reasons which I shall discuss later on, is an unstable and in many ways hackneyed term. As for "tragedy", from which *tragic* derives, it is one of numerous Greek words that have entered the lexicon of many languages with divergent meanings. The term "tragedy" has undergone several semantic shifts across the different periods of history and has been the object of much discussion. However, the starting point of any discussion has always been, explicitly or implicitly, the definition Aristotle gives in his *Poetics*, where he talks of tragedy as the "imitation of events that awaken pity and terror and which purify these emotions". I think that the attempt to formulate a modern theory of tragedy would lead us too far away from our central concerns. If we think of a continuum along which to position the various definitions of tragedy, we might place Hegel at one extreme – he saw the conflict at the heart of tragedy as a contradiction that has been overcome – and Schopenhauer at the other; for him the conflict remains insoluble.

Let us stick then to the current, everyday meaning of the term: "tragic" is a word which is usually associated with loss, severe pain and sadness, as well as reflecting the never-failing presence of guilt. I decided to use the term with Unamuno's title *The Tragic Sense of Life in Men and in Peoples* at the back of my mind, and because the point of view I was trying to name does not deny the tragic dimension of life – whatever its ultimate meaning.[1] *Awareness* of the tragic dimension is an essential part of overcoming guilt, whereas *the sense of the tragic* can be felt by a Nazi and is something that can lead to paranoia.[2]

There is, however, at least one important reason why the choice of the word "tragic" fails to be completely satisfactory. Once an individual has overcome the pain and the more or less intensely catastrophic feelings experienced during the period in which he changes his perspective on reality, his state of mind is not necessarily one of depression and anxiety.[3] The term *tragic* is one that is overloaded with negative associations: "the hero of tragedy must suffer," commented Freud, "he had to bear the burden of what was known as 'tragic guilt'."[4] The dimension I am seeking to describe, however, does not exclude joy, pleasure, even intense pleasure and, above all, a certain peace of mind. These are, of course, all things that are not generally associated with the adjective "tragic" as it is used in everyday language.

To go back to Unamuno: although this complex personality, who was strongly influenced by Pascal and Kierkegaard, is not the most obvious supporter of the case I am making for this meaning of the term tragic, in *The Tragic Sense* we do find this extraordinary passage:

> The man who does not really know why he acts as he does and not otherwise feels the necessity of explaining to himself the motive of his action and so he forges a motive . . . uncertainty, doubt, perpetually wrestling with our final destiny, mental despair and the lack of any solid and stable dogmatic foundation may be the basis of an ethic. He who bases or thinks he bases his conduct – his inward or his outward conduct, his feelings or his action – upon a dogma or a theoretical principle which he deems incontrovertible, runs the risk of becoming a fanatic, and moreover, the moment that this dogma is weakened or shattered, the morality based on it gives way.[5]

The leap that allows us to transcend the logic of guilt can initially be the cause of deep anxiety.

Can this vantage-point be reached by going through what Melanie Klein calls the depressive position – and then coming out the other side, as it were? What is certain is that it is impossible to escape or repress the sense of guilt with impunity. But there is another equally important question to ask: what do we mean when we say "going through the sense of guilt"? In Chapter 3 I tried to give a concrete demonstration of what this means by describing sessions with the patient L.L., but this description still leaves some questions open.

Many fear this journey through guilt as something that will plunge them into the depths of despair. The corrosive scepticism of Chamfort's Maxim xxiii can be taken as an example of a common opinion on this point:

> How wonderful is the allegory in the Bible of the tree of knowledge of good and evil that leads to death! Surely this symbol means that, once we have penetrated the essence of things, the loss of all illusion will lead inevitably to the death of the soul, in other words to the complete disintegration of what touches and concerns others.[6]

In general, as Freud's insight teaches us, the pangs of unconscious guilt remain outside consciousness precisely because they cause suffering. What might make us face up to them? Before trying to answer this question, it is perhaps worth making it clear that many people die without ever having really faced up to guilt. A person might live his whole life thinking he is a sinner, experiencing the burden of guilt and suffering the acute pangs of depression, but this does not mean that he has really confronted guilt. It is difficult to say what originally drove L.L. to the discovery that, year after year, he had harmed the son he loved so much. Equally, how can we tell what induced G.G. (the patient who married without feeling love) to stop deluding herself about her decisions? Was it a need to repair the damage done; was it a search for truth? Possibly, but such answers seem somewhat inadequate. It might also have been a search for coherence upon which to build a more solid sense of identity and a fuller life.

As I see it, working through the sense of guilt also means showing up the deceptive nature of certain uses of the terminology of guilt and sin whose sole purpose is really to disguise and not to reveal. An example is when people say that we are all guilty, that we are all sinners (which is the opposite of making someone into a scapegoat: then only that person is guilty or a sinner). In reality, this inflationary use of the term is a form of denial which makes everything indefinite and vague and tends only to create confusion. As the twentieth century drew to a close we witnessed a series of apologies: Helmut Kohl apologised for the Nazi atrocities, Tony Blair for the famine in Ireland in the nineteenth century, Elizabeth II half-apologised for the 1919 massacre in Amritsar, Chirac for Vichy, Pik Botha for apartheid in South Africa. Even Pope John Paul II joined in.

I referred earlier to the fact that psychoanalysis not only deals with the sense of guilt but also with what is called "objective guilt". Now I must remind the reader that by adopting these terms we are using vocabulary that belongs to the logic of guilt.

We saw that Nietzsche talked about "debt"; from a psychological point of view, we need to focus attention on "harm" or "injury". Biting a breast, a bang on the head are "harm". For me, working through guilt means getting to the point of reflecting on this harm. When L.L. stops accusing his son and starts accusing himself, he manages to attain a balance and reaches an understanding of the harm he (together with others, even together with his son himself) has done to his son. And he achieves this by taking on real, not omnipotent responsibility; a responsibility which severely limits the scope of his reparative claims, but which at the same time awakens hope for his creativity.

The analyst has to use his own containing capacity, as well as his interpretative ability, in line with the strategy he has adopted. Personally I think that trying at too early a stage to make a patient feel concern for the people he loves or ought to love, in other words trying to bring about hasty reconciliation, premature reparation, however sincere it may be, can cost the patient dear, as he sees himself forced to sacrifice self-fulfilment. Hate, anger and violence towards the object that rejects or persecutes one should be relived to the full (this also applies to transference neuroses) before moving on to reparation.

Preparing the ground for a dispute

One route we can take in our search for answers is to look at the theoretical investigations into the sense of guilt carried out by some psychoanalysts working in Great Britain during the extremely creative period that started in the late 1920s. Our discussion will not be linear, but will rather compare what they wrote with their personal relationships. Should we find that the theoretical on the one hand and the historical and personal on the other are at variance, this might give us some useful pointers. Far from taking us away from the scientific approach, the history of personal involvement will enable us to move on to more firmly grounded hypotheses. After all, psychoanalysis differs from other sciences because its aim is to clarify human relations and the way they impinge on all kinds of activities.

We said earlier that the ability to leave behind the logic of guilt represents a valuable but seldom achieved stage in the process of growing to maturity. It would be interesting to find out more about this. Let us start again from a question we posed a moment ago and underline one aspect of that question: does Melanie Klein see the depressive position as the final stage of maturation in human beings? We shall see later that her answer is no. In Melanie Klein's view, when the child moves out of the "pathological" position *par excellence* (the paranoid–schizoid position) and is able to progress to the new mental and emotional state (the depressive position), some important maturational phenomena occur.[7]

Taking our cue from Klein's comments and following on from Bion, we could say that the individual's very way of perceiving or thinking is transformed. In the paranoid–schizoid position other people are experienced – and often used – as a *function* at our service. In other words, an aspect or a function (or several aspects and several functions) of what one normally experiences of another person is effectively seen and dealt with as if it corresponded to the whole person.

In the depressive position, the other progressively changes into and becomes an individual with his or her own autonomy. To use Klein's own terminology: the "partial object" becomes a "whole object". Here we have another leap. The mother, to take a customary example, no longer only exists as the breast that nourishes and provides a soft comforting cushion, or as the container of anxieties we would not otherwise know where to put, but is transformed into a human being with her own demands. If she is not present, that does not mean that she is bad or that she neglects us (as we would feel in the paranoid–schizoid position): she could be at work, ill or engaged in other tasks.

The partial object of the paranoid–schizoid position, I would add, does not have a true story; it lacks the needs or desires a real person might have. It has no past, no future (or rather the problem does not pose itself). These are the qualities that belong to a complete person, a whole object.

The adult who remains entrenched in the first position continues to look at the other much in this way. So a partner, spouse or lover will think it right that his/her companion is there for his/her own benefit. The wife, companion or lover can be considered only as a cook (the nourishing breast), as responsible for order and cleanliness (the caring mother), as a person who should not inflict the pain of abandonment and jealousy, or as an object whose sole *raison d'être* is to allow impulses to be discharged, a *remedium concupiscentiae*. Each reader will no doubt be able to come up with numerous examples of his/her own.

At this point a digression on the subject of the relationship with the partial object might help us reach a deeper understanding, in phenomenological terms, of Melanie Klein's contribution. I would also like to use this digression to comment indirectly on some of the important points we have emphasised so far. We should also take note of the fact that cultural ideologies (one need think only of authoritarianism) can reinforce an approach to human relations where men and women use others as if they were mere functions.

As we shall see when we comment on the ideas expressed by Winnicott in "The use of an object", the use of the other is not necessarily to be considered as pathological. It is perfectly normal and is at the basis of relations between friends and collaboration between colleagues; "maestros are there to be plundered", as a famous conductor once said. It should not be rejected on moralistic grounds. In fact, if the capacity to use others is absent during growth, growth itself can be arrested. It becomes pathological when the use of the other is coupled with the need to control the other, when there is exploitation which limits the other's freedom and when the relationship is not based on reciprocity.

This phenomenon can also acquire symbolic associations. So we can have a mother who is proud of her Don Juan son and who rationalises his activities by thinking that "men are hunters" (the suffering of a Don Juan, however, has its roots in his early inadequate relationship with the mother). For this mother her child could unconsciously represent a phallus to display to other women. So she will admire and support her son, providing he continues to embody this "value", and so long as he does not fall genuinely in love with only one woman and thus free himself from her apron strings – which would put an end to his function.

Obviously this type of narcissistic investment on the part of the mother (though it can also be on the part of the father) can involve other areas, not only the conquering of women. Very often it concerns success in studies or at work, popularity in competitive sports, the acquisition of social status, fame and so on.[8] It is easy to see how a daughter, too, if she is good-looking, can come to stand for a phallus. One need only think of the pitiful spectacle of mothers accompanying daughters to beauty contests. This sort of tie, the sort which often binds politicians to their protégés, the various types of barons to their vassals, can take on slight, serious or even grave pathological forms.

An imaginary mother, faced with a failure on the part of her son or daughter, feels disappointment and resentment towards him/her, and at this point her guilt can come out into the open. In her rancour she may also accuse or blame the child. What does she blame him/her for? For no longer wanting to be her child-phallus, for failing to meet her narcissistic needs? This is extremely unlikely, if not impossible. If for no other reason than that, her desire must remain unconscious. Were it to find its way into her consciousness she would experience great suffering which she would not be ready to face. So she accuses the son or the daughter of some other misdeed, or shifts the target. To cite a common example: so as not to attack him or her she will accuse other people whom the child is attached to (one of the variations of the complaint about children who get into "bad company"). Lacan thought that the goal of analysis was to help the patient to distinguish and to disentangle his/her own desire from the desire of the other, the mother, the father, and so on. This topic forms part of the whole question of the narcissistic use of the other.[9]

The son can then feel this guilt weighing down on him like some unjust and confusing accusation (the persecutory sense of guilt), or, depending on the way he is blamed, as a vague curse, an unreachable ideal, or something else. In his turn the son may to a certain extent become aware of this narcissistic investment on the part of the mother (or the father), may realise that he is being manipulated and thus develop in his turn aggressiveness and rancour. This rancour is mixed with guilt and fear, on account of the hatred that quickens within this feeling and the fear of breaking his tie with the parent, whom he needs.

At the beginning, this child (but the same applies to the mother in relation to the son) had had an exceptionally good mother who flattered and appreciated him – a perfect mother. Now he is faced with this malignant, avid figure who makes use of him. First the mother-witch was somewhere else: split off and projected onto other figures, mostly but not always women. This pernicious figure who returns in the mother starts to be attacked verbally, practically or only in fantasy: in fantasies that can be removed from consciousness.

For Melanie Klein a situation like this is a revised version of an unresolved childhood problem. Rather than considering the interaction between mother and child as I have just done, Melanie Klein tends to concentrate her attention on the son or daughter. This child – as we have seen – was someone who has not worked through his depressive position. In other words, there was another moment in his childhood when another mother appeared, side by side with the mother idealised as exceptional, and this second mother was wicked and terrifying. At a moment like this, the mother can be experienced as wounded, harmed, brutally mutilated. According to Melanie Klein, wicked fantasies at this level of virulence arise out of destructive impulses which the child feels towards the mother and which are fed by the death instinct.

If the child, while fighting against its own hate, manages to recognise that the person it hates is the same as the one it venerated (because that person fed it, took care of it and loved it); in other words, if it realises that the fairy and the witch are two sides of the same mother; if it starts to recognise all of this, then it can move on to the depressive position. As far as I can tell, no mention is made of the mother who uses her children narcissistically – which was our starting point.

One of the consequences of working through the depressive position is that the other becomes a separate object and potentially has his or her own individuality and independence. But there are other consequences: the omnipotence that characterises the child's fantasies diminishes and it becomes aware that it no longer occupies a position at the centre of the universe but rather a limited space in a vast surrounding world. Others live and move independently from your desires and needs. However, there is another side to the coin: this frustrating collapse of illusions is "worth the journey". The upside is that, if someone loves you, if someone looks to you and desires you, they do so because they want to, because they want you more than anyone else.

Given these changes, it is easy to understand how this can produce a very different ability to enter into relations with others. To understand what is involved in this transformation, we need only recall that concern and all the other positive feelings that one can feel for another person become feelings towards the other person as such, the other understood as an opportunity offered by life and not only in terms of what he or she can provide. To go back to the technical terms we have already used: no longer the *narcissistic use of the other*, but *object love*. The transition to object love was described by Melanie Klein in 1935 in a book where she also makes the following point: "through this step the ego arrives at a new position, which forms the foundation of the situation called the loss of the loved object. Not until the object is loved *as a whole* can its loss be felt as a whole. With this change in the relation to the object, new anxiety-contents make their appearance and a change takes place in the mechanisms of defence."[10]

A true restructuring of personality takes place which is not sudden but fluctuating and progressive.

Melanie Klein as seen by Winnicott

Melanie Klein's language is highly technical and at times dramatic. Her analysis of children gave her an increasingly accurate picture of their internal world. She described it in terms of madness, suffering and death. This hell-like image stood in opposition to the tradition that depicted childhood as paradise, a period that human beings could look back on only with nostalgia. Melanie Klein thought that the child oriented itself towards the objects that surrounded it by projecting its loving impulses, but also its avid and aggressive impulses. Later it re-introjected these objects which then took on the characteristics of precisely these projected impulses. For her the world within each of us hides a potential for destruction and self-destruction. It is understandable therefore that she decided to show the reader the psychotic anxiety which she saw as convulsing the internal world of each individual.

Compared to the language previously used in psychoanalysis, her style appears initially crude and threatening, merciless and cold. D. W. Winnicott wrote Melanie Klein a succession of letters, trying to warn her and the Kleinians against becoming isolated in the scientific debate through their use of coded language. Let us take two passages from Klein (where some of the problems that I have just discussed are mentioned):[11]

> Anxiety-situations of this kind I have found to be at the bottom not only of depression, but of all inhibitions of work. The attempts to save the loved object, to repair and restore it, attempts which in the state of depression are coupled with despair, since the ego doubts its capacity to achieve this restoration, are determining factors for all sublimations and the whole of the ego-development. In this connection I shall only mention the specific importance for sublimation of the bits to which the loved object has been reduced and the effort to put them together. It is a "perfect" object which is in pieces; thus the effort to undo the state of disintegration to which it has been reduced presupposes the necessity to make it beautiful and "perfect".

In the second excerpt, we find a reference to guilt, but also the term "responsibility" and a remarkable definition of love:

> As I have pointed out before, the ego comes to a realization of its love for a good object, a whole object and in addition a real object, together with an overwhelming feeling of guilt towards it. Full identification with the object based on the libidinal attachment, first to the breast, then to the whole person, goes hand in hand with anxiety for it (of its disintegration), with guilt and remorse, with a sense of responsibility for preserving it intact against persecutors and the id, and with sadness relating to expectations of impending loss of it. These emotions, whether conscious or unconscious, are in my view among the essential and fundamental elements of the feelings we call love.

However accustomed psychoanalysts thought they were to dissecting all the noble sentiments which have accompanied men and women through the centuries of their history, the language Klein used to describe the central place given to anxiety and guilt was to meet with resistance and opposition, despite the fact that Klein's thinking was to have an enormous influence.[12]

Winnicott, who besides being a psychoanalyst was a respected paediatrician and child psychiatrist, first moved close to the London group of analysts headed by Melanie Klein but later detached himself from them. I have chosen Winnicott for the purpose of a theoretical and personal comparison rather than other psychoanalysts who opposed Klein's theories, such as Anna Freud, Edmund Glover or Margaret Mahler, because Winnicott also developed theoretical positions *vis-à-vis* Klein on the subject of guilt. The comparison between their positions will allow me to clarify some points I consider important. My interest in Winnicott in this context also stems from the fact that his relationship with Melanie Klein is well documented. His critical positions appear, at least at first, imprecise, and this sort of confusion is probably closely connected to his dramatic personal situation. Winnicott was probably never a total adherent of Klein; the conflictual relationship with her strong personality must have been one factor that led him to pursue his own path.

Winnicott is often seen as a Klein disciple who later came into theoretical conflict with her. This idea is based on accounts of the intertwining of their professional lives and the fact that for a long time Winnicott described himself as a member of Klein's group; then again, she was also his supervisor. Some argue that the signs of Winnicott's potential originality were visible from the very start. His theories were founded on very specific experiences: his work with children and mothers, as well as with borderline adult patients.[13]

According to Phyllis Grosskurth, in 1952 an editorial committee met to select contributions for a volume in honour of Melanie Klein.[14] Winnicott brought along an article he had written on what he called "transitional objects". Melanie Klein asked him to modify it and to make clear reference in it to her own ideas, but Winnicott did not accept this and, saddened, left the meeting. He was later said to have told his wife: "Apparently Mrs Klein no longer considers me as one of hers". This was very probably true. From his point of view Klein was not wrong because Winnicott – who was always to remain grateful to her – seemed to waver as a thinker, at least in some of his works, between undoubted originality and a dependence on Kleinian models, models which he reworked with an arbitrariness that cannot have met with her approval – as he himself admitted.

A short example will serve to demonstrate the delicacy of the situation. Melanie Klein placed great value on the mother's breast, the first object that elicited the child's capacity to enter into relationships; in this connection she insisted on the distinction between the breast and the nipple.[15] Her acute observation showed many analysts that the characteristics of the breast can be disjoined, split. In some serious pathologies it can be seen how the "giving" characteristics (the breast's ability to provide milk), which depend on the nipple (the organ of feeding), cannot be accepted by the baby as being in the same person together with the typical function of the breast, namely to provide softness. Now Winnicott, in his attempt to build a bridge between the positions of Melanie Klein and Anna Freud,[16] goes so far as to equate the breast in a perfunctory way with maternal care as such. So he treats the breast, which Melanie Klein had subjected to a precise analysis, as if it were a metaphor. Obviously Winnicott had every right to criticise Melanie Klein, but what he is doing here is not criticising, but distorting an important concept and pushing it in a direction which Klein could not follow. It should come as no surprise, then, that, in her eyes, Winnicott was superficial and ambivalent. Later, after leaving the Kleinian group, Winnicott was to write more coherently.

On the subject of the sense of guilt, Winnicott did work within the Klein group, not as an outsider like Fairbairn. But the group's work did not totally convince him. He tried to pursue its objectives, use its techniques, but there came a point where he felt ill at ease. He felt that he had to take a new direction, one which previously he had not clearly understood. There came a point where he began to see things which had been left as a deposit, as it were, by the wide variety of his experience. He felt the need to leave an atmosphere where guilt, for reasons he did not entirely understand, played a role he did not believe it to have.

It is possible to follow him along this path, examining passages taken from some of his more famous contributions. A possible starting point is the article which he took along to the editorial meeting and which he refused to modify. This article appeared in the following year, 1953, under the title "Transitional objects and transitional phenomena". Following on from this, he wrote two more which engage more directly with the theme of guilt.[17]

The transitional object was a great success. It was a powerful concept which caught the imagination, and in a short time entered the collective imagination – or at least that of the readers of Charles M. Schulz's *Peanuts*. The "comforter" from which Linus refuses to be separated has become the prototype of the transitional object. The infant's transitional object can be a teat, a teddy bear or, indeed, a blanket.

Winnicott described the paradox of this phenomenon in a style which was only superficially clear: in his view the transitional object is not an internal object (which is a mental concept): it is a possession. And yet for the child it is not even an external object. Winnicott formulates a complex theory: the small child can use a transitional object when the internal object is alive, real and good enough – not too persecutory. He believes that the qualities of this internal object depend on the existence, the vitality and the behaviour of the external object (breast, mother figure, care of the general environment). If the latter is bad or lacking, this leads indirectly to lifelessness or the persecutory quality of the internal object.

If external lack of success persists, the internal object fails to take on a meaning for the child, and then, and only then, does the transitional object too lose meaning. Probably this precise description of the importance of the external object marks the beginning of Winnicott's detachment from

Melanie Klein. The transitional object can mean the "external" breast, but also the "internal" breast. "The transitional object is never under magical control like an internal object nor is it out of control like the real mother."[18]

For Winnicott this is a paradox: the transitional object is at one and the same time a "created" and a "found" object. An interesting detail is that he adds the "care of the general environment" to "breast" and "mother". More causes come into play. The main factors that create aggressiveness in the child, he argues, are not simply a question of the death instinct, but depend on the vitality, the quality and the behaviour of the mother – and also on other contributing causes, such as the environment.[19] By illustrating how the situation external to the child can influence internal objects, and thus the Super-Ego, making it persecutory, he touches upon the problem of guilt.

Winnicott seems to modify the crude drama of Melanie Klein's writings, pushing her ideas in a direction that recalls the theories of Rousseau. For him cultural influences are of vital importance, but they can be studied as a superimposition of numerous personal models: "in other words, the key to social and group psychology is individual psychology" (a statement which not all would agree with today). Those who are convinced that morality must be inculcated "educate their children in accordance with this con-viction, and by doing so preclude themselves from the pleasure of observing morality developing naturally in their children when they grow up in a positive atmosphere provided for them personally and individually". He concludes: "in fact we have no reason to suppose that any individual who is not mentally retarded is constitutionally incapable of developing a moral sense".[20]

Is this position over-optimistic? Winnicott is peering into a darkness where it is difficult to discern firm parameters. He confirms the need to broaden horizons; he cites cultural influences, and ascribes vital importance to them.[21] Thus far all he seems to be doing is diluting Freud's concept of the Super-Ego.

The next point Winnicott makes calls to mind Rousseau's *Letter on Providence*, where Rousseau argues that the evils that afflict men are the product of a distorted historical development and the institutions that derive from it. Once the child has been guaranteed a good enough mother in a positive environment, argues Winnicott, there is no reason to suppose that it will not be able to develop a good moral sense. This is a clearly stated and important position because it sees morality, and thus ways of dealing with the sense of guilt, as depending on interpersonal relations, the environment and the family atmosphere surrounding the child. This is a position shared by many, both inside and outside psychoanalysis.

But Winnicott goes beyond this: he suggests that the original condition becomes tinged with despair and anger because legitimate expectations are frustrated or left unfulfilled. Does psychoanalysis contain an implicit theory of legitimate expectations?[22] Probably we are dealing with a level of need and response to need which is in many ways innate; ethology seems to confirm this view.

What remains from Melanie Klein's theory is the important role played by the early relationship with the mother (a role which no-one in psycho-analysis would now contest).[23] Again Winnicott underlines the fact that the mother can be good enough (that is, functional), but can also not be good enough, or even bad (non-functional). And this is the case independently of the child's instincts.[24] It is no surprise then that Winnicott was impatient with Melanie Klein and her group.[25]

At one point, when talking about his personal relations with Klein, he described how she put him into analysis with someone "near and dear to her". He then added: "it should be made clear that I never had analysis by her, or by any of her analysands, so that I did not qualify to be one of her group of chosen Kleinians".[26]

His second analyst was Joan Riviere, whom Winnicott saw as one of the leading supporters of Melanie Klein, together with Paula Heimann and Susan Isaacs. Is the implication that one becomes a Kleinian by direct initiation? And what about his impatience with her theories? When he talks about this question he defines himself as independent. This is the same adjective that was used to describe the group of London analysts that he joined and of which he later became a leader. There came a point when he realised that his ideas were beginning to diverge from Klein's: "in any case I found she had not included me in as a Kleinian. This did not matter to me because I have never been able to follow anyone else, not even Freud. But Freud was easy to criticise because he was always critical of himself."[27]

There are some very precise questions here which Winnicott fails to address directly: does Kleinianism, in one way or another, require an acritical, faith-like dependence? Does Kleinianism exemplify the typical closure of orthodoxy, or are the Kleinians defending basic scientific dis-coveries which they cannot give up and which Winnicott is betraying?

Psychoanalysis, as a therapeutic process, seeks to emancipate the indi-vidual, aiming to provide him/her with the means for becoming, within the limits set by the talents of each individual (including the analyst), as creative and as free as possible. Every communication that contains a trace of authoritarianism would seem to compromise this purpose. The problem could be reformulated: is Winnicott projecting his own personal conflicts or does he have a clearer picture of real problems than other members of the group he is working with? At one point he wonders whether Melanie Klein is capable of understanding him:

> Klein claimed to have paid full attention to the environmental factor, but it is my opinion that she was temperamentally incapable of this. Perhaps there was a gain in this, for certainly she had a powerful drive

to go further and further back into the personal individual mental mechanisms that constitute the human being who is at the bottom rung of the ladder of emotional development.

Winnicott uses the word "temperamentally". It is not clear what he means by it, given that temperament is a term used to refer to secret dispositions of character to which philosophers, doctors and psychiatrists have given a variety of different meanings. If he does not express himself clearly, it is perhaps so as not to hurt Melanie Klein, whose undoubted merits he always recognised. In a note in *On the Shoulders of Freud*,[28] I emphasised the importance of bearing in mind the possible extent to which subjective elements can impinge significantly on the creation of theories of personality: "We cannot rule out a priori the possibility that Melanie Klein might have unconsciously used Freud's theory of the death instincts in order to counter the charges levelled publicly against her by her daughter Melitta, as if to say: 'It is not the evil mother, but the death instincts which make the child destructive'". We shall be returning to the subject of the external world in Klein later.[29]

". . . you should meet Melanie Klein"

One of the discoveries made by psychoanalysis concerns the way in which the personal story of each individual influences his manner of thinking and pursuing knowledge. Is it possible to identify some of the formative events in Winnicott's own past? His first analyst, James Strachey, was very close to the anti-conformist Bloomsbury group – whose members included not only Virginia Woolf and John Maynard Keynes, but also Strachey's elder brother Lytton. James Strachey kept Winnicott in analysis for ten years (a decidedly long time for that period) and at a certain point said to him: "If you are applying psychoanalytic theory to children, you should meet Melanie Klein . . . she is saying things that may or may not be true, and you must find out for yourself for you will not get what Melanie Klein teaches in my analysis of you".

Today we know, or ought to know, that comments of this kind are not very "analytic". For all his extreme caution, Strachey failed to realise that the suggestion he made might have (one is tempted to say: was to have) a significant influence on his patient's later choices and on his conflicts with Melanie Klein. Evidently, Strachey had a rather imprecise idea of how transference works. But at that time this was the "style" of many analysts, and one has to say that this is perhaps one reason why – viewed with hindsight – so many analyses failed. Nowadays the emphasis is on not making suggestions or giving advice, but only on helping the patient to understand himself, to understand what he wants from life and to try to achieve it.

If we forget this side of things for the moment, we can recognise that Strachey's remarks were impressive on two counts: for one thing, they contain a humility that comes across as authentic and for another, they express an invitation to put the emphasis on the search for the truth, wherever it may come from. *Tragically*, however, these two qualities clash with the neutrality he ought to have maintained. The message Winnicott received from Strachey was a very pragmatic one. It is probable that he appreciated Strachey's "secular" intent, since he was to recall it much later. It was, of course, during this period – the end of the 1950s – that Bertrand Russell (1957) published, to much outcry, *Why I Am Not a Christian*. One of the points Russell made was that as a rule people adopted the religion of their family, or of the group into which they were born.

To gain a clearer idea of the ambiguity behind the questions that Winnicott tried to pose, we must look more closely at the intellectual climate that prevailed at the time when he was collaborating with Melanie Klein. On the one hand, Melanie Klein could exude a kind of Judaeo-Christian pessimism, seeing guilt as something one inherits phylo-genetically together with one's instinctual endowments, a kind of original sin. Klein's descriptions and theories lend themselves to such accusations. They recall the nagging doubts of Augustine of Hippo when he asked himself questions about his sins as a child at his mother's bosom. Winnicott can, from this point of view, be considered a neo-Pelagian, opposed to original sin. But was this really the basic dispute between the two of them? It should not be forgotten that Klein was the same woman who had, in her original, revolutionary way, investigated the process of idealisation.[30]

Idealisation combines with splitting to maintain on the one hand a completely good being, all love, altruism and justice, and on the other a totally bad being, all hate and deception. This produces many dichotomies: the fairy and the witch, the angelic woman and the wicked whore, the heroic lover and the poor husband, the male rapist and the man-child, one's loyal friends and treacherous enemies, and so on. But this insight also throws light on the much more solid and rooted idealisations at the heart of both monotheistic and polytheistic religions.

Without his apprenticeship with Melanie Klein and an understanding of projective identification, Winnicott would also have been unable to write passages as decidedly radical as this (again from the year 1962c):

> man continues to create and re-create God as a place to put that which is good in himself, and which he might spoil if he kept it in himself along with all the hate and destructiveness which is also to be found there.
>
> Religion (or is it theology?) has stolen the good from the developing individual child, and has then set up an artificial scheme for injecting this that has been stolen back into the child, and has called it "moral education".[31]

He keeps his eye trained on the child, but at the same time he does not take it off the environment. And he also keeps on simplifying, in one way or another. One suspects that Job, if he could have spoken as a lay person and not in a state of submission, would, in his heart of hearts, have agreed with Winnicott about the goodness of his God. The environment that Winnicott speaks about, as Freud suggested, is reflected in the Super-Ego, in the ideals and ideologies of the adults of the family.

One can add here that only a hasty reading of Freud would suggest that he put the emphasis on parents over environment: "The institution of conscience was at bottom an embodiment, first of parental criticism, and subsequently of that of society".[32] And in lesson 31 in his *Introduction to Psychoanalysis* we find: "the past, the tradition of the race and of the people, which only slowly yield to the influences of the present, to new changes, survive in the ideologies of the super-ego and, as long as they act through them, play a powerful part in human life which does not depend on economic conditions" (the reference to Marxism is evident).

When Winnicott talks of the facilitating role of the environment, he refers to something specific: "the environment does not make the child grow, nor does it determine the direction of growth. When it is good enough, the environment facilitates the maturational process."[33] Hence, when it is not good enough, it hinders the maturational process.

"Pining", "concern", and "responsibility"

Winnicott's article on the capacity for concern is considered to be the most important in his theoretical development. Here is a passage from it, again not immediately easy to understand:

> The word 'concern' is used to indicate the positive aspect of a phenomenon whose negative aspect is indicated by the word 'guilt'. The sense of guilt is anxiety linked to the concept of ambivalence and presupposes a certain degree of integration of the individual into the ego which enables it to keep both the good imago of the object as well as the idea of destroying it. Concern involves further integration and further growth and is linked positively with the individual's sense of responsibility, in particular with regard to relations where instinctual drives come into play. Concern refers to the fact that the individual cares, or minds, feels and at the same time accepts responsibility.[34]

Winnicott sees guilt and concern as two sides of the same phenomenon, although he thinks that concern requires a higher level of maturity. He clearly realises that the question is complex and feels the need to give a practical example. According to the Freudian theory of development, "Caring could be defined as the basis of the family: during sexual intercourse – beyond the pleasure of the act itself – both partners take responsibility for the outcome".

With his concept of concern, does Winnicott break away from Klein, who saw caring for the other as dependent on guilt? He does not say so explicitly. He does not seem to want to claim originality for what appears to be a new concept that stands in opposition to guilt.[35] But very probably he is wrong, and in fact he broke away from Melanie Klein not only on the question of the importance to give to the role of the good-enough mother but also because of his different conception of guilt and concern. But the terms of the clash, when put in this way, seem even clearer. Winnicott gives the impression of someone whose pupils are only now starting to dilate and who is making his way as best he can through a darkness that is centuries deep. What is more, he is moving across terrain that is mined and fraught with intense anxiety – for all involved.

Winnicott was interested in the atmosphere surrounding the small child, and consequently also in words. He thought that the terms "depressive position" and "paranoid–schizoid position" were both "bad". His basic Rousseauesque spirit made him feel ill at the very sound of the words. Was this why he thought it better to talk of concern?[36] A further digression will take us briefly away from these questions.

We know that it is best not to believe blindly in the proof value of etymology, even when it appears to be correct and in no way bizarre. Nevertheless, it can offer clues and at times reveal some fragments or hidden veins of truth.

We saw that Winnicott dedicated an entire lecture to concern. Melanie Klein (1940) often spoke about the feelings of "sorrow and concern" and while she talked about pining for the loved object on only a few occasions, she was convinced of the importance of this emotion.

> When the depressive position arises, the ego is forced (in addition to earlier defences) to develop methods of defence which are essentially directed against the "pining" for the loved object. These are funda-mental to the whole ego-organization.[37]

What is meant by "pining"? The basic meaning is "yearning", "longing"; it is suffering with "longing", a feeling which seems to cover a wide range of emotions from desire to nostalgia. So the term Klein chooses is over-determined. The word comes from the Old English verb *pinian*, to torment, which in turn derives from late Latin *pena*, a variation of *poena*, meaning punishment and at the same time suffering, as is still the case in some Romance languages. *Poenas expetere* meant to "take revenge". The Italian *pena* and the French *peine* suggest a feeling of pity at the sight of the suffering of others. So the term "pining" takes us to the very heart of the logic of guilt.

Klein's term "concern", according to Winnicott, seems to point in a different direction. Again, etymologically it comes from a Latin word: *concernere*. In the second-century Latin of Gellio and the fourth/fifth-century Latin of Augustine of Hippo it meant to "mix". In medieval Latin, as in Middle English, the meaning was "to establish a relationship with". At the same time it covered another nuance of meaning: "to distinguish". To be in relationship with, to mix, but keeping oneself distinct? This meaning has been kept alive in the Italian "concenere". The English meaning is "to worry about, to care about, but also to stand in relationship with", "relate to", and "to regard".

Another good choice. The term has made its way across the centuries, starting from the meaning of "mixing" and finally reaching "differentiation"! But in this case the logic of guilt and its attendant punishments seem to be excluded.

After this etymological digression, let us try to see whether it is possible to summarise Winnicott's position: while good-enough mothering and a facilitating environment create guilt, they also produce the capacity for concern; and concern leads to responsibility, and in turn to maturity, which seems to be founded on the capacity for being responsible. At this point the question that arises is why this courageous thinker did not emphasise the point that, in addition to the two positions upon which she constructed her whole theory, Melanie Klein also included a third moment in human development. And why did he not draw any consequences from the fact that Melanie Klein only mentions this third moment, and neither describes it nor constructs a theory about it? Indeed, more than once in her most famous works, Melanie Klein does speak about overcoming the depressive position when she mentions the normal working-through of mourning.[38] What exactly is this process of overcoming? Why did no one talk about it, and why is it ignored even today?

Chapter 5

Responsibility

The point in his development at which Winnicott began to address the question of guilt seemed to coincide exactly with his attempt to establish his autonomy of thought. Since this was also the moment when he was trying to become independent from Melanie Klein, it is worth looking back briefly at the legacy left by Klein.

In talking about an inner world based on the paranoid–schizoid position and one based on the depressive position, Melanie Klein was, according to Money-Kyrle, describing two types of "moral world" which tend to develop in succession in every human being as a result of innate programming. Each child's earliest Super-Ego is fed by its own projected destructiveness which turns against it. The same is true of adults who have remained fixed in that position: the more aggressiveness we harbour, the more our Super-Ego persecutes us. It should be remembered that Melanie Klein saw the death instinct as being effective from birth.

The internal world in which these forces move is, consequently, a delusory construct akin to the serious psychoses of paranoia and schizophrenia. What it has in common with schizophrenia is especially the use of splitting, and what it shares with paranoia is the need to project onto others. This Super-Ego, as described by Freud, acts like a primitive god practising the punishment of retaliation.[1] "This is not ego-syntonic," commented Money-Kyrle, "and a major aim of analysis is to weaken it."[2]

When the child is about four months old, the gradual appearance of the depressive position offers the possibility of a different "morality" – one which is more bearable, no longer in the form of a paranoid delusion but centred on the depressive guilt we feel on realising the injuries we have inflicted, either in reality or in our fantasy, on loved objects. To the extent to which these loved and injured people are *mourned*, they are felt to come alive inside us. They become trusted presences that come to our aid and support our ego in its battle against any remaining bad internal objects, as well as against our real external enemies.

Melanie Klein was immediately accused, more or less openly, of *inducing* a moral schema in her analysands. The defence against this accusation was simple: Melanie Klein believed that she was describing what she found before her. Even at that time, however, the idea that the observer was not neutral was already beginning to spread among psychoanalysts. At any rate the criticism persisted, so that Money-Kyrle, in his *Introduction* to the first volume of Melanie Klein's *Writings*, felt the need to defend her against these insinuations, as indeed others had already done.

In his view, Melanie Klein did not use moral pressure to "foster this kind of morality in her patients". When her analytical work succeeded in laying bare "the delusions behind the archaic morality" and the various mechanisms with which we defend ourselves against guilt (whether persecutory or depressive), the second type of morality tends to dominate of its own accord: "This change was considered [by Melanie Klein] as one of the factors indicating a change towards integration and maturity".[3]

Even after he had left the group for good, Winnicott maintained that Melanie Klein's contribution should not be disregarded, although he did criticise her for constructing a child psychology which ignored the contribution made by the environment. This criticism touches a delicate nerve: disregarding or underestimating the influence of the environment or seeing drives as the only causes of the sense of guilt (and – one might add – of other forms of suffering) could be tantamount to locating the cause of guilt in the child (and the neurotic adult). This is precisely because the ethos of guilt follows a dichotomous logic: either I'm guilty or you are. If it is not the environment (and the parents), it's the child. A possible reply to this is to argue that everything depends on the analyst's ability to interpret. But is it really enough to interpret with consummate skill to ensure that the analysand does not feel guilty?

Even though the tendency today is no longer to see theory and practice as intimately connected, it seems fairly obvious that this theoretical model continues to exert a strong influence, especially when decisions have to be made under emotional pressure, which is often the situation the interpreting analyst finds himself in.

Winnicott added other charges connected to this first criticism: he felt unable to agree with the use that Melanie Klein made of the theory of the life and death instincts and her attempt to formulate infantile destructiveness in terms of inheritance and envy. Finally, he was in disagreement with Klein about placing the origin of depressive guilt at four months. He thought this was too early; he wondered whether it was really important to put a time on it at all. However, as we pointed out above, he did give Klein full credit for having emphasised the importance of *concern*. Talking about the supervision he had with her, he wrote: "Klein was able to make it clear to me from the material my patients presented, how the capacity for concern and to feel guilty is an achievement, and it is this rather than depression that characterizes arrival of the depressive position in the case of the growing baby or child".[4]

Some writers have wondered whether Winnicott's position on the capacity for *concern* can be distinguished from Klein's, which, according to Winnicott "relates in a positive way to the individual's sense of responsibility, especially in respect of relationships into which instinctual drives have entered".[5] The word "responsibility" is of great significance here and needs to be examined very carefully before we carry on.

Melanie Klein, too, talks about *responsibility*. Talking about Ilse, a patient analysed in Berlin before 1932, she wrote: "Her way of dealing with her sense of guilt . . . was to reject all responsibility for her actions and in a very hostile and challenging attitude towards her environment".[6]

Let us look briefly again at the passage where Winnicott explains what he means by responsibility (the italics are mine):

> At the genital level in the statement of the theory of development, *concern* could be said to be the basis of the family, where both partners in intercourse – beyond their pleasure – *take responsibility* for the result.

The idea of the "responsibility" of love-making parents is in some ways very touching. This invocation of a moment that each individual ought to experience in its immediacy risks, however, being misleading. Psychoanalytically speaking it appears to explain very little. The motivations of the parents are not only highly complex, as are those of every human being, but also multi-layered: not only the conscious but also the unconscious is at work. Psychoanalytic experience recalls how *beneath* the type of "acceptance" which Winnicott mentions, there can be other conflicting motives. Clearly, this is always true and precisely for this reason the definition of terms such as "responsibility" is never easy.

All adults who have wanted their love-making to produce children are aware of the extraordinary emotion we are talking about. Alongside this emotion there is certainly the feeling that we are taking responsibility. But this does not exclude the possibility that our motivation could be spurious and ambivalent. A woman, to continue along the line of the examples given so far, can be absolutely certain that she wants a child from her partner, and common sense might say that she wants and desires it, yet at the same time she may have unconscious motives: she might want a child so as not to be abandoned by her man (on the principle, at least I'll get something from him) or to demonstrate to herself that she is a woman, or to reassure herself about her capacity to procreate, or to compensate for an unconscious castration wound. A man can take *responsibility* for the (hopefully male!) child and yet, without suspecting it, want it unconsciously in order to be able to realise through him ambitions he has not been able to fulfil himself, or to offload onto him his undesired parts, as in the case of the patient L.L. These are only some of the cases in which the child is used narcissistically; all contradict Winnicott's somewhat ingenuous idea of "responsibility".

Students of depression have long known that human beings can overload themselves with tasks: *formally* they take on a lot of responsibility, in a manic effort to boost their dwindling self-esteem. It is easy for a psychiatrist, or a psychoanalyst, to see that this is a defensive manoeuvre because such people are unlikely to find the time to seek treatment, even when they are in a bad psychological state. And if they do, very often it is because there is someone close to them who is suffering and whom they don't know how to look after: a son or a daughter who has become a criminal or a drug addict or who is extremely depressed or even suicidal. And this can be a son or a daughter who was in many cases "responsibly" wanted. In this context one could talk about pseudo-responsibility, but this would not help us to find a new definition of the term.

Winnicott's attempts to help us reach a better understanding of this multifaceted concept do not seem to be particularly clear.[7] Nevertheless, he recalls and intuits the central importance of responsibility at significant moments: clearly, this idea is at work inside him.

I personally believe that one characteristic of authentic responsibility is conscious and in some ways calculated risk-taking; responsibility implies that the individual is to a certain extent aware of his qualities, his gifts and his knowledge. A therapist, a psychoanalyst can look after a patient for various reasons: because he needs to earn money; because having a patient allows him to do training supervisions (an obligatory step towards obtaining a higher qualification, but also towards entering the profession); he can also want to cure others because this allows him to deny that he or she also needs to be cured. In all of these cases (and the list could go on) the therapist can count on what he has learned, on what his more senior colleagues can teach him and in this way he can take a series of risks. But can we truly say in each of these cases that he is taking a "responsible" risk? Analysts who use their patients to deny that they themselves need help (a not infrequent case) have marked the cards, as it were, in such a way that it is difficult to talk of an initial assumption of responsibility. Ultimately these are manic or hyper-manic states based on denial.

And yet this does not exclude the possibility that later such an analyst might progressively become more responsible. As he proceeds he will gradually have to weigh things up, to assess the progress he is making in his training. He will try to remedy things; he might undergo a new analysis and will try to look for other ways to grow. In other words, he will strive to become a sensitive therapist who is as aware as is humanly possible of what he is doing. This process of becoming progressively responsible is not exclusive to this path of professional training and indeed it will not always happen. Responsibility can be nipped in the bud, as it were; by cynicism, for example, or by madness. I make this point to emphasise how the path towards responsibility may merge with the broader path of the tragic.

If not on the basis of this emphasis on subjective responsibility, how then does Winnicott's view differ from Klein's? On the subject of guilt we could cite the objective *responsibility* for the good growth of the child which he attributes to the mother and the environment. It is important, however, to give this expression a precise meaning. The idea of objective responsibility does not refer to someone who is aware and free to decide about the consequences caused by his decisions. We are talking about a person who can be either conscious or not conscious, free or not free, who has objectively produced (or helped produce) certain consequences. There are then two very different meanings of the word "responsibility", each with very different psychological connotations. Our interest is necessarily also in the subjective meaning of the term.

We have now reached the watershed between the logic of guilt and the logic that transcends guilt. The former (which tends to influence us unconsciously all the time) often blurs this basic distinction; it is taken for granted that we are talking about the objective meaning of responsibility and instead we find ourselves talking about subjective responsibility. Or rather, when we speak of this subject we often alternate between the two meanings without realising that this is what we are doing.

I said earlier that one of the advantages implicit in Winnicott's idea lies in the fact that the explanation of the child's destructive aggressiveness towards the mother no longer depends principally on a concept like the death instinct, but on concrete and real human relations. The extent to which these relations are also influenced by drives is only one aspect of the problem, albeit an important one.

If we invert the sentence that we looked at earlier, what is the implication of what Winnicott is saying? He is in effect saying that two parents who bring a child into the world without wanting to look after that child are "irresponsible". In line with the theoretical model which he gradually built up on the basis on his experience, we can draw the conclusion that this "irresponsibility" very often negatively affects the emotional development of the child and can produce future sufferings. This is an idea that is shared not only by psychoanalysts: the vast movement which supports responsible conception fully upholds the same view.

So we should use the quality of human relations rather than the evocative power of words in order to understand more precisely what meanings to give to certain concepts.[8] This is another reason to investigate the term "responsibility" more fully. Put this way, the question may seem complicated to the point of incomprehensibility. In order to find a way out of this impasse I intend to shift the focus of my investigation to the private lives of the two leading figures in this case. Perhaps we shall find more convincing explanations if we look in that direction.

A letter to one's analyst

We can take as our starting point a paper entitled *Envy and Gratitude*, which Melanie Klein presented at the beginning of 1956, and which was published in a revised version the following year. It expressed the idea that the capacity to experience gratitude and envy are innate. On 3 February 1956, Winnicott wrote a letter to Joan Riviere about it:[9]

> Dear Mrs Riviere,
> After Mrs Klein's paper you and she spoke to me and within the framework of friendliness you gave me to understand that both of you are absolutely certain that there is no positive contribution to be made from me to the interesting attempt Melanie is making all the time to state the psychology of the earliest stages. You will agree that you implied that the trouble is that I am unable to recognize that Melanie does say the very things I am asking her to say. In other words, there is a block in me.

We already know what these things are that Winnicott would like Klein to say: he wants her to talk about the active role played by the external world, in particular by the mother, in the creation of the child's pathology.

In this work Melanie Klein, after recalling that the state preceding birth brings with it a sense of unity and security, pointed out that "how far this state is undisturbed must depend on the psychological and physical condition of the mother, and possibly even on certain still unexplored factors in the unborn infant". Then she added: "External circumstances play a vital part in the initial relation to the breast. If birth has been difficult and in particular if it results in complications such as lack of oxygen, a disturbance in adaptation to the external world occurs and the relation to the breast starts at a great disadvantage. In such cases the baby's ability to experience new sources of gratification is impaired and in consequence he cannot sufficiently internalise a really good primal object."

Up to this point, however correct Klein's opinions may have been and however easy it may have been to concur with them, she does not seem to be providing answers to the specific questions that Winnicott was posing. In the following passage she becomes much more explicit:

> Furthermore, whether or not the child is adequately fed and mothered, whether the mother fully enjoys the care of the child or is anxious and has psychological difficulties over feeding – *all these factors influence the child's capacity to accept the milk with enjoyment and to internalize the good breast.*[10] An element of frustration by the breast is bound to enter into the infant's earliest relation to it, because even a happy feeding situation cannot altogether replace the prenatal unity with the mother.

This passage seems to bear out what Riviere and Klein were suggesting to Winnicott: Melanie is already saying what you want her to say! You are the one who has no ears to hear!

A little later in the same book came a sentence which complemented (but did not replace) what had already been said: "The struggle between life and death instincts and the ensuing threat of annihilation of the self and of the object by destructive impulses *are fundamental factors in the infant's initial relation to the mother*. For his desires imply that the breast, and soon the mother, should do away with these destructive impulses and the pain of persecutory anxiety."

Klein went on to postulate "an innate conflict between love and hate", basically between the life and death instincts. Furthermore she described how envy can be at work in situations of deprivation, *but even in situations of gratification*, and interfere with normal gratitude. The effects of envy, in particular envy that has remained unconscious, influence the formation of personality and character: "I am implying that the capacity both for love and for destructive impulses is, to some extent, constitutional, though varying individually in strength and interacting from the beginning with external conditions".

Melanie Klein makes many statements about the importance of the environment and in her formal and conjectural descriptions she always includes external experience. She can rightly be considered more interactional than she is thought to be, as I pointed out in my Introduction. But she put a great deal of emphasis on endogenous factors and did not work out a detailed theory or phenomenology of interaction, or of how the actions of the external object affected the Self, other than in the general statement that bad experiences exacerbate anxiety and good experiences alleviate it.

But it was precisely for this reason that Winnicott felt unable to agree with her. He argued that the effect of the external world is more decisive, far-reaching and subtle: in my view, the concept of an innate instinct of death and envy takes up a large part of the area occupied by interpersonal relations. What he did not say, but implied (as we have seen, others will suggest it) was the view that these theories fail to create a "facilitating" atmosphere.

On the question of "responsibility", Winnicott would probably have said that Melanie Klein hypostatised a death instinct and innate envy so as to be able to draw the consequences she wanted to draw. These consequences ultimately obscured the extent to which the "not good enough mother" has an impact on the child's conflicts. Melanie Klein did not deny this, but preferred to steer clear of it. According to Winnicott, both Melanie Klein and her followers, in this case Riviere, tended to close up on this point and refused dialogue.

We need now to go back to Joan Riviere's letter in order to draw some conclusions. Winnicott felt that he was being interpreted (it is not clear how openly) as having a block with regard to Melanie Klein. The observation hurt him, but later he still felt able to discuss the question with Riviere (who was his analyst): "This, naturally, concerns me a lot and I really hope that she will give me a little of her time. I would gladly come to her, if she doesn't feel like writing a letter."

The tone is regretful and deferential. Very probably the part of him that was still dependent on her was upset but he wanted to separate his personal analysis from the scientific discussion. He enclosed a series of notes on the paper that started off the whole debate and briefly summarised three points he felt deserving of criticism. They are points we already know: two regard the concept of innate envy and the third relates to Klein's psychology of early infancy ("problems which are far from being resolved . . . the formulation of a concept that is very easy to disprove"). After recalling Melanie Klein's merits, he went on in a tone of irony that verges on sarcasm: "It is not surprising if a work which puts these three subjects together confusedly should not produce a good discussion. All that can happen is that those of us who want to support Melanie produce, as each of us could do, clinical material or quotations from the Bible in favour of her theses."

The bitterness Winnicott displayed here echoes a similar bitterness shown by Wilfried Bion. At a congress of psychoanalysts in Geneva, a few months before Winnicott's letter to Riviere, on 26 July 1955, Bion wrote to his wife Francesca about feeling somewhat dejected about Melanie Klein and her entourage: "To be a little irreverent, all this reminds me of stories that a friend told me about Marlene Dietrich, who, he said, used to surround herself with a team of handsome young men – handsome in the Teutonic sense, of course – who hastened to satisfy her every wish and to drive away anyone who looked like an intruder".[11] On the one hand Bion, an expert on groups, offered a picture of what he thought went on around Melanie Klein, but on the other, by comparing her to Marlene Dietrich, he paid her an "aggressive" compliment which Melanie, even if she had known about it, would not necessarily have been offended by (at least in her heart of hearts). If this really was the atmosphere created by Melanie Klein, then it is legitimate to doubt whether it was an environment that facilitated individuality.

In the last phrase I quoted Winnicott doesn't mince his words; he moves almost inadvertently from a scientific to a personal discussion. But he does so in private with his analyst and after expounding his scientific reasons. The other two, on the other hand, seem to have used analytical interpretation as a way of rebutting him: "I want you to know that I do not accept what you and Melanie implied, namely that my concern about Melanie's statement of the psychology of earliest infancy is based on subjective rather than objective factors."

Apparently Riviere and Klein had replied to him in this way (or perhaps only Riviere – the expression "what you implied" fails to clarify this point).

This is a key point that allows us to understand the entire question. Rodman made the following comment: "Even if Winnicott's theories were related to his own conflicts, it would have been a mistake to regard them as invalid on that account. He certainly could not have replied to such accusations in kind. Riviere had the advantage of having analysed him, while he did not have the corresponding one of knowing the intimate details of Melanie Klein's childhood." According to Rodman, any author's theories have an independent value and they should be accepted or rejected on that basis alone, no matter how interesting or even neurotic their origins may be. "Attempts at devaluing ideas by *ad hominem* references to unanalyzed conflicts are hardly unknown in the public and private deliberations of psychoanalysts of various schools. But we rarely have a chance to identify such instances in written form, or in cases such as that of Winnicott, in which a deliberate effort is made to crush potentially major contributions."[12]

To bring this sketch of the problem of responsibility to a close and to pass on to a saying from pagan Rome, I would like to recall a celebrated passage from the Book of Job:

> Again there was a day when the sons of God came to present themselves before the LORD, and Satan came also among them to present himself before the LORD. And the LORD said unto Satan, From whence comest thou? And Satan answered the LORD, and said, From going to and fro in the earth, and from walking up and down in it. And the LORD said unto Satan, Hast thou considered my servant Job, that there is none like him in the earth, a perfect and an upright man, one that feareth God, and escheweth evil? and still he holdeth fast his integrity, although thou movedst me against him, to destroy him without cause. And Satan answered the LORD, and said, Skin for skin, yea, all that a man hath will he give for his life. But put forth thine hand now, and touch his bone and his flesh, and he will curse thee to thy face. And the LORD said unto Satan, Behold, he is in thine hand; but save his life. So went Satan forth from the presence of the LORD, and smote Job with sore boils from the sole of his foot unto his crown. And he took him a potsherd to scrape himself withal; and he sat down among the ashes. Then said his wife unto him, Dost thou still retain thine integrity? curse God, and die. But he said unto her, Thou speakest as one of the foolish women speaketh. What? shall we receive good at the hand of God, and shall we not receive evil? In all this did not Job sin with his lips.[13]

There are any number of reasons for looking at the story of Job in a book about guilt (and this is probably clear from the number of times I have mentioned his name). One possibly even more relevant reason can be found at the beginning of Chapter 9, where I speak about the double bind.

If I have cited the Biblical passage about the pact between God and Satan at the expense of Job, it is in order to suggest that in the Judaic tradition (and subsequently in the Christian tradition, too) the problem of guilt always involves the children. If the passage is read in terms of the family, God (the Father) lets Himself be incited by one son, Satan, against the other, Job, and accepts the challenge that Satan in his envy puts to Him: He places Himself almost on a par with Satan. God the Father makes clear distinctions between Cain and Abel, between Jacob and Esau, who sends a malign spirit to deceive with falsehood the (godless) king Ahab of Israel so that he will die at Ramoth-gilead (1 Kings 22: 20). But this does not shock the readers of Kings, as Finkelstein, the great Jewish theologian, commented.[14]

In this tradition the parents are to be "honoured", not loved, and just like God the Father, they seem to be able to do everything without their omnipotence being called into question.[15] Freud concentrates on Oedipus, not on Laius and Jocasta; so the tradition whereby the analyst–parent calls into question the patient–son or –daughter and not himself or herself will probably have seemed natural to Melanie Klein.

It should be added that Freud is not stingy with his human sympathy for the "sons". One need only remember how, through the words of Goethe, he makes his "moving accusation" against parental "heavenly powers":

> You put us into the world
> You let the poor man become guilty,
> Then you leave him to his punishment,
> For every guilt is expiated on earth.[16]

Arguing "ad hominem"

The point made above by Rodman deserves further comment. The theoretical conflicts we are trying to reconstruct here can be contaminated by personal and even ideological factors. These factors can distort or paralyse the scientific method, meaning that they can obstruct research as well as interrupting dialogue.

What Rodman is referring to is a singular practice that dates back at least to Roman times. Instead of arguing against certain ideas, theories or hypotheses, the debater points out the limits and human weaknesses of the person who holds them. Typically this expedient – which goes by the name of arguing *ad hominem* or *ad personam* – is adopted by those who feel short of arguments, but this is not always true: the authoritarian personality tends to use it constantly. The authoritarian personality has his own particular ways of dealing with his sense of guilt, just as he has a particular way of treating his pupils and disciples. Generally he considers them as if they were appendages to himself who lack the capacity for independent choice or thought. The use of *ad hominem* arguments is a feature of fascism, according to Bollas.[17] Obviously there are varying degrees of authoritarianism.

Ad hominem arguments are mostly used to divert attention away from the subject under discussion towards the person whose ideas one wants to reject. In this case the purpose is fairly evident: if the other person lacks sufficient intellectual ability, then clearly his arguments also have no value. If, on the other hand, a writer uses episodes from the private life of a writer and personality traits as part of a critical look at a scientific idea, a delicate operation is set in motion whose sole purpose is to gather information. In brief: I do not think that Sigmund Freud can be accused of an *ad hominem* attack when he writes about President Wilson.

Among jurists and politicians, in other words, in discussions that take place in the public sphere, in the *agora*, it is considered an unfair practice. I wouldn't say that it is practised by all psychoanalysts, but it is certainly more frequent: mistakes must have been made in their training if analysts consider the use of *ad hominem* argumentation a "normal" mode of reasoning and don't even realise they are using it. This practice does not, however, seem to have been passed down to the younger generations of analysts.

It must be remembered, of course, that psychoanalytical interpretation has only one correct location: inside an analysis agreed upon on the basis of a contract. In other words, a person who is not well requests an analysis and this request is accepted by a therapist who thinks he is capable of relieving this suffering and takes on responsibility for doing so. Beyond this context, even among analysts, between the analyst and the analysand outside the setting or after the end of the analysis, analytical interpretation can prove to be a destructive act, precisely because it is then tantamount to *ad hominem* argument. Its use implies unresolved problems in the person who adopts it. For those who share this point of view, it is a thousand times preferable to use insult and vulgarity in scientific discussions than to make comments that refer to intimate aspects of the personality of one's interlocutor.

The use of *ad hominem* argument can easily be confused with a position which in some ways resembles it. In this book, for example, I have suggested hypotheses based on features of personality or episodes from the personal lives of some figures, hypotheses which could be considered very close to the *ad hominem* form of argumentation that I am censuring.[18] The reader might think that I was not practising what I was preaching, that I was criticising the use of *ad hominem* but then adopting an *ad mulierem* argument myself about some aspects of Melanie Klein's personality; this objection could be made (and indeed some readers have raised this very point, adding that she could not "defend herself"). This is a crucial point in my entire discussion about guilt, and so I feel I should set the record straight.

Independently of the possible validity of his arguments, the historian is called upon to gather his facts and expound his theses from a point of view that should *transcend guilt*. To think that Melanie Klein would have been offended by the arguments put forward in this context amounts to saying that she would not have been able to grasp the difference between the logic of guilt and a logic which takes into consideration the tragic, ineluctable aspects of human existence, in other words our shortcomings.

In my opinion, for it to be legitimate, and even desirable, to discuss personalities, we must avoid an *ad personam* attack: the personalities who are being "interpreted" must have acquired a certain historical importance (otherwise it becomes especially difficult to gather reliable biographical information); they must be no longer alive and an appropriate period of time must have passed since their death. Furthermore, the personal or private aspect of their lives must be part of the construction of a critical argument.

Such personal facts are not the same as gossip. Gossip contributes to the manipulation of history and should be ignored. Straightforward biographical information about important individuals, however, as well as descriptions of their particular characteristics, can help us to understand their mental state at a certain point in their lives and the influence that this may have had on their theories.

Donald Winnicott was born in Devon and grew up in the non-conformist tradition of John Wesley, the founder of Methodism, a man who was more interested in ethics than in dogma. Later, as a student of medicine, Donald converted to Anglicanism, but this did not prevent him from having a fundamentally non-religious attitude to everything he did. He took Joan Riviere to task for the dogmatic closure she betrayed in her introduction (Riviere, 1952) to a book by Melanie Klein, where she expressed the idea that Klein's system of thought had taken everything into account, and so all that was left to do was to broaden the application of her theories.[19] Winnicott, in a letter to Klein herself dated 17 November of the same year, said he was sure that not even she would approve. We come back once again to Winnicott's letter to Riviere: "My problem, when I start to talk to Melanie about her theory of early childhood, is that I feel I am talking about colours to someone who is colour blind".

Winnicott felt that there was an insurmountable barrier between them but he also believed that he saw things that she could not see. Klein maintained that she had not forgotten the mother and the role played by the mother, but Winnicott thought that she had given no proof of really understanding the function which the mother has at the beginning of life: "I say this very emphatically despite the fact that I have never been a mother, whilst Melanie naturally has".

He sees an example of this in Klein's statement "that there is a 'good breast' and there is the child, and this leads to an attachment to the breast".

For Winnicott this was too little; it was not a theory of early infancy. His main argument ran thus: "The 'good breast' is not a thing, it is a name given to a *technique*". It is the name given to the way in which the breast (or the feeding bottle) is presented to the child. For Winnicott the paediatrician it was a very delicate matter, which at the beginning of the child's life should be handled "sufficiently well":

> the mother must be in that particular state of sensitivity which for the moment I call a "state of primary maternal concern". If at the beginning she is not capable of identifying totally with her child, we cannot say that that mother "has a good breast". The simple fact of possessing the thing does not mean anything to the child.

Winnicott's position with regard to Klein becomes clear. But this explanation could also be taken as an example of the *quality* of human relations that might help us to understand the concepts we are using.

Winnicott's way of arguing gives us a broader basis for continuing our discussion. On the level of pure survival, it does not matter much to the child whether he has had a sensitive mother or not. What matters is that a minimum of protection and milk is provided – whether it is provided by a nipple or a feeding bottle is of little importance. But if – and this is the perspective of the preventive treatment of child psychoanalysis – we want the child to live and grow up with as little suffering as possible, then Winnicott's qualification becomes extremely important.

A first possible conclusion to be drawn from Winnicott's words could be as follows: we can only talk about a "good breast", about an "envious attack on the good breast", if the good breast has really fulfilled the child's needs.

One must not overlook how the tragic dimension also extends to this situation: in at least one respect, the dialogue between Winnicott and Klein is a dialogue between the deaf. There is a misunderstanding between Klein, whose attention is focused *primarily* on the phantasms that fill our unconscious, understood as products of our drives, and Winnicott, whose attention is *primarily* on the effect that reality can have on phantasms.

Winnicott believed that the mother ought to find herself in a special state of sensitivity towards the child she is suckling. This point (which Bion was also fond of emphasising) may seem simple, but it is not. What is he referring to? This state of sensitivity depends on numerous factors and many different circumstances. It depends on the psychic conflicts within the mother, but also on her state of weakness after the birth, on the repercussions the child's bad health may have on the mother. I recall the case of a child that cried for the first six months of its life for reasons that the mother simply could not fathom. The mother's sensitivity also depends on her ability to cope with tiredness and her ambivalence towards the sick child.

The discussion about the role that external reality can have on the individual was affected by Freud's discovery years earlier that the stories he was told by some of his patients about sexual molestation at a very young age (these were mostly patients who were hysterical or considered hysterical) were not true. Freud came to understand that the outbreak of neuroses was not necessarily caused by a dramatic and specific external event (typically for that period, patients talked about seduction by an adult), but could also be the result of internal drives.

This qualification opened the way for later discoveries which brought about an understanding not only of the pre-Oedipal roots of neurotic conflicts, but also of psychotic conflicts which had previously been impossible to interpret. In other words, an understanding of the complexity of a child's or an adult's psychic life needed to start from the acknowledgement that some events in his past had not in fact taken place and that the power of fantasy is at least equal to that of reality.

It is important to add, however, that Freud never gave up his theory of seduction (that is to say, to put it in more general terms, the pathogenic role of real people); what he did was simply to correct it.[20] Perhaps he veered too much in the latter direction, but he did maintain the theory.[21] Today some analysts would add: these events may not have happened precisely as that person believes and recounts, but still they are often based on some real external occurrences.[22]

Melanie Klein never gave up her theory of the role of the external world, as we saw above, and yet many psychoanalysts would agree with Winnicott that she was not really interested in this area. And her recourse to the much debated idea of the death instinct makes this tribute paid to external reality even more fragile.

Every day in his paediatric practice, Winnicott observed the interaction between anxious children and parents and this led him to place significant emphasis on the role of reality over and above the role of fantasy. "His own sense of reality and perhaps even his sense of fairness, demanded it of him".[23] Rodman felt that he possessed a particular sensitivity towards issues of guilt and justice. But to Melanie Klein, Winnicott resembled someone who was "obsessed by the fear of penetrating ever deeper into the unconscious and finding themselves, so to speak, in mid-air: far from reality and from real people".[24]

Winnicott's and Klein's positions might become clearer if we examine them in the light of the perceptive comments, expressed in simple and direct language, made by another London analyst, John Bowlby. He believed that psychoanalysis should study not only the way in which children are treated in reality by their parents and the effects this treatment produces upon them, but also the internal representations of the parents within the child or within the adult undergoing analysis. The main aim of the science of psychoanalysis should be to understand how one thing interacts with another, how the internal world of a person, made up of impulses, desires, feelings, representations, expectations, hypotheses and fantasies, interacts with the external world. Bowlby included here the intolerance one feels towards events to which one is and has been exposed, events which are often completely beyond one's control.[25]

As a psychoanalyst, Bowlby was concerned with one of the most important modern questions: the relationship between nature on the one hand and culture, society and history on the other. He anticipated one of the great turn-of-the-millennium themes: DNA versus education. Our genes push us towards certain environmental experiences and away from others; different behaviour patterns in a child elicit different reactions in parents.

Initially, Freud thought that the experiences of each one of us in our early relationships determine our future sufferings; later, without giving up his first hypothesis, he was particularly struck by the role of drives and fantasies.

To focus on the central question to which we are trying to find a more adequate answer: do the sufferings of the patient (as of all human beings) and his pathological behaviour depend on drives, on the unconscious fantasies that these express, or are they the result of a negative (pathogenic) or insufficient relationship with the figures of his early infancy? To put the point in a more extreme form: those who tend to "accuse" the drives stress the ambivalence which (in Freud's *Totem and Taboo*) children feel towards fathers; the advocates of the second position put the emphasis on the children's tyrannical and violent father. Reality lies in their complex interaction.

There are two important corollaries to all of this. The first is implicitly very much present in Freud: if the causes of a psychic phenomenon are multiple and interact with each other (which is what a person thinks when he views things from the vantage point of tragic responsibility), every time we, for some reason or other, do not give due consideration to new factors which are brought to our attention, we leave behind scientific research and move towards something more akin to orthodox religion.

The second corollary: Winnicott had suggested that, if we want to talk about an envious attack on the "good breast", we first need to ascertain whether the mother (with her breast) really responded well enough to the complex needs of the child. But then – considering the fact that this situation is repeated in transference during psychoanalytic treatment – one can say that in order to talk about envy in relation to the analyst's interpretations, there really needs to be a good enough interpretation by the analyst. All these qualifications would appear to seriously call into question the central role that Melanie Klein gives to the death instinct.

For Winnicott, his failure to get Melanie Klein to accept this point, or indeed to consider the point worthy of serious debate, was a "cause of great pain". He spoke of "pain", the word used by patient L.L. It is difficult to know whether, when he wrote these words, he was also considering another possibility: the equally painful, equally tragic idea that Melanie Klein *could not* accept his arguments, that something prevented her from doing so. It is true that he compared her to someone who is colour blind, but the insistence with which he continued – at least for a long period – to look for dialogue suggests that he thought (wishfully?) that he would eventually manage to convince her.

The central point about the dynamics we are looking at here is that Winnicott was induced by Klein and Riviere to feel guilty because he had experiences and ideas which differed from those of Klein. The cultural environment of the dispute made him not so much into a possibly fallible thinker as into a *culprit*.

A responsible rejection

In 1932, that is, after finishing his analysis with Strachey, and some years after Strachey had suggested he contact Melanie, Winnicott began a supervision with her. Klein began to send him patients and offered to supervise the analysis that Winnicott was doing with Eric (Eric Clyne), her son. Winnicott turned the offer down.

According to Klein's biographer, Phyllis Grosskurth, there was mutual esteem between the two: Winnicott asked Melanie for a supplementary analysis, which she did not grant him and she persuaded him to analyse her son. When this was finished, she wrote to him: "I don't know how to express the gratitude that I feel for all you have done for Eric". The analysis had lasted from 1935 to 1939 and, during that period, Eric had married and had a son, Michael, who later became very important in Melanie's life. At the age of eleven Michael Clyne went into analysis with Marion Milner. This time his grandmother was the supervisor.[26]

Years later, Marion Milner said how upset she had been by the scornful comments Melanie made about her son Eric; Milner had not realised that it would have been better to exclude her from her grandson's analysis. It seems clear that in the London psychoanalyst scene at that time there was an implicit hierarchical system whose mechanisms Milner, unlike Winnicott, was unable to escape.

Klein herself recognised that she was not a natural-born mother. Winnicott, on the other hand, who is said to have had a relatively happy childhood, apparently had a strong maternal identification. It is well known that Klein suffered from deep depression. Her face itself seems to me to betray signs of this depression. The photograph that appears on the front cover of her collected works bears touching witness to it: two eyes laden with sadness and eyebrows that are not arched but fall sorrowfully.[27]

According to Grosskurth's reconstruction, Klein in Berlin before 1932 had "analysed" her two sons Eric and Hans, and perhaps also her daughter

Melitta. This was common practice among many analysts at the time: Freud analysed his daughter Anna, and Abraham, who was Klein's second analyst, analysed his own daughter for some time, following Freud's own instructions.[28] These analyses were called "preventive" and at that period Klein still conducted them according to the principles laid down by Freud. Many, including Melanie Klein, were full of enthusiasm for Freud's still fresh discoveries, and engaged in what Klein herself was to call a manic denial. That is to say, they denied that the delicacy and complexity which marked the relations between parents and children far exceeded the possibilities of psychoanalytic technique and theory – which was true both then and now. What counted for them was doing analysis, no matter who with; it could even be with one's father or mother, just as long as it was psychoanalysis.[29]

With hindsight we can see that, in circumstances like these, the sense of guilt could not be worked through or interpreted unless by implicit reference to Freud's typically cold schemas based on the shift towards biology and myth, or by drawing on the debatable concept of the death instinct, as Klein did. But my impression is that in these cases the guilt remained frozen, or was transformed into something else. There was every chance that analysis might end in failure, and very often it did.

In the pioneering phase, the possibility that the psychoanalytic process might conclude negatively (not simply because it had not lasted long enough; after Freud's *Analysis Terminable and Interminable* (1937b), the interminability of analysis was considered to be in the nature of things) or that analytic treatment might not produce results was not really envisaged. It would probably have been seen as a sign of unacceptable defeatism.

Of Melanie's three children, her daughter Melitta later underwent analysis with Horney, with Sharpe and with Glover; Hans was analysed again by Simmel and Eric went to Happer, Searl and Joseph and, before Joseph, as we said, to Winnicott.

Even at that stage people were trying not to ask the embarrassing question as to whether it was right for a parent to send his or her own child into analysis. From the very beginning, analysts had realised that there was something deeply unnatural about this. What was it in these pioneers, both men and women, that deprived them of the basic common sense that would have advised them against it? What state of exhilaration, what rigidity, what illusion clouded their vision and prevented them from seeing the violence implicit in such an act?

If the messianic illusion promoted by psychoanalysis was to continue and the project of these analyses to be realised, one idea had to be kept at a distance – namely, that the parents might have caused their children's suffering, as we pointed out earlier when we referred to the Book of Job.

It was very difficult to face up firmly to the idea that the suffering of the children was produced not so much by "natural" circumstances (as we might describe the Oedipus complex), circumstances that have been repeated in an unchanged and ineluctable manner since the beginning of time; but rather by that complex itself, but now understood as a series of specific acts which could be attributed to the limitations of the parents, to their personalities, their blindness. If the idea had become conscious that one's own jealousy or possessiveness, one's own sadism or inattention, might have produced or even simply helped to produce one's child's neurosis, it probably would have led to beneficial crises and doubts. But – and this too is important – it would also have helped these pioneers to work through the disturbing idea that not all parents are equal and that, if some have a pathological influence on their children, others have no such influence at all or certainly much less. But this brings us back to guilt and to the ways in which to work through the sense of guilt.

The focus on counter-transference highlights the experience of the analyst, and thus also his responsibility and his sins. This is possibly why Freud and Klein considered it dangerous. Winnicott framed a general hypothesis that explained the "incestuous" aspect of these analyses very well: he focused attention on a phenomenon he called "intrusion". The term referred to the tendency of some mothers (but obviously this could also apply to fathers) to interfere in the development of their children, acting in ways that obstructed their growth. Surely he must have been thinking of Melanie Klein, who asked him if she could supervise his work with her son Erich after having "analysed" him herself. And if Winnicott had accepted her supervision, what would have happened to the aggressive fantasies that Erich harboured about his mother? How would he have had to interpret them to him? In terms of the death instinct or the deprivations and frustrations he suffered? And what would have happened to the rancour that Marion Milner felt Melanie nursed towards her son? Would she have been able to deal with this situation – supervising the analysis of her son Erich carried out by another – with detachment? And if she denied the usefulness of the analyst (and thus also the supervisor) recognising and using his or her own emotions towards the patient, on what basis would she have done so?

Supposing that Winnicott had gone through with this supervision and had accepted Klein's overriding idea that destructiveness and envy are the result of the death instinct, would he have managed to resolve Eric's conflicts without subtly inculcating in his patient the idea that, if not he himself, then at least his "biological" destructiveness was the ultimate source of those unconscious fantasies, those feelings that had to be "treated"?

We have no choice but to leave these questions unanswered; not without remembering, however, that apparently Eric was an unwanted child. During the pregnancy, Melanie was extremely depressed; the bereavement she suffered soon after his birth left her in such an anxious state that she was forced to go to Ferenczi for help. Very probably Eric would have felt the effects of this in the form of mounting tension between his parents.[30]

It is highly unlikely that any analyst today would challenge Winnicott's refusal to accept Melanie's supervision or deny that his decision was the mark of a more mature collective consciousness, an example of concrete, collective responsibility.

The unavoidably tragic dimension to this whole question might also reveal other unexpected depths if we accept that Klein, focused as she was on her titanic research efforts, in some remote corner, somewhere deep in her heart, was to some degree self-aware. Remember her words:

> whether the mother fully enjoys the care of the child or is anxious and has psychological difficulties over feeding – all these factors influence the child's capacity to accept the milk with enjoyment and to internalise the good breast.

Did her depression mean that she was not able to fully enjoy suckling Eric?

Given that she so admirably describes the manic mechanisms which we all adopt to deny depression and guilt, highlighting among the defences one she calls "control", can we be so sure that there was no self-recognition in this act of asking her younger colleagues to supervise the case of Eric and her grandson Michael?

In one of her most important essays, she emphasises that what is "specific to mania" is the attempt to control and dominate others. When we are terrified of someone and want to avoid feeling this terror (in other words, when we deny it), then we use our *"sense of omnipotence* for the purpose of *controlling and mastering* objects".[31] Something similar happens when we want to conclude the process that Klein herself called "false reparation" (repairing a person previously imagined as destroyed or smashed to pieces). Now, the question arises: did she know that, by analysing and supervising the cases of her own children and grandchildren, she was expressing a desire to engage in reparation in some way? Is this a confession, or to what extent is it a confession?

The ideas she expresses here about "reparation" are nothing if not clear: she refers to false manic reparation, carried out to avoid feeling guilt and melancholy; she explains that this type of reparation is nearly always impracticable and unattainable.[32] This is the deepest thorn in the side of her depression; how did she react to these words? The fact that she considered the supervision of her son Eric *practicable* and that later she actually *practised* the supervision of her grandson's analysis demonstrates that that she never had the least doubt. Perhaps this is another reason why her depression became so acute and became the other cancer of her old age. But these are only conjectures.

A woman of exceptional creativity and insight – in this respect she was equalled perhaps only by Freud himself – Klein saw into some of the jealously kept secrets of the human soul, enabling future generations, including many of her disciples, to understand and to overcome their limitations once they had achieved the right degree of detachment. It is very possible that she did not consciously realise, or at least was unable to fully work through the fact that, driven by some profound, magical, hopeless need for reparation, she needed to control the analyses of the members of her family. Nevertheless, "control" was precisely what she understood and theorised about. And we should be grateful to her for this. Each one of us, I believe, reaches the truth we can afford. However, some find themselves in that state of grace which allows them to hit upon truths which would be beyond their reach as simple human beings.

The chance it offers to create antibodies against one's own infection – which, though it may not be unique to psychoanalysis, is probably rare elsewhere – is certainly one of the most fascinating and comforting aspects of Freud's science. However, not all those united under his name seem capable of putting these antibodies to work.

Chapter 6

The dilating pupil: counter-transference

Melanie Klein descended further into the depths that Freud had only begun to explore. This took her on a journey through largely uncharted territory. To undertake this voyage into the heart of darkness she had, it is true, followed the maps and techniques of her masters, Freud and Abraham, but on the harshest stretches she was essentially on her own. This was partly because she was unable to hear those, like Winnicott, who suggested that she reconsider some aspects of reality. So she had to rely on her own personality, with all its talents and limitations.

Before Klein no one had explored guilt and depression in such a resolute and crude manner. By tuning into her wavelength we have learnt the extent to which destructiveness, even when it is only fantasised, is linked to the basic categories of anxiety, guilt and panic. Margaret Little, Paula Heimann, and in some ways Winnicott too, criticised her from the inside. She was wrong to think that their direct or indirect objections were only an expression of unresolved neuroses. But equally it is very probable that the climate that grew up around these divergences helped psychoanalysts identify new strands of research and discover new dimensions. Generally, when our pupils start to dilate in the dark, we see new things which we had previously not been able to make out. There were two main escape routes from the particular problem area we are talking about here: the first, and more popular, was through *counter-transference*; the second, "the one less travelled by", was through *ideology*.

There were several psychoanalysts who more or less simultaneously took up the question of counter-transference – Heinrich Racker, Paula Heimann and Margaret Little. I would like to look first at Paula Heimann. One reason for doing so is to be able to remain in London, in contact with the same group of thinkers; Racker was Argentinian and Margaret Little was less concerned with certain important issues. This does not mean that the thinking of these two authors was any less interesting than that of Paula Heimann. Racker's (1968) work remains a classic in the literature of psychoanalysis, and Little (to whom we shall return shortly) went so far as to argue courageously in 1951 that counter-transference *was an essential part of every analysis*. Today this is a statement which *in theory* almost all analysts have accepted.[1] The fact remains that Paula Heimann was the most influential writer on this subject.

Even her very first work testified to a decided need for freedom of thought. In Berlin she had undergone a "classical" analysis with Theodor Reik, a curious and open-minded man with a vast range of interests, who made a profound and original study of the masochism of modern man, guilt and the preconscious attention of the analyst, which he called *listening with the third ear*. These are all topics which I am trying to re-examine here. At first Heimann was close to Melanie Klein in London as a patient (until her analysis was discontinued) and friend, as well as an authoritative member of her group. Eventually Heimann joined the *Independent* group to which Winnicott also belonged. There are various explanations for the cooling of relations between the two analysts. King mentions that Melanie asked Heimann to withdraw her article about counter-transference.[2] Grosskurth (1986), however, recounts a more complicated episode which acted as the trigger. I quote this version because I think it raises an issue that is relevant to our discussion of guilt. In my view, the value of such stories should not be overestimated. There is always the risk that one is forced to take sides, to belong to either the orthodox or the infidel camp. Anecdotes serve, however, as an index of a climate of unrest, and they can also reveal mentalities and, as we shall see later, ideologies.

> The events of 1953 culminated in the definitive break between Klein and Heimann, a break which however did not become public knowledge until 1955. Klein was very upset about the state of her health, and also because of the bother of having to move house. Anyway, she managed to find a nice spacious first-floor flat in West Hampstead, at number 20 Bracknell Gardens. She sold her lovely house in Clifton Hill, where she had lived for twenty years.
>
> A few days after the move, Heimann's daughter, Mertza, gave birth to a son. It was a difficult birth, and Heimann was not allowed to see her grandson for more than a week. Precisely during this period Melanie Klein demanded that Heimann accompany her to choose curtains and carpets for the new flat. Paula Heimann was in a terrible state: she was terrified that she was not being allowed to see the baby because it was abnormal, and going on a shopping expedition was the last thing she felt like doing. Mertza Heimann says that her mother never forgave Klein for this demonstration of egoism and total lack of understanding.[3]

It is difficult to tell whether Grosskurth maintains the necessary distance of the historian here; the way the story is told and quotations are used seems to show that she wanted to highlight Klein's egocentric arrogance. On the other hand, we should not forget that it cannot have been an easy task

writing the biography of such a complex and controversial personality as
Klein: so determined, and with such great charisma.

Even if this particular episode was in fact apocryphal, it illustrates one of
the more naïve principles of the logic of guilt, the idea that if one person is
guilty, the other must be innocent: Grosskurth emphasises Melanie Klein's
arrogance and insensitivity, although she does admit that it came at a
moment of serious crisis. She puts less emphasis on Heimann's position,
which appears, to say the least, acquiescent. Why did she not explain,
gently but firmly, to her elderly analyst that she had absolutely no desire to
help her with her shopping, because she had serious worries of her own? To
what extent did this compliant attitude lead to breaking off the analysis?
Why did Paula suffer, why did she make no effort to turn down a demand
she found excessive? Did Klein brook no objections? Was she easily
offended? We know that in depressed people this is quite common. At the
same time other hypotheses should be kept open. We might well ask to
what extent Klein's character traits were encouraged and kept alive by the
yielding behaviour of some members of her entourage.

My feeling is that questions like these can help us find other openings,
other passageways into the world of the logic of guilt. If it is true that
Heimann began to think about the idea of improving the relationship
between analyst and patient, she must also have come up with some answers
on this point.

Firstly, she opposed what had been called the "theory of the analyst as
mirror", which Little had already called a myth. In its most banal interpretation (the one we have been using here), what Freud was saying was
that the analyst should *reflect* the conflicts of the patient and not reveal any
of his own. Heimann started to investigate counter-transference, in other
words, precisely those "responses" to the transference of the patient which,
according to Freud, the analyst ought not even to feel. He saw counter-
transference as a minefield but, at the same time, a tool of fundamental
importance for the analyst.

The analyst's feelings, precisely when they are connected to the patient's
experience, can prove to be a device for getting to know the most hidden and
otherwise incomprehensible elements of transference. On the question of the
potential danger involved, Heimann is implicitly making an important
statement: counter-transference which is not decoded can lead the analyst to
attribute to the patient mental states which belong in fact to the analyst
himself. An analyst who has worked through his conflicts and childish
anxieties in his own analysis and has established a ready contact with his
own unconscious "will not impute to the patient what belongs to him".
She uses one of the verbs typical of the world of guilt and judgement: *he will
not impute*.

Although expressed in an understated manner, the idea that the analyst
can introduce into his patients a pathology which is extraneous to them and

which belongs to the analyst himself was a kind of Copernican revolution, at least in psychoanalytic circles.[4] So not only might an analysis fail – in other words, produce no positive results – but it could even have damaging effects! To put it in the terms of the logic of guilt, the analyst could be *guilty* of adding to his patient's suffering. So it was not a question of the analyst perhaps not healing but at least doing no harm, or even a question of the analyst feeling guilty because the patient wants to make him feel guilty, but simply: the analyst *can be objectively responsible* for imputing to the patient things that do not belong to him. In this way psychoanalysis acknowledged what in medicine is called iatrogenic behaviour.[5]

Heimann's paper was never presented to the British Society. It contained no references to Melanie Klein or her thinking, and yet was included as an essential part of Kleinian literature and was often used in authoritative fashion by psychoanalysts of this school when talking about the analysis of complex and serious cases. For Melanie Klein the counter-transference, as it was initially for Freud, was, as we have said, an interference. The psychoanalyst Tom Hayley told Grosskurth that Melanie had repeatedly told him that, if one feels emotions towards one's own patient, one should carry out a rapid self-analysis.

Paula Heimann, on the other hand, dignified the emotions with which the analyst responds and elevated the counter-transference, if not yet to a *via regia*, then at least to one of the main keys to "an understanding of the patient's unconscious".[6] The fact that she recognised its positive value justly assured her a place in the history of psychoanalysis. All later elaborations of the concept of counter-transference necessarily started from this insight. Melanie Klein at any rate never disavowed counter-transference, and she has always been seen as the person who forced psychoanalysis to face up to the problem of counter-transference.

The loss of the notion of the analyst as mirror was to have far-reaching consequences. Margaret Little, who had met with Klein's disfavour precisely on the point of *reparation*, which Klein had been the first to identify, thought that, if the analyst could rely on attaining self-knowledge and maturity (and on the patient's own drive for health, the same force which helped him to decide to undergo analysis in the first place), then he would be able to supply enough of that *something* which was missing from the patient's early environment and which he needed so badly: namely, a person who would allow him to grow without interference or excessive stimulation.[7]

Little also argued that the analyst who is working to the best of his ability and who is self-confident must always be able to become aware of counter-transference, at least sufficiently to realise whether he is causing the patient to progress or to regress.[8] In other words, he should be aware of the need for a kind of systematic monitoring of his own reactions. In taking up this position Heimann was also subscribing to the idea, so important to Winnicott, that something "was missing" in the patient's childhood environment.

The mirror-analyst: first cracks

> *Je ne veux avoir ni amour, ni haine, ni pitié, ni colére. Quant à la*
> *sympathie, c'est différent: jamais on n'en a assez.*
> [I want to feel neither love nor hate nor pity nor anger. As for
> sympathy, that's different: one can never have enough of that.]
> (Gustave Flaubert)

Is it possible for the analyst to act as a mirror and not reveal anything of himself? This wish is one that goes back centuries. Seneca used the metaphor of the mirror when talking to his august pupil Nero about the proper attitude of a teacher. At times the analyst betrays aspects of himself involuntarily: for example, when he makes a mistake (he gets the time of the appointment wrong), or when he lets himself be carried away by an emotion of counter-transference (when he fails to "contain", as I shall explain later). But in addition to these episodic communications, he continually reveals himself "through his way of being and living . . . through his deepest and most genuine essential and human quality". One need only think of the furnishing of the room, his way of dressing. But we can also consider other factors: how this mirror-analyst responds with his body language, the rigidity of his features, the inflection of his voice, how often he speaks, on what occasions he chooses to interpret. Then of course there is also the ideology hidden, as it were, between the lines of his interpretation. All these not strictly verbal communications form part of what Jung called the *personal equation of the analyst*. Patients register it, although with varying degrees of intensity and sensitivity.

Probably every analyst sees this rule of the mirror in his own way. At the time when I was training, a famous remark by Anna Freud was doing the rounds: "many years ago we used to offer our patients tea to keep them in analysis".[9] Acting like a mirror might simply mean not taking tea and biscuits with one's patient at five o'clock in the afternoon. But the choice of the metaphor of the mirror is revealing. How many times does the effort (and basically that is what it is, although it is not perceived as such) the analyst makes to appear without emotion come to impact on and twist the already fervent imagination of the patient? The model was in itself a terrifying one.

Assuming that it is possible to embody a being that has no emotional responses, such a person would necessarily use defence mechanisms such as repression, suppression and isolation. He might then be perceived by the patient as an impenetrable oracle, a deity who possesses both incontrovertible truth and boundless will. The vaguely oracular pose (a kind of *ipse dixit*) adopted by some psychoanalysts tends, according to Fairbairn, to repress onto a deeper level the persecutory spirit that the therapist emanates

– partly thanks to transference – through his attitude. Clearly the therapist does not create the patient's conflicts out of nowhere; he can, however, make them worse and even make them impossible to analyse. He might elicit what appears to be a spirit of authentic collaboration in the patient, but which is in fact propitiatory. At worst, this attitude can become a barrier and turn into a general rejection of the analysis. If every objection or disagreement is then interpreted as resistance, this can lead to resistance to resistance: the so-called "negative therapeutic reaction", which is then attributed to the patient's death instinct. But the excessively distanced analyst can also produce different reactions: to patients who have regressed to a lesser extent or to patients who have kept a sense of reality he can give the impression of being insecure and worried.

The idea of the mirror was later taken up again by psychoanalysis to refer to other questions, among others by Lacan (for whom the first mirror is the actual mirror) and by Winnicott (for whom the first mirror is the mother).

The metaphor of the mirror-analyst had been suggested and favourably received in an age when the idea that the analyst might have a negative influence on the patient had not yet been entertained. Freud thought that mistaken interpretations did not cause any damage. This idea is linked to another of his convictions. Freud gave vent to all his fears about counter-transference in a work published in 1910: if the analyst "fails to produce results in a self-analysis of this kind [he] may at once give up any idea of being able to treat patients by analysis".[10] This view is as radical as it is disquieting. Does this mean, then, that the analyst cannot enter into dialogue with the secret voices of his soul, with his fears, his bewilderment, his anger, in response to the "influence of the patient"? Was Freud afraid of the sense of guilt? Was the inability to work through the sense of guilt the main reason why he too was never able to be free of certain moments of depression? The depressed person feels guilt but, as Freud himself realised, he does not know the real reasons behind it.

Heimann's view was that analytical interpretation is something that happens between patient and analyst, something they feel as mutual and reciprocal.[11] This statement is of considerable importance in the history of psychoanalysis: it is antithetical to the idea of the oracular analyst, the analyst who reflects without participating, the analyst–God dealing with the patient–Job. It represented a new way of understanding the analyst–patient relationship, which later many tried to adopt. In actual fact it was a project that was by no means easy to understand, let alone put into practice.

This new, "more equitable" way of relating to the patient aroused concern among many analysts. The danger they saw was that such an approach might prove to be demagogic; in other words, that instead of being an attempt to face up to problems, it reflected a tendency to avoid problems by entering into an alliance with the patient for the purposes of self-defence.

Some analysts started to realise that the pioneers around Freud, as well as many of their own number, had in fact entered into such a *mésalliance* with their patients. If we read Célia Bertin's remarkable biography of the Princess Marie Bonaparte from this perspective, we can see the extent of the collusion between Marie Bonaparte and Freud.[12] The analyst knows that most patients prefer to think of themselves as being in an adult, equal relationship with their analyst, because, if the patient accepts that there is a part of him that has childish needs (a need to *depend*), all the anxieties and persecutions experienced during the first period of dependence – on the breast, then on the mother and soon also on the father – are bound painfully to come to the surface.

It was to take decades to devise a model of understanding, but also a technique and an appropriate form of vigilance capable of making this project based on reciprocal emotions into something feasible. The analysts who left Melanie Klein all tended to move in this more "equitable" direction.[13]

Melanie Klein apparently did not want to get personally involved, or at least not in public. There are "confessions" which suggest that she continued in her self-analysis.[14] She talks about working through her grief at the death of her son Hans in April 1934, a death which led her to go into analysis with Sylvia Payne for seven months.[15] Probably the rule that applies to all psychoanalysts also applied to her: when formulating theories, one exploits what one knows of oneself (mainly her unresolved problems with the breast). However, we cannot always exclude self-deception, nor can we use our counter-transference for the benefit of the patient.

Let us turn once again to one of the leading figures in this story and look at a closely related question. Joan Riviere had made a very wise point in 1936(a): she warned against an excessive insistence on the analysis of aggressive impulses (the main source of guilt, according to Klein's theory), because she thought that nothing was more likely to lead to the failure of therapy, to deadlock, than the kind of analysis in which the analyst focuses only on aggressiveness. In my view, this insistence is frequently to be found in therapists who have insufficient experience in working through counter-transference and who tend to adhere rather rigidly to the models that they have learnt. Riviere added that not all negative reactions to therapy are attempts by the patient to bring about the failure of the analysis. But again such views were only partial visions, as we shall see later.

The patient's criticisms

Among second-generation Kleinian analysts, Herbert Rosenfeld stood out as someone who looked squarely at one of the most important aspects of the relationship between analyst and patient. In his last work, published posthumously, he wrote that sometimes analysts prove to be *insensitive to criticisms* from their patients and "in so being will miss significant communications".[16]

Rosenfeld was in no doubt that it is necessary to consider *the contribution of the analyst to the success but also to the failure of treatment*. In this context, he cited, among others, the American analyst Robert Langs, who had made acceptance of patients' criticisms of the analyst his central concern. The title of the book by Langs that Rosenfeld refers to is *The Therapeutic Interaction*, in other words the interaction between analyst and patient. For Langs it is fundamentally important to realise that a *spiral of communications* is set in motion between the therapist and the patient which involves interaction on both a conscious and an unconscious level. This spiral of communications forms the very heart of the therapeutic process; it is here that agreement is needed if the therapy is to be successful.

When the analyst is guilty of "distortion" (in other words, when he commits a mistake, or makes an observation that is incorrect or out of place) normally the patient responds with a masked comment that is buried under the material that he brings to the analyst. Even though this coded comment is unrealistic, it can still be *relevant*. The patient's criticism, if it is not realistic, adds a new distortion (the beginning of a negative spiral); but it is not so if it is based on a series of valid unconscious perceptions. The patient may have realised the mistake, the deviation, and thus his criticism of the analyst may be justified.

Analysts who are able to tune in to the frequency of these coded communications from patients know that they do occur. Much more frequently than one might think, the patient not only collaborates, but also insists on trying to correct the analyst. During the supervision of colleagues in training, this phenomenon becomes evident and is often corrected, consequently unblocking a therapeutic impasse. But at first, many young analysts find it hard to accept criticisms coming from the patient; most probably the ability to do so presupposes experience and confidence in one's own skills. Again the big obstacle to overcome is the sense of guilt.

Once he can open himself up humbly to criticisms from the patient, the analyst can acquire a tranquillity which he would have previously found unthinkable. Accepting justified criticism ceases to be a reason for a narcissistic wound or a sense of guilt, and is progressively perceived as the expression of an inner solidity, a solidity which, generally, patients, even seriously ill patients, can easily perceive, although their reaction to it is ambivalent.

So one needs not only to be vigilant towards counter-transference (self-monitoring), but also to pay close attention to the *possible* external monitor that is the patient himself.[17] Paula Heimann's definition of interpretation as something which happens in the emotional interplay between patient and analyst seems to lay the foundation for a clearer formulation of this theory.

If we adopt this new perspective, we must also extrapolate from and reformulate a phrase used earlier: before offering the patient the interpretation that he is resisting, or attacking dependence, or telling him that he is showing ingratitude or envy, the analyst needs to be certain that he has not overlooked valuable "significant" criticisms that the patient may have levelled at him, possibly even on several occasions.

Chapter 7

The devil with breasts: an interlude

Should the reader be troubled by the idea of an interlude at this point, I would invite him to skip this chapter – which he can treat as an appendix to the book – and to come back to it as and when he wishes. If, on the other hand, the reader would like to take a rest and to step back for a moment from the demanding material I have forced him to wade through so far, I would not want him to think that we are straying too far off the beaten track: this interlude also concerns guilt. The devil combines at least two relevant characteristics: he is a *tempter* – who induces us to commit wrongs – and, at the same time, he is the being from whom we have to expect *punishment* for these wrong-doings, at least when we come to find ourselves in his place of residence.[1]

Looking at some of the devil's mostly neglected characteristics may help us to understand what has been called "primary paranoia", a concept that might prove useful as part of a strategy that seeks to alleviate the patient's sense of guilt. So although this story is a digression, it contains a clinically important core. And like all fairy tales, it has a moral.

So let's talk about the devil. The image that most people have is of a limping figure with horns and a tail, with the hoofs of an animal and with wings and hairy thighs. Many will know that there is in fact a monument to the devil – which, interestingly, is to be found not in a land of infidels but in *El Retiro* in Madrid, the capital of the deeply Catholic country of Spain – where he takes the form of a beautiful young man with angels' wings. But perhaps fewer are aware that the same demon can have a woman's breast. Attentive readers of Sigmund Freud, however, will probably remember. Talking about the seventeenth-century painter Christoph Haizmann in *A Seventeenth-Century Demonological Neurosis*, Freud analysed some of his paintings and discovered what he called a "reference to sexuality".[2] The devil had appeared to the painter for the first time in the form of a respectable gentleman. But then in its second appearance it was naked and deformed, and had "two pairs of female breasts. The breasts, sometimes only a single pair, sometimes two pairs, appear in all the subsequent apparitions. Only in one of them does the devil display not only breasts but also a large penis with a snake at its end."

Freud wonders whether this emphasis on female sexual characteristics contradicts his theory that the devil represented a substitute father for the painter. "This way of portraying the devil is unusual", he adds. When *devil* is a concept that indicates a whole species of beings, when, that is, several devils appear, even the representation of female devils is by no means disturbing. "But as far as I know," he continues, "it never happens that *the* Devil, who is a great individual, the lord of hell and the adversary of God, is depicted as anything other than a male, and in fact as a super-male with horns, a tail and a snake penis."

For once, Freud proves himself here to be not very well informed.

We have already said that Klein places the early manifestations of guilt in the breastfeeding phase.[3] She was criticised because, it was argued, it is the adult who *a posteriori* ante-dates events.[4] Despite these criticisms, the myth would seem to prove her right. Unless, that is, the myth is guilty of ante-dating too.

Of Greek origin, the word "daemon" (*daimōn*) referred to genies who occupied an intermediary space between men and the gods. In the course of history, the term has taken on very different and even divergent meanings. From the earliest period of Christianity, apologists also used the word "devil" (from *diàbolos*, the slanderer, the defender of falsehood) as a synonym for daemon.

For the sake of convenience we shall use the word "demon" to include all the various other meanings and names, such as "devil", "evil spirit", "daemon", etc., because this term was the first to be used in demonology.[5] We should, however, note that while at the moment we use these terms as synonyms, from the point of view of the sciences that deal with demonic phenomena, such as sociology or ethnology, this is incorrect and can cause confusion.

In Mesopotamia, in the Assyrian and Babylonian empires, and in ancient Egypt, fears of demons were very much alive, as were practices to exorcise the devil, that is, to drive it out with formulas and sacred rituals or by the laying on of hands. Even Hinduism has its demons, which it has passed on to Buddhism. The presence of demons in Tibetan beliefs, and in all the forms of primitive religions known to us, seems to confirm that the need to create demons exists in all peoples.

Yet demons do not necessarily have negative characteristics: they can be either malevolent or benevolent. In ethnological literature *demons*, considered malign, are at times distinguished from *spirits*, held to be benign. But we also speak of the "spirit of evil". Apparently, where there are malevolent spirits there are also benevolent spirits. We can see here in action that process of splitting we have examined at some length.

However, when we encounter devils and consider them from the viewpoint of our culture and according to the patterns dictated by our prejudices, this can easily set off a chain of errors. The great French anthropologist, René

Guénon, a scholar of western and eastern symbologies, warned against distorting the image of the Chinese dragon, for example, which is considered by westerners as a persecutory figure. The figure of the snake, which Guénon shows as emerging from the dragon, is also misunderstood by those who are influenced by the archetype of the tempter, the Biblical snake. The dragon in China is the symbol of the Word as creator.[6] Similarly, terrifying figures in Chinese or Japanese Buddhism have the function of defending and protecting both individuals and sacred places from hostile influences. One need only think of sculptures from the Kamakura period in Japan.

But let us go back to the Greek tradition. In the version of Herodotus attributed to Hesiod, there were three orders of powers: gods, heroes and demons. Unlike gods and heroes, demons were not individualised powers and did not possess a cult of their own or engage in ritual practices.

Their function was intermediary: they were mediators between gods and mortals. In Manichaean thought, as in Jewish and Christian thought, the demon is no longer an intermediary. In Christianity this function was passed on to the Son, to the prophets and to other figures, as we recalled at the beginning. Intermediation became *intercession*, which is simply the entreaty that (punitive) treatment be benevolent.

When it loses his role as an intermediary, the demon seems predisposed to become the receptacle for projections of everything that human beings cannot stand about themselves and their lives – or to put it more simply, everything they cannot or do not want to know fully. Let us turn to a figure closer to home: Hesiod is from the eighth to seventh century BC, Herodotus from the fifth century BC. Pausanias, on the other hand, lived in the second century AD.[7] Pausanias talks differently about demons: he brings them out of the state of constant anonymity in which they were mostly portrayed. Demons were not a specific category for the Greeks: demonic powers lived at the margins of the political world or in the interstices of people's activities.[8] Nevertheless, they did eventually acquire particular names. And this is precisely the point I am getting at: first comes the name and then the sex.

For Pausanias, Euronymous is always a demon of the night, with rather curious characteristics: he is capable of taking on any form. He is recognisable by his bronze foot, a clear sign of mutilation. He feeds on human flesh, preferably women or children. To entice his victims he can also assume the form of a beautiful woman. Lamia is another demon who specialises in devouring children; she was a bugbear for mothers and wet-nurses, and was already a synonym for "witch" in the eighteenth century.[9] Another female demon, who was occasionally identified with Lamia, was Mormo, who was also invoked to threaten naughty children. The punishment she was said to inflict on children was to bite them and also to make them lame.[10]

All these antecedents of the demon are female; they move through the realm of darkness and exploit people's terror of being persecuted and devoured.

This is the kind of atmosphere that can be found in a large number of fairy tales, from Red Riding Hood to Hänsel and Gretel, which mothers tell their children even today, usually when they are trying to help them go to sleep in the evening.

Did these plots and stories that reflect the fantastic layers of the unconscious start to take shape at the time of the child's early conflict with the breast and the mother? We have seen that the mother who, for some reason, frustrates the baby at her breast, becomes, through the process of splitting, the wicked mother whom we can consider the matrix of all witches, and of all ogres and ogresses. So, if the connections I am suggesting here have any validity (and remembering that we must also bear in mind all the transformations caused by the many other frustrations of life), the mother becomes the matrix of all kinds of demons.

As we have seen, there is no agreement among psychoanalysts about the origins of all this. Many factors, including our drives, come into play. The situation is complex partly because mothers (and those fathers capable of showing tenderness) often feel affectionate cannibalistic impulses towards their children. We have all seen mothers taking excited pleasure in tickling their child's tummy, nibbling at it and threatening it by saying things like: "I'm going to gobble you up". And the child's reaction is to laugh blissfully.

From Homer onwards we find the spread of the cult of instigating and protective demons. The *daimōn* in Socrates is the inspiration of moral conscience. Around sumptuously laid tables in homes and in cities, some cults are integrated into what at least seem to be benign belief systems. Besides the cult of Zeus the Provider, we meet the cult of the Good Demon.

The myth of Metis and Athena marks a significant appropriation by a paternal figure – Zeus, king of all the gods – of prerogatives which were once exclusively maternal, and of features and skills that were typically female. Zeus possibly did not realise that by swallowing Metis, who was pregnant with Athena, he was not only coming into possession of the ability to give birth but also of the terrifying, dark side of nature that belongs to mothers. In the same way the Biblical God became the *creator* of sons and daughters. At the cradle of the screaming baby, the *babau* originally was female, maternal, and later was to become male and paternal.

Now we have reached the crucial point. At the very moment of birth, every child and every mother runs the risk of death, and this is the source of strong persecutory anxieties which fuel guilt, with all its need for omnipotence. We now know that the origin of many serious mental illnesses can be traced back to a lack of – or deficiency in – a mother's care, or to an excess of engulfing possessiveness in early infancy.

In the attempt to reclaim the terrain of the early relationship between the mother and the child, a powerful paternal figure comes into play. The father – unconsciously – takes on a double function, both protecting the family and acting as a kind of lightning conductor: I will relieve you of these anxieties. Fornari called this process (which he did not see as a sign of illness) "primary paranoia". For him this meant that the unconscious persecution that is part of birth leaves the relationship between mother and child, and is placed instead inside the figure of the father. The father thus acquires "the function of the shock absorber and guarantor in the face of dangers which threaten the birth of the man's child".[11]

Myths contain traces of their history and elements of these – very often mutually contradictory – ambiguities. To come back to the serpent referred to by Guénon, both Zeus the Good Demon and Zeus the Provider appear in the form of a serpent, a phallic symbol, and thus, a paternal symbol, as people would now say. But the serpent is an ambiguous figure in numerous popular and religious traditions. In the Sumeric saga of Gilgamesh, as indeed in the Bible, the serpent represents the diabolical, the enemy that drives people to sin, but in the Cretan tradition it refers to the ability to cure, to heal; probably because of its ability to change its skin, it evokes the idea of rebirth after illness. This tradition also provides the inspiration for the myth of Asclepius (the god of medicine described by Hesiod and praised by Pindar) who chose the serpent as his symbol.

Zeus the Provider and Zeus the Good Demon are no exception to the ambiguity of myths and their connection with food and the need to be fed reflects their links with maternal demons (the mother is the first food provider). Their place is in the larder, in the storehouse, where staple foods are kept. And after they have eaten, Zeus' table companions drink a grateful toast to him with pure wine.

But the female, the terrifying maternal component of the original demon, always seems destined to return, with the vehement force of the repressed; strangely, however, this escaped Freud's notice. The mythological tradition exploits this theme in a spirit of great vitality, producing a vast number of phantasmagoric creations. The Musée des Beaux-Arts (on the first floor of the Palais Rohan) in Strasbourg contains a polyptych by Hans Memling (1435–1494) depicting demonic figures with enormous voracious jaws, but also with clearly female breasts, withered and careworn. Strasbourg, incidentally, is the city where the first edition of *Malleus Maleficarum* – the fundamental work on witch trials – was published.

Mouth and breast (the distinctive signs of orality) are represented in connection with the demon and hell in many other prints, paintings, drawings and tapestries. In a German woodcut of 1525, an anonymous Protestant artist depicted the pontiff being handed over to the Demon. An angel bears him in flight close to the mouth of Satan, who not only has wanton female breasts, but inside whose mouth there is a fully laid table with five guests.

Entry into hell has been associated with the mouth from the times of the translations of the sacred texts – one need only think of Isaiah (5:14): *Therefore hell . . . has opened her mouth without measure*[12] – and it is confirmed by lesser works such as the splendid miniature of a *Book of Hours* of 1450 kept in Utrecht, the extensive series of woodcuts for *Epistola Luciferi* by Matthias Huptutt (*c.* 1507–1510) and the celebrated *Adoration in the Name of Jesus* (also known as the *Dream of Phillip II*) by El Greco (*c.* 1577). The list could go on.

Michael Pacher was an Austrian painter and sculptor who lived between 1435 and 1498. In his altarpiece *The Devil and St Wolfang*, kept in the Alte Pinakothek in Munich, he painted a mouth in the place of an anus. It is one of the many portraits of the devil with a face instead of buttocks: in the witches' Sabbath his subjects had to kiss it (the so-called *osculum infame*).[13]

Finally, some depictions of Dante's *Inferno* can be found in the Campo Santo cemetery in Pisa. One of these bears the inscription

QVESTO+ENINFERHO+DEL+CHAPOSAHTO DI PISA

Here Satan, complete with horns, stands out at the centre of four *bolge* (pits), surrounded by sumptuous tables and voracious jaws. His head has three mouths, out of which emerge the bodies of three great traitors; between his thighs, in place of the genitals we find something that Dante does not describe: a mouth out of which comes a human body, pulled down by its arms by an animal-like demon that acts as a midwife. The equation mouth–vagina (one need only think of the dreams of toothed vaginas) is well known. I do not think there can be any doubt that what we have here is a representation of birth. When Dante comes before God, what is the only image that he thinks capable of describing this scene?

> There is no babe that leaps so suddenly
> With face towards the milk, if he awake
> Much later than his usual custom is . . .
> As I did . . .[14]

The child turns towards God as a giver of milk; in other words, a mother. We know that Pope John Paul I maintained that God was a mother before being a father. Behind the Devil and behind God, both the artist and the poet seem to find the wicked mother who devours and destroys and the good mother who feeds and cheers up the child.

Turning from the particular to the general, from the devil to the demon, at the end of the eighteenth century and in the pre-Romantic period, under the influence of the Enlightenment and of poets such as Schiller and Goethe, the *positive* aspect of the demon returns and grows stronger, coming to represent the irrational force of man, the creativity of the artist.

Plato's *Symposium* taught us that the art of divination, the sacerdotal art of sacrifice, of spells and every sort of magic – in other words all knowledge that seems to transcend human limits – passed through a demonic being.

But also guilt – and this is the point I am trying to get across – pushes man beyond human limits.

The devil became definitively virile in the patrocentric religions of Judaism, Christianity and Islam, or in those which were almost mono-theistic such as the Mazdaism of pre-Islamic Persia. Later he was to become more explicitly and openly female – through demonic possession, a kind of symbiotic fusion, or through the sexual act.

Chapter 8

Ideology and guilt

When I think of the subject of guilt in connection with ideology I am reminded of a rather Gothic remark made by a shrewd old friend of mine: "ideology is like the blade of an axe whose edge is steeped in guilt". Just like an axe, ideology makes clear divisions: on the one side lies truth, on the other, falsehood; here stand the innocent and the good, there the guilty and the bad.

I have always been fascinated by the subject of ideology and its relationship with psychoanalysis, partly because it seems to me to be a topic which, despite its centrality, has received little attention. I hope to demonstrate its importance in this and the next chapter. In order to understand the potentially interfering role of ideology, however, we need first to take a few steps back.

Freud was aware that certain risks could arise during psychoanalytical therapy. He saw counter-transference, for example, as a threat to the scientific nature of psychoanalysis.[1] And a further risk was the indoctrination of the patient by the analyst.

Some analysts, instead of responding to the conflicts of the analysand and trying to reach a clearer understanding of how these relate to their own theoretical models in a way which serves the interest of the patient, reverse these priorities: the patient is asked to serve the theory and to satisfy the analyst's need for reassurance. What emerges from the patient is used to confirm the validity of the analyst's theoretical models and to lend legitimacy to his actions, to confirm his supposed ability to help others. Freud was not necessarily thinking of these specific dangers, but his warnings seem to point in this direction.

The metaphor that Freud used to explain how to avoid this risk is well-known: the analyst should proceed like a sculptor – taking away, chipping away at the marble, removing the clay until the statue takes shape. While the "wild" analyst imposes *his* ideas and *his* norms of behaviour on the patient rather than investigating the latter's unconscious, the well-trained analyst, in Freud's view, should not do this. He believed that this is not difficult for the analyst, simply because he has no need of a "vision of the world", no need of a *Weltanschauung* whose emotional usefulness stems from the fact that "trusting in it, one can feel secure in life". The analyst should be satisfied with a scientific *Weltanschauung* whose sole aim is the "search for truth".[2] *Weltanschauung* is a term which is very close to 'ideology' – the word that largely replaced it, before itself entering a period of relative decline.

Freud comes up with some perceptive insights on the subject of a person's *Weltanschauung*. He sees it as being the result of childhood influence; he can see that there is something analogous to religion in it: science "is convinced that those who are unaware of its applications expose themselves to harm". However, he underestimates the difficulties involved in trying to flush out ideology from all the recesses where it is hidden.[3] In this respect he was the victim of an illusion.

The image of the analyst who removes without adding may be very appealing, but unfortunately it has proved to be erroneous. It is not enough for the analyst to take away conflicts and complexes, to break down a patient's defences and resistance; he should also provide the patient with something that enables him to think about himself in a more useful and practical way; he should lay the groundwork for the process of healing old wounds. The analyst must help the patient understand how he can resume or initiate a process of separation and individuation; in a word, maturation. This is undoubtedly a noble and arduous task, because it requires sensibility and care, as well as maturity – the sole guarantee that the analyst is not exploiting his patient.

Freud himself not only deployed the technique of removal, but adopted a rather directive approach. He confessed that he had "never found it easy to direct the attention of my patient" and that he exercised a certain amount of influence ("Now, I should like you to pay close attention to the exact words you used"). Moreover, his approach to the material provided by the patient was didactic ("I'll explain that to you presently").[4] But most importantly, he was unaware of how ideology might unconsciously suggest some decisions rather than others.

Willy Baranger was probably the first person in psychoanalysis to look at the question of ideology.[5] Previously, under Freud's influence, psychoanalysts had seen ideology as uninteresting, something that belonged rather to philosophy, sociology or the history of ideas. Even now, after many authoritative works have been written on the subject, most analysts continue to see it as a topic of no importance, irrelevant to clinical practice, even irksome.[6]

Baranger pointed out that, generally speaking, the analyst was supposed to "engage in what one could call ideological abstinence" during therapy. It was one thing, he said, to assume a pedagogical attitude, but quite another to be motivated by an ideology, although the two can merge into one another. The case I shall refer to shortly of "the nourishing father" falls into the category which Baranger calls pedagogic.

In Baranger's view, even saying to a patient something like "this behaviour of yours is masochistic" is not so much an interpretation as a call to the patient to stop behaving that way. If, on the other hand, the analyst offers an interpretation along the following lines: "you are trying to harm yourself because of such and such a situation which happened in the transference and by doing so you are repeating the model of a situation from your childhood", this is no longer didactic. However, the apparent objectivity of this interpretation does not make it non-ideological. The idea underlying this interpretation, namely that the blamed behaviour is masochistic, neurotic and thus to be avoided, remains intact. "In many cases this implicit judgement does not create many problems, but in others it does", Baranger commented.

The rule of ideological abstinence goes something like this: the analyst "must avoid exerting any type of influence on the analysand that is ideological in nature", that is to say, he must avoid making comments to the patient which are based on his own religious, political or ethical beliefs.

Well, went on Baranger, *this rule is inapplicable.* In support of this outspoken (and still shocking) statement he lists several arguments: first of all, this statement presupposes that we can isolate a whole area of the analyst's personality outside his analytic activity. Secondly, the "scientific" ideology of the analyst (the psychological principles and concepts which he uses in his interpretations) cannot be independent of his other ideological conceptions. But he went further: the principle adopted in the treatment in itself implies a normative attitude.[7] And fourthly, this interpretation looks both forwards and backwards. That is to say, it not only explains the patient's past, but expresses a purpose, namely "to modify something in the inner world of the patient; in other words, to modify his intentions and their future realisations".

His final point is that psychoanalysis is itself an ideology, in both the narrow and the broad sense of the term. In the broad sense, "if we define ideology as a systematic set of representations, psychoanalysis is an ideology like any other science". In the narrow sense, it is an ideology in that it implies "a certain perspective on the world, norms of behaviour, values which can govern behaviour. There is such a thing as a psychoanalytic ethic." All these theoretical arguments, concluded Baranger, are confirmed by a very simple observation: "during the course of analysis, ideological changes take place in the analysand".

It seems to me difficult to agree with everything Baranger says; his definition of ideology probably needs to be examined more closely and from a more specifically psychoanalytic point of view. However, what he says is extremely courageous: for one thing he does not demonise ideology, but points simply to the undeniable element of planning that it contains, thus rightly introducing a basic note of doubt into the quiet lives of colleagues who continue to think they are immune from ideological influence.

George Downing, in his *Il corpo e la parola* (*The Body and the Word*), looks at the possibility of a therapeutic approach which combines psycho-analysis and body-therapy. He makes the strikingly obvious point that even the words "Say what comes into your mind", with which the analyst is traditionally supposed to start the first session (irrespective of whether this phrase is still used or not), contain an element of ideological bias. By asking the patient what comes into his *mind*, "we tacitly invite him to neglect his bodily experience: to look inside, to be receptive, to find 'what comes'"; we narrow his perspective. "Implicit in what we say is the suggestion that the patient should stay on the level of knowledge and image. We ask him for thoughts, words and images; we exclude bodily experience." In other words, we take for granted that the most important thing to do if we want to make him feel better, to change (and also to communicate) is to influence his purely mental activity.

One could argue that feelings, and talking about feelings, are still "mental events". But Downing's observation does point to a still very common idea, namely that the mind is the place where there is no body and that it is antithetical to the body.[8]

I shall describe how ideology comes to interfere in the relationship between two people by looking at a variety of examples. We shall start by analysing fragments taken from psychoanalytical sessions whose common theme is the identity and gender of the analyst. I shall then make some observations about the need that people feel to idealise mythical figures and also try to understand how this need can produce stereotypical commonplaces. As we know, commonplaces, like prejudices, reflect blind patches.

We shall be looking especially at how ideology creates the sense of guilt. Perhaps my friend was right: *all* types of ideology (in the negative sense of the word) have the tendency to create guilt; *they use guilt to govern*, to exercise power over others. The first examples involve patients and analysts, but as we go on, especially as our third case unfolds, it should become clear that what emerges has a general import. These are complex problems and so I shall try to tread as cautiously as possible and limit myself to a few simple observations.

In this first fragment a male analyst offers the following interpretation to a patient: "You have to eat something every day before coming to the session because you cannot stand the idea that a *good father nourishes you* with his interpretations". The question of whether this interpretation is correct or not does not interest us here, only the words that I have high-lighted in italics. The second episode takes place before the actual analysis begins, but does have an influence on it. This case takes us back some decades, to a time when many psychoanalysts asked patients who needed to be referred to colleagues whether they preferred to have a male or a female analyst.

General experience confirms that this is still done today, although perhaps less often than in the past. In the next chapter, we shall look at a much more intricate situation – where a patient is "co-opted". To conclude this overview of ideology we shall then re-examine the Judgement of Solomon.

The nourishing father

When an analyst defines himself in an interpretation as a good father (or a good mother, or simply a good analyst), what he is doing is first and foremost exerting pressure on the patient. He is introducing a positive judgement about himself and what he has done for the patient. He leaves behind the "neutrality" of psychoanalysis and enters the field of manipulation. Without being conscious of doing so, he is influencing the patient in an authoritarian manner and in a way that tends to make the patient feel guilty.

Let us suppose that the analyst has understood correctly that the patient eats not out of hunger, but for some defensive reason. His interpretation suggests that the patient eats something before coming to the session, not because he is anxious (although this is probable) about the idea of depending on someone (and so running the risk of repeating those childhood moments of great suffering which I have already emphasised), but because he does not want to recognise the good parent that he is lucky enough to have in the person of his analyst. The expression "cannot stand" could sound like a kind of indirect accusation that he is somewhat envious: I am good, I help you and you cannot stand it!

But let us come to the second part of the expression: the nourishing father. Here it is easier to see the element that we have called ideological. I believe that nowadays there are probably very few people in our culture who would be taken aback to hear that a father feeds a son or a daughter. In a psychoanalytic relationship, however, it is not common sense that matters. When a patient reveals his fear of not being self-sufficient and of having an unconfessed need to depend on someone who accepts him and nourishes him (and this is true of all analyses), this usually points to the reawakening of a conflict which has its roots in the oral phase. *At its origin* lies a problem relating to the first time we were fed, as we all need to be.

The influence that early relations between the child and the mother have on adult psychic conflicts is manifested through what we have several times called the genetic factor – something which is very similar to what ethologists call *imprinting*. But, if suckling the child is a maternal role, then the expression "the good nourishing father" does not correspond to what is reproduced in the transference.

Why bother with such subtleties? First of all, because the expressions we are analysing create confusion and also because such interpretations often reveal an unresolved conflict in the analyst. If the analyst is a man, this conflict may be due to a fear of losing his virile characteristics if he embodies a female or maternal role. Clearly, the conscious or unconscious idea or fantasy activated by the patient's request is enough to trigger the analyst's defence process.

Our therapist could thus belong to the category of analysts who see themselves as being of the masculine gender in their relations with the patient because they are men, or of the feminine gender because they are women. In this case, a maternal function becomes paternal only when the person performing it is a man. Freud himself was honest enough to declare openly the difficulties he experienced when acting as the maternal transfer object and when eliciting pre-Oedipal conflicts in his patients, just as he also confessed his uneasiness with negative transference. But Freud had on his side the fact that he was a pioneer. On other occasions – and here the level of pathology is higher – the male analyst does not even think what it must be like to exercise a maternal function because he has left his conflicts with his own mother unexplored. He has left them encysted inside himself and no-one has helped him to explore them.

The second case I have chosen allows us to go more deeply into the questions raised by these preliminary reflections.

Accepting and containing

The second situation is one where the analyst asks a patient looking for analysis whether he or she prefers to be analysed by a man or a woman. The need to ask this question seems to be based on the confusion between male and female gender and male and female function we discussed above. This confusion can manifest itself in various ways. I outline this case not so much to tell a particular story, but because I hope that this will allow us to understand better the various ways in which ideology can influence the analyst's behaviour and the repercussions this may have on his sense of guilt.

For centuries, in many cultures including our own, function, sex and gender were experienced as one and the same thing: on the one hand, there were masculine activities, to be carried out by men; and on the other, there were feminine activities, to be carried out by women. The dividing-line was clear-cut, never to be crossed over or called into question. We should also not forget that there are many societies where this is still the case. The various forms of collective unconscious seem to reflect this fact. The function of giving birth, suckling and taking care of children was an exclusively maternal/female function, and so was looking after the house and house-work. The function of procuring food and other means of sustenance, by hunting or non-agricultural work, was paternal/male, as was engaging in politics or fighting wars. Today we know that either sex can perform all these functions, excluding some connected to conception, gestation and birth.

Up to 1901, that is, up to the case-history of Dora, Freud believed that transference developed because of some real characteristics in the analyst, but later most psychoanalysts began to realise that this view was mistaken and that, on the level of the unconscious relationship, the gender of the analyst did not have any great influence on the transference. When, as occasionally happens, the male analyst and the female patient fall in love with each other and act on this emotion (courting, sexual relations, etc.), I believe that this can be seen as a sign of something much deeper: the incapacity of the analyst to contain and deal with certain primitive anxieties and violent needs in the patient. This also applies to *acting out* between a woman analyst and a male patient. This is a complex issue that would lead us beyond the confines of our subject. What I am trying to suggest is that, although things might be different at the beginning of the analysis, the sex of the analyst only matters when the analytical couple finds itself in an impasse.

Usually this impasse occurs because the analyst has engaged in such deeply-rooted defensive practices (for example, taking part in the erotic transference, when sexual relations are involved) that he is unable to deal with the tensions and demands which the "enamoured" patient or "seductress" addresses to him the analyst *as to a mother*.

The patient, while he regresses on the couch, tends to project *onto* or *into* the analyst *all* the figures that people his interior world: his father, his mother, his brothers and sisters and so on.[9] During therapy he has to be put in a position to do this; if the analyst is not able to provide a stage for all the performances that the patient feels compelled to put on, proper psychoanalysis cannot take place. It is precisely in order to facilitate this dramatic projection that the life and personal characteristics of the analyst should remain unknown to the patient.

A hysteric, for example, if she knew a lot about the reality of her analyst's life, would not be able to act out one of her recurrent behaviour patterns, namely treating her analyst as a seductive, inadequate and violent parent one moment and, *a moment later*, as a son who has a deep need for protection and who elicits maternal self-sacrifice. An extraordinary example of such repeated sudden changes comes in the famous monologue *La voix humaine* by Jean Cocteau. If we interpret the manifest content, we find that the lover who has left the protagonist is first experienced as a cruel mother, and then immediately afterwards as a child that should become emancipated and go off and fend for itself, even though the mother (the protagonist) will die from the pain. It is right that she sacrifices herself . . . no, it is wrong! And once again everything starts *da capo*.

This happens – with some variants – with hysterics of both sexes in their relations with analysts of both sexes. But this behaviour pattern only follows this "natural" sequence under certain conditions: the analysis must be carried out within an appropriate setting and the analyst must have reached a certain degree of maturity and cohesion.

Basically the setting must be kept consistent and caring and not too rigid. It may seem a paradox, but the looser (or the more rigid) the setting, the more the sex and the real characteristics of the analyst himself or herself come to the fore and interfere with the patient's fantasies, altering them, or making them so indistinguishable from reality that it becomes impossible to interpret them. What is projected becomes confused with reality. As long as the analyst sits quietly in the auditorium, as it were, attention will be paid to the music that is being played. Obviously, as we know, absolute silence in the auditorium is impossible to achieve.

But this type of setting cannot simply be created and maintained by whoever wants it and plans it. Experience, especially experience gained from the analysis of seriously disturbed patients over the past few decades, has highlighted a previously unsuspected phenomenon: the patient directs much of his destructiveness against the correct and necessary maintenance of the setting, if for no other reason than that he wants to keep his analyst – to whom he attributes so much power and transference meaning – under control. What I am saying about the *setting* applies even more to what I shall call the *internal setting*; in other words, the analyst's ability to contain. There is a positive aspect to this: the patient tests the therapist's ability to contain, and only if he passes the test will the patient have sufficient courage to place more trust in him.

In order to ward off these attacks, the analyst must be able to accept a variety of projections, each of which will be accompanied by a range of different types of aggressive behaviour. He must then be able to work through these behaviours and give them back in the form of interpretations which are not too intellectual and are therefore easy to digest. This is by no means an easy task, but only in this way will he avoid making the patient feel guilty.

By "accept" I mean taking in with one's whole self – body and mind. I would not want the addition of the word "body" here to go unobserved. Wilhelm Reich, who alone rediscovered millennia of oriental knowledge, also understood that inhibitions, defences and conflicts lie hidden within the body (in the tense or relaxed, hypertonic or atonic state of the muscles, etc.). These body states could interfere with the mind activity which, according to recent research, is located in the body.[10]

Drawing on the intellectual and rational abilities which many of us possess, it is relatively easy to accept the consequences of transference, especially when one comes from an open, non-repressive culture. (Once again the paradox is only apparent: someone who comes from a culture that is not open is normally incapable of accepting this even when he intellectualises or rationalises.) It is by no means easy to accept – genuinely and non-defensively – that one will be "transformed", for example, into a depressed and deadly mother or into a scornfully judgemental father. This is especially true in situations of extreme tension, when the patient offloads onto the analyst the whole of his primitive wish to destroy. It is certainly not easy for a man whose unresolved relationship with his own parents has left him with deeply-rooted and unexplored prejudices about his maternal parts.[11]

But this ability to contain can prove extremely difficult to acquire *even for a woman* if she has not resolved these conflicts. In the most severe cases, appropriate containment can turn out to be impossible for analysts of either sex.

Let us consider the example of a patient who tries to deny feeling any need for the analyst, who denies the emotion felt by the small child he once was – the child who needed his mother and was not given sufficient attention. This type of patient can elect to defend himself through a reversal of roles: by taking on the role of the mother and trying to put the analyst in the role of the child. If the therapist stops at this first stage, that is, if he *accepts* this situation, the analysis is unlikely to turn into a harmful sado-masochistic relationship (one where the analyst does not come out with utterances such as "you're the one who depends on me, not me on you"). Even if he reaches this level of acceptance, however, he will still end up in an impasse. It is by a process of working through (in other words, the process of decoding and comprehension that the analyst must be capable of if he is to interpret correctly) that the analytical relationship can resume and the patient can enter into contact with his own denied needs.

I have now moved on from talking about the ability to accept to talking about the *ability to contain*. This is the technical expression used currently to refer to this difficult process. The ability to contain children is typically and primarily a female ability, connected as it is to female organs and functions – the vagina, the uterus, the womb – but also to the capacity to embrace a child.

Those who are able to do this spontaneously and naturally probably have difficulty imagining how hard it can be for a therapist to contain emotions and the parts of the self (in the above example, the unwanted child) or the internal objects (the deadly mother, the scornful father) that the patient places within him. We have considered feeding as a maternal/female function; but a paternal/male function can also fall victim to a similar destiny. We shall be examining this in the next chapter.

Let us return to the analyst who asks his patient if he prefers to have an analysis with a man or with a woman. Such a question is likely to strengthen the resistance of the person who has turned to psychoanalysis for help. A kind of hidden agreement can be reached between the "referring" doctor and the patient: i.e. let's leave aside certain problems relating to your psychosexual identity; let's leave aside some of the persecutory family objects you have repressed. This kind of complicity will have negative repercussions for the therapy – and these repercussions will be serious if the patient's pathology is severe.[12] So, for example, a very violent mannish young woman whom I had occasion to observe over a period of many years, the daughter of a depressed alcoholic mother who had abandoned her and an (only apparently) considerate father, might choose a male analyst, in her desire to avoid confronting her psychic pain and the difficulties connected to the development of her endangered femininity, as well as the sense of guilt inevitably connected to her relationship with her mother.

Assuming that all this makes some kind of sense, I think that, when an analyst has to refer a patient to a colleague, he should, in the interests of the patient, ask himself whether the male or female colleague he is considering has sufficiently developed and integrated the male and female parts of his or her personality. This applies especially to those maternal and paternal aspects which need to chime with the demands of the patient. However, there is no point in asking the patient, who would not ask himself, let alone give a reply.

As pointed out before, for centuries sex and role have largely coincided and in many cultures this equivalence continues. The distinction between sex and function is a relatively recent breakthrough, and the determining factors in this development have been the feminist movement and a certain type of psychoanalysis. Suckling a child to ensure its survival, to go back once again to an unequivocally maternal function, can also now be carried out by a man, the father; even by a brother or a sister, a boy or a girl.

This form of suckling may not be identical to breastfeeding by a mother. The difference will be registered as a lack by the child who has not experienced the real nipple and the real breast; but the man or the woman who bottle-feeds the baby will also feel a loss, because they will never know what it is like to have a child suck their breast. The specifically female or male functions (one thinks of the suckling nipple penetrating the mouth, or the penis penetrating the vagina) are unique, but the partial, or basic, functions which are performed as part of each of these specifically female or male functions (the ability to penetrate, for example) are not exclusive to one sex.[13] This can help the analyst, and all sensitive people, of the other sex to understand the functions which are not part of his or her biological make-up. Psychoanalytic technique does not expect the analyst to perform specifically parental functions in all their complexity, but only the part that relates to an understanding and working through of what has happened and all its consequences. Direct experience probably enables many people to fine-tune the skill of identification. Complete identification, however, must always be beyond reach.

Chapter 9

The double bind and guilt

Excited and bursting with enthusiasm, a five-year-old boy comes up to his grandmother, a very important person in his life, to tell her what has just happened to him. Gently but firmly she interrupts him by saying "*pomme poire*", going on to explain: "I am listening, you know, carry on, but be careful, you have to say '*pomme poire*' so that your mouth stays small. I'm telling you for your own good; one day you'll be grateful to me." (Incidentally, the old lady had a very large mouth, while the little boy's mouth was perfectly normal.)

On the surface it would appear that the old lady is merely showing concern for her grandchild, but in fact what she is doing is something much more complex: for one thing she interrupts him, and then – from an objective point of view – she communicates to him that what he is telling her with such joy is not as important as certain other things that affect him. Finally, she unexpectedly forces him to pay unsolicited (and slightly delirious) attention to his body at a moment when he is busily engaged in expressing himself. She brings him to a halt. What we have here is, to say the very least, an example of inconsistency.

Before trying to look more closely at the relationship between ideology and guilt and before going on to examine our next clinical case, it might be a good idea to clarify a concept which we have referred to on several occasions: the *double bind*. This is the most successful discovery in the human sciences made by the Palo Alto Group, one of the few ideas formulated by this school which has been taken over by a wide range of psychoanalysts. At the heart of this phenomenon lies a kind of "logical perversion". Initially the expression "double bind" was used to refer to a characteristic type of interaction in families in which one member was diagnosed as schizophrenic. The parent of the schizophrenic is perceived by the patient as someone who sends out contradictory signals. This inconsistency becomes more evident when the behaviour of a parent half precedes and half follows an act by the patient. For example, the parent can ask the child to express an honest opinion and, once he has expressed his opinion, can accuse him of being disobedient, lacking in affection, ungrateful and so on.[1]

Later the concept was extended to include many types of human relations. In an important work entitled *Pragmatics of Human Communication*, an attempt was made by Watzlawick to identify the main characteristics of the double bind. Firstly, the relationship in which the communication is made must be intense; the point then is that (a) the message says something, (b) it contains a comment about this first statement, (c) the two statements – the assertion and the comment – are mutually exclusive. Finally, (d) the person who receives the message discovers that it is impossible for him to get out of the emotional situation – he cannot comment on the message, he cannot ignore it, and he cannot clam up.[2] Basically he finds himself in a very complex kind of trap.

Let us try to apply this sequence to the case with which we opened this chapter. The grandmother who recommended saying *pomme poire* says: "I'm listening to you, you know, go on"; then she adds, "but be careful, you have to say '*pomme poir*', so that your mouth stays small. I'm telling you for your own good, one day you'll be grateful to me." The consequence of a double bind devised along these lines is that the order must be disobeyed in order to be carried out. If the child in our example says *pomme poire*, he cannot carry on saying the things he is saying with the same enthusiasm.

When the underlying hidden trick is not understood and exposed, the double bind produces paradoxical behaviour which in turn is inconsistent. The model is perpetuated in a spiral and – on an individual level – can produce psychic or psychosomatic disturbances. *Every time it generates guilt, it also generates persecutory guilt.*

Later the Palo Alto school was to argue that some double binds are harmless while others are pathogenic to varying degrees. The double bind can communicate on two levels, one verbal and the other non-verbal. By this I mean the bodily apparatus which produces communication through inflexion, tone of voice, rhythm, and so on, and which manifests itself in gestures and bodily expressions. One level can contradict the other and thus belie it. A parent can constantly encourage his or her adolescent child to be "adult" and "responsible", or to do more competitive sport and, at the same time, be sceptical about his or her chances of success, either verbally, perhaps jokingly, or simply using facial expression. He can of course also employ open derision.

When I talked earlier about the hidden trick and the need to bring it out into the open, I was referring to something which is in fact very difficult. Those who have grown up in an atmosphere of double binds are usually unable to avoid them because they fail to recognise them. The double bind is all the more pathogenic when certain other conditions are fulfilled: the communication will usually take place inside relationships (such as those involving parental affection) which have very high "survival" value; double binds are repeated all the time and are aimed at someone who has not yet achieved the maturity necessary for independence of judgement. In these cases all that is needed is a brief memory of the original sequence to produce a reaction of panic or anger.[3]

The woman we shall shortly discuss realises that something has gone wrong, mounts strong opposition to the double bind she has been subjected to, but has to turn to her analyst in order to shed light on a tangle of messages and behaviours which she cannot quite understand.

There are very few escape routes available to someone trapped in the impasse created by a double bind if they also want to continue what they see as a positive human relationship. Sometimes the person who has received the message is able to point out the contradiction to the "transmitter". But often the "transmitter" is not aware that he is communicating through double binds, and generally has deep-seated and powerful reasons, which are also conflictual and ideological, for brooking no objections.

If he does accept the criticism, the *insight* is usually only very short-lasting. Mostly these are people who are not capable of steadily working through a sense of guilt or of adequately containing primitive persecutory anxieties. In other words, the double bind reveals a form of pathology which – although encysted – exerts a strong influence. Accepting criticism is very rare; the sender of double bind messages normally responds with rationalisation and self-defence.[4]

The studies underpinning the theory of the double bind have been examined closely and carefully on several occasions. Some writers have reached the conclusion that the double bind is a necessary but not sufficient condition for the outbreak of pathology.[5] On this point most psychoanalysts would probably agree.

We now come to the case of the "co-opted" patient, whom we could call the "child-senator" to highlight the inconsistency of the situation in which she is placed. V.V. is an experienced middle-aged manager. During one session towards the end of her analysis, she tells her analyst about a situation in which she found herself. One of the associations she belongs to (a culturally prestigious charity) has a council of "elders", a kind of "senate". Every now and then new members join this council, nominated from among people who have long been known to the "senators". The new member is co-opted and V.V. is the last person to have been elected. However, some of the "elders" are younger than her.

Some time after being co-opted onto the council, V.V. goes along to a meeting. Several members are late, and while those present are waiting for a quorum to be reached, the chairman asks V.V. to talk about a subject on which she is quite knowledgeable and which is of interest to various members of the council. Later, when the quorum is reached, the chairman brings this digression to an end and opens the meeting. V.V., present at such a meeting for the first time, participates actively and naturally without feeling ill at ease because she is in the company of people who have been her friends for some time.

Thus far the background. The patient then goes on to tell her analyst about the main point: the day after this episode, a member of the council (who, incidentally, had been the first to put forward V.V.'s name for co-optation) met V.V., took her aside and told her: "If I may give you an uncle's advice: yesterday you made a bad impression. I wasn't there, but people have told me that you didn't let anybody else speak! And it was your first time at one of our meetings!"

Would Franco Fornari's theory of affective codes make psychoanalytical sense of this episode?[6] In this situation maternal and paternal components put together, piece by piece, an ideological mosaic which tends to engender guilt.[7]

Seen from a purely sociological point of view, the "philosophy" of the "uncle-senator" does not appear to be the product of a group with a vertical power structure that selects executives for co-optation (in other words, on the basis of an unquestionable decision made by those who are already members).[8] He appears rather to be the advocate of a two-stage initiation rite whereby the newcomer is accorded a particular space or function over time. First stage: election and entry; second stage: a period of relative silence.[9]

His exaggerated accusation – "you didn't let anybody else speak" – is a way of saying that the new member should have shown deference or symbolic submission towards her colleagues on the council by talking as little as possible, since it was the first time she had attended one of their meetings. But there were no such explicit rules. Apparently, this is the practice in some Masonic lodges but there the rules are evidently made clear to new members. Such "unspoken" rules about the type of behaviour that is "expected" remind one of children who assume that if they are talking to a stranger, he or she will know names and places that are familiar to them. It is difficult for a child to conceive that when he says "Max", the stranger he is talking to does not understand immediately that he is referring to his dog. These are residues of omnipotent thought.

The hyperbolic "you didn't let anybody else speak" is likely to trigger a sense of guilt. The origin of two-stage rituals such as the one implied by the committee-member lies in the unconscious desire to avoid distressing either the long-standing members or those who have only just joined the group. But why should the members of this "senate" be distressed if a new member behaves like someone who has been a member for a long time? What balance is disturbed? What unconscious spectres are raised?

The usual reply (the true reasons are unconscious and remain so) would be to argue that the behaviour suggested by the patronising councillor is "natural". Ideologies create their deception using two techniques: they present themselves as reality, and not as an arbitrary construction; and they treat the social and cultural causes of the phenomenon in question as if they were natural.

Despite his advanced age, the "senator" had not realised how important it was for a person who had struggled hard to achieve maturity – as in the case of his friend V.V. – to develop and maintain a sense of equality. Perhaps he was unaware of the importance of having a healthy degree of "contractual power" which allows people, depending on the individual situation, to avoid being abused, getting lost in empty rituals, or simply not experiencing the disadvantages that ensue from inhibition or reverential fear. Failing to understand this, he is also unable to appreciate the talents of a friend he esteems and is very fond of. Ideology fogs the mind and prevents the flow of positive feelings. It prevents one from enjoying good human relations to the full.

As with all initiation rites, the one practised by the older committee member might have found its formal expression within the association. The fact that the chairman asked the newly-elected member to speak while waiting for the quorum to be reached suggests, however, that this idea of the symbolic subjugation of the new member (a subjugation that does not serve the real interests of the council) is only practised by a small sub-group: the elderly committee member, the person who reported the episode and perhaps one other person.

It is worth adding that V.V., who was getting on in years, and the senator, who was only a few years older, are fond of each other and have enjoyed a long-standing friendship, tempestuous perhaps but basically good and pleasant. The patient has no doubts about her friend's "good intentions" or about the affection he has previously always shown towards her. Ideology disregards all this; as Freud appreciated, it has its roots in distorted past relations which have somehow become fossilised and encysted.

This story came out in an analytical session during which the patient revealed her deep unease. Now it is up to us to come up with some ideas about her particular communicative problems and intentions. The psycho-analyst knows from experience that everything, or almost everything, that he is told has some kind of hidden content which corresponds to an unconscious fantasy and discourse which has to do with the relationship between the patient and the analyst himself. So what is the subtext to this story? Here the points made by Baranger are extremely useful.

Let us take the case of an analyst who discovers *what is behind the story* in a routine way, according to a narrow, repetitive model, without worrying about anything else. Let us imagine that he thinks his task is merely to investigate the impulses and aggressive fantasies that have been released in the patient. In the case we are looking at it is very probable that V.V. entertains aggressive impulses and fantasies towards her friend. The analyst will easily be able to interpret the anxiety and the unease which V.V. showed in the session in the light of her aggressivity. In other words, his line of thought will run more or less like this: you are now anxious (or unconsciously you feel guilty) because – according to the law of retaliation – you feel aggressive.

If the imaginary analyst happened to share the ideology of the "uncle-senator", there is every likelihood that he would interpret the behaviour of his patient as that of someone who takes a slightly irreverent attitude towards parental figures, who has behaved with adolescent haste, narcissistic exhibitionism – and more besides. If he has a limited view of transference, he will almost certainly find a way of interpreting everything that has happened in terms of a conflict between the patient and the analyst, based on some actual episodes that have happened during the analysis.

I do not agree with this interpretative approach. I tend rather to think that comments like this on the part of the analyst are not emancipatory, nor do they offer a genuine way out. In fact, I fear that this approach may be responsible for some of the consequences which I have been describing throughout this book; for example, the tendency to identify with the aggressor, or – in the extreme case – the "Job syndrome".

I share the belief that transference almost always happens underneath most of what patients tell their therapist, and I also believe that the ideology of the analyst can lead him to interpret it mistakenly. By doing so he can do more harm than good. Before going into more detail about this case I would like to add that, if the criticism of the patient V.V. revealed a pattern of behaviour on the part of the analyst similar to that of the avuncular senator, one would hope that this criticism (whether explicit or implicit) would be taken into account and not rejected in the way that Freud ironically described: heads I'm right, tails the patient is wrong.

It is no accident that V.V. asks the analyst whether we can expect rules in life to be "explicit", at least in emotional relationships. Or, to put it more clearly, whether it is possible to have reliable parents and brothers and sisters.[10] What the patient – in her disappointment – seems to be saying is that the elderly councillor is a good person but he is not "honest", because he does not have the courage to play the game fairly; in other words – if it is not a personal problem – because he does not know how to challenge the reality of society and its institutions.

We mentioned the fact that there is something in what the patronising old councillor says to the patient *which makes her feel, or is supposed to make her feel, guilty*. The patient has failed to submit herself to an initiatory rite according to a rule she knew nothing about. Obviously she had been brought up to follow other rules (and this proved in her analysis to be a reason for gratitude towards her father). Let us try to understand more about the technique used to induce feelings of guilt in her.

For one thing, this rule is presented as if it were a universal truth (the impersonal comment "you made a bad impression" makes this quite clear), as if it were a law of nature: everybody knows that the sun sets in the evening and water flows down to the valley.

Codes and guilt

This detail recalls the structure of taboos as studied by anthropologists. Rules based on taboos proscribe rather than prescribe action: do not enter that area, do not talk in the temple, do not kill that animal, and so on. Those who obey these restraints do so without knowing the reasons for them. They know that if they break the rule they will be punished and chastised. But unlike the ideological impositions which the "uncle-senator" would like to see in force, taboos can be precisely explained and this instruction is an integral part of the initiation into the sacred world. In some cases the taboo is even revealed (to the males) after the initiation.[11] The rule adopted by the elderly senator, on the other hand, is a double bind, to the effect: if you join us, you must first know how to behave, if you don't join us, you'll never know.

When the ways of thinking such as those shown by the "uncle-senator" catch on (in the sense that they become *the* organising principle or a basic assumption, in Bion's sense of the word) inside an institution or a grouping of people, they tend to create a spiral of double binds more than actual taboos.[12]

V.V. is probably asking for clarity from her analyst so as to be able to maintain or increase her degree of freedom, or perhaps to test her reliability at a moment when the analysis is about to come to an end. Likewise, a daughter or a son wants their parents to confirm that their rules are "valid" and that they must be prepared to fight to defend them. However, this confirmation can be a transference request.

The probable reason V.V. is talking about this with her analyst is that she feels threatened; but it is also likely that she wants to talk about the fact that her old friend has disappointed her and that losing her old image of him also amounts to losing the trusting part of herself. In his magisterial account, Grinberg has put events such as this at the centre of the working through of grief.

I would like to use this case to clarify a point I see as extremely important. We shall never know exactly what deep-seated motivation induced V.V. to tell her analyst about this episode. My explanation is based on a network of clues and reflections. There does, however, seem to be one firm point in all of this, one which represents the other side of the question: in my view, the analyst ought to be able to recognise the value of the hypothesis that I have just put forward of a "need for confirmation". If his vision of the world does not embrace this hypothesis, any interpretation he gives his patient might easily not only perpetuate anger and a sense of guilt but also leave a sense of solitude in the wake of disappointment that is not easy to dispel. Certainly the analyst should also consider the possibility that the bad treatment his patient received at the hands of her friend was not a conscious act but, at the same time, his behaviour was also not an isolated instance of a double bind. What we have here is the logic of institutions. This is something that has to be accepted as part of the tragic reality of things (although, obviously, accepting it does not necessarily mean adapting to it).[13]

We can simplify the analysis by looking at three roles or functions. Fornari talked in this context of *codes*. This term has the advantage of occupying a space at the intersection of various disciplines – law, linguistics, biology, philology – all of which talk about codes. According to Fornari, parental codes help the child and the human species to survive (with the least possible amount of suffering, I would add); the fraternal code is designed for the democratic implementation of parental codes in a situation among equals, as in our council, where – by explicit definition – discourse should take place *inter pares*.[14]

The *maternal code* is based on the principle of *belonging*, while the paternal code is based on *selection*. Without having to offer anything in exchange apart from his smile and the appeal of his tenderness, every child needs to be nursed, cared for and fed; he needs to be welcomed by comforting arms and to be assured of secrecy when he has to unburden his hidden torments and anxieties in private. He has a natural right simply because he belongs to a mother. Here we are coming close to the deep-seated roots of what is known as "distributive justice" and "equity". The functions that are related to the correct responses to these needs are the tools and content of the maternal code.

The *paternal code*, on the other hand, has to do with the ways in which the individual is gradually enabled to deal with the inevitable frustrations that arise in groupings of people, political and civil society, the encounter with others in the agora – everything that occupies the public arena.[15] Metaphorically speaking, only the son or the daughter who has the ability, the strength, the knowledge and the necessary tools – such as the mastery over the bow and arrow, the ability to follow footprints, knowledge of the rules, of language, of the law, of regulations and so on – can follow their father either into the woods to hunt or into the agora to be a politician.

To guarantee survival, the paternal code *is forced to select*: if it doesn't, the son, the daughter and the community all run serious risks. A healthy society, just like a healthy family or institution, should, where possible, be able to combine the two parental codes in a dialectical relationship, as it searches for low-risk equitable solutions. I would add that, on another level, the two codes also ought to monitor each other. In the words of Isaiah Berlin, the complete liberty of the powerful and the able is not compatible with the fact that the weak and the less able are also entitled to a decent life. Clearly, this is extremely difficult, but it would be cynical to argue that it is always impossible. In order to heal, the psychoanalyst should understand these rules, which are connected to our longing for justice.

To promote the emotional maturity of their sons and daughters, the codes of both parents should be deployed *at the right moment*, that is, at particular ages and moments in the life of each individual. Dealing with the psychological approach to illness, as Alexander Mitscherlich (1966) argued some years ago, means dealing with "the context of values which provoke it".[16] And values change. Let's take a well-known example: according to Plutarch, the ancient Spartans took deformed newborn babies who would be incapable of pursuing a future military career to Mount Taigeto and left them to die. The Spartans selected (according to the paternal code) between those suited and those unsuited to the military, and did so not only in this drastic manner but also at an age that would be inconceivable in a Christian culture like ours. From this point of view (but only from this point of view), we could talk about the perverse use of the paternal code and, consequently, of an attack on the values of the maternal code (which wants to see all children survive, whether deformed or not). The analyst who has been brought up within this value system (again this is the idea of analytical ideology we found in W. Baranger) will think it a perverse use, and one to be avoided.

Similar situations to this one in ancient Sparta can also be found in other cultures. In his history of ancient Australia, the anthropologist Geoffrey Blainey writes that infanticide was practised throughout the land. Mothers normally suckled their children for three (or sometimes up to six) years because there was no animal milk to be had on the whole continent and easily digestible food was not available during some months in the year. As the mother is not able to nourish several children, "if too many pregnancies occur too close to each other, and one child follows another in the space of eighteen months, the newly-born child will probably be killed".[17] Is this an exception to the maternal code, or a perversion of it?

Examples of the perversion of the emancipatory purpose of the paternal code are easy to find, both in the family and in society. When selection, which is the characteristic activity of the paternal code, does not occur naturally, it can be practised on the basis of judgement. Sometimes, the judgement factor – in other words, the assessment of merit and talent – is threatened, but simply as a way of exercising control over the other, not as a way of helping him to mature. When our credit is low, or when we think we do not have sufficient authority, we turn to punitive, persecutory father figures. The mother who exploits the father by saying things such as "wait and see what happens when your father finds out!" is a kind of primordial model of this perverse use.

In some extreme cases we can even witness something which resembles a practical joke. In cultures where the rules of the agora, of open debate, do not apply, where the secret rules of corridors, ante-chambers and *camerae caritatis* prevail, something very strange can happen. The locution *in camera caritatis* is of medieval origin, and in some ways denotes the opposite of agora. It refers to the place where power is exercised with *caritas*, in other words with comprehension and flexibility. The expression is still commonly used for reproaches like that uttered by the "uncle-senator", given "in a spirit of friendship" and not meant to be divulged. The everyday emancipatory function of the paternal code is disregarded and circumvented, and judgement, which should be its operating instrument, is not only brandished for its striking, anxiety-creating effect, but also deferred till the moment of death, or after death, when its emancipatory function (at least from a lay perspective) ceases to exist.[18]

Let us return to the parental functions. From our present-day perspective, each individual who is capable of applying both codes, maternal and paternal, ought to be able to use both to provide children and adolescents with the parental functions which real mothers and fathers can give.[19]

In our episode, the "senator" who reproaches the patient *in camera caritatis* sees himself as "avuncular", that is to say, corresponding to a family figure who belongs to the generation of the parents and to the sex of the fathers. At the moment when the patient symbolically (that is, by becoming a member of the council) becomes a sister to the senator, the latter seems suddenly unable to tolerate the situation and thrusts her back into the ranks of the children, while he takes on an explicitly parental role. The fact that they are all members of a council, the fact of being *inter pares*, recalls the equal relationship between brothers. This status either exists or it doesn't: emancipation *in two stages*, such as the elderly councillor would like to see, is very close to being unlawful, an act of arbitrary violence not sanctioned by the norms which govern the public affairs of the council. It is precisely into these recesses that light needs to be shed.

The "uncle-senator" seems to want to reassert an artificial generation gap; usually an attitude of this type is called "paternalistic". But is this a paternal code? He says that V.V. has been judged negatively on account of her behaviour. Once again, this statement seems to refer to her as a "daughter"; she has been a bad girl because she talked too much when she should have been quiet. She did not show respect to her parents, to the adults, so she does not deserve respect. In this way the "senator" tries first to cast the new colleague in an infantile role, and then to provoke her anxiety and guilt.

Again, this is a double bind: the "uncle-senator" accepts the council's fraternal code (already visible in the way the chairman treated V.V. on a par with the other council members), but at the same time unconsciously he attacks the very nature of the council by not accepting the principle of equality and open debate. He has proposed her candidacy, so he must see her as "elderly" enough to serve the interests of the association, but the first time others treat her as a full member of the council, he feels the impulse to treat her like a child.

We have already made the point that this type of communication, if repeated inside a family or institution, can create (or reinforce) serious pathologies. Anyone who has experienced life in an institution knows that those who suffer from persecutory anxiety often try very hard to join associations and groups in which ideologies of this nature are prevalent. People have asked the reason for this phenomenon: it would seem that "philosophies" based on the double bind also exercise a protective role. A persecutory reality makes it easier to project internal persecutions outwards and thus fosters the illusion that pressure is being lifted.

If we wanted to make another distinction between religions and ideologies in the context of guilt, we could add that, while monotheistic religions seek to partially internalise guilt, ideologies tend mostly to project guilt more directly and "operatively" onto the enemy or more generally onto the "different" other, onto "outgroups", to use the terminology of American psycho-sociology in the 1950s and 1960s.

Earlier we wondered whether our avuncular–paternal councillor was really behaving like a father. Was he complying with the paternal code, or was his behaviour more maternal? The "senator" had said that he wasn't present when the patient behaved incorrectly; he had been told about it. If we observe carefully, we discover that in this way he applies certain principles: he states implicitly that what counts is not the agora; in other words, the arena of public discussion where the best ideas can be chosen, where V.V. could also have been asked to speak less and to leave more room for the others if her behaviour had been perceived as interfering with the council's work. What seems to count here is politics behind closed doors, comments exchanged in the corridor: hearsay, the currency of a private world where no right of reply is granted. Here we are in the atmosphere of a *camera caritatis*; we are witnessing a characteristic feature of the maternal code being applied at the wrong time.

Modern child psychology is more or less agreed on the fact that there is a long period in the life of every child when it is important to belong to a mother capable of deciding what is good and what is bad (without the need for agreement from the child, which it would not be able to give). There is an extended period during which it is important to have someone to whom we can unburden ourselves in private, someone who listens to us, who presents us with their point of view, who tells us off when need be, in a reserved, confidential manner, who consoles us secretly, out of an understanding of the heart's secret impulses. But all this runs its course; there comes a moment in everyone's life when the extraordinary generosity of the maternal code should no longer be freely available. We know how important it is to be able to ask for and obtain this kind of comfort, but opinions (not advice) should not be imposed with the excuse of friendship or kinship.

To make the point a little more clearly: the basic attitude of willingness to help has to be the same towards the child as towards the adult. Respect for the freedom of the other person is important in both cases: the comment by the patronising councillor would have been equally incorrect, and very probably much more harmful, if the recipient of the message had really been a child.

In the case we are analysing it is important that the parents, in particular the mother, know that they should step aside to allow the son or the daughter to cope on their own. If they don't, they are interfering and controlling, as Winnicott and Klein would have argued. This could be the point of connection between the episode involving the newly elected councillor being treated like a child and the question which her analyst was presumably called upon to clear up.

In theory, all analysts ought to be sensitive to these needs, but how many are able to appreciate the ideological predisposition underlying their own behaviour and words that also underlies the behaviour of our elderly council-member? How many analysts and therapists chose their profession in order to be able to pursue their compulsive need to make others dependent, their unspoken desire to mould people? How many contribute to the creation of taboos within their institutions or analytical setting without realising it?

There is a widespread belief that it should be the father that, so to speak, severs the child's maternal apron strings. This is unfair towards those mothers who know when they should give and when they should withdraw, who know, that is, how to release their children. And these are not two "periods" that come one after the other but two alternating modalities. Children need to be emancipated from the cradle on. The idea that the father emancipates the child from the mother obscures the fact that even men, as in the case of the patronising councillor, can behave "paternalistically", that is, like a *mother* who doesn't want to let her child grow up.

King Solomon

The paternal code led us to look at the question of judgement. If it is true that all types of guilt can be traced back to judgements, then judgement is closely linked to guilt and the sense of guilt. Even when unconscious guilt is brought out into the open, we discover that judgement is involved. Guilt without judgement (without motive), as happens in some forms of very primitive persecutory sense of guilt, shades ever more into what is called nameless anxiety.

Perhaps because judgement is of cardinal importance in the dynamics of the codes that govern everyday life, it has deep roots in mythology. In Judaeo-Christian culture, the progenitor can be found in the Judgement of Solomon (1 Kings 3: 16–28). The story is well known:

> Then came there two women, that were harlots, unto the king, and stood before him. And the one woman said, O my lord, I and this woman dwell in one house; and I was delivered of a child with her in

the house. And it came to pass the third day after that I was delivered, that this woman was delivered also: and we were together; there was no stranger with us in the house, save we two in the house. And this woman's child died in the night; because she overlaid it. And she arose at midnight, and took my son from beside me, while thine handmaid slept, and laid it in her bosom, and laid her dead child in my bosom. And when I rose in the morning to give my child suck, behold, it was dead: but when I had considered it in the morning, behold, it was not my son, which I did bear.

The accused mother denies the accusation and claims that the dead son is the son of the other and that the living son is hers. And so they argue in the presence of the king. Solomon orders a sword to be brought to him and delivers the famous sentence:

And the king said, Divide the living child in two, and give half to the one, and half to the other. Then spake the woman whose the living child was unto the king, for her bowels yearned upon her son, and she said, O my lord, give her the living child, and in no wise slay it. But the other said, Let it be neither mine nor thine, but divide it. Then the king answered and said, Give her the living child, and in no wise slay it: she is the mother thereof.

Most interpretations of this passage draw the same conclusion: the real mother (the Bible tells us who the real mother is, but we should remember that Solomon didn't know) speaks with the voice of nature that cries for the preservation of the child; the coldness with which the other accepts the king's sentence reveals the fact that the child is not hers. There are no witnesses, so there is no way of deciding the question by following the usual procedure of weighing up their statements. Solomon relies on a "new expedient, but appropriate to the case, founded on his knowledge of the human heart and the realm of nature".[20] It is this episode more than any other that made Solomon famous, to the point of transforming his name and his judgement into metonymies to be found in many languages.

Solomon, who according to the Bible "pronounced three thousand sentences and wrote one thousand five hundred songs", will be recalled also for constructing a temple and for having replied to all the insidious questions asked of him by the Queen of Sheba. But it is for this "exemplary" episode that he has become the embodiment of the impartial judge, the incomparable administrator of justice, although in more recent times some have added that, as a judge, he was "both too rigid and cold".[21]

I would like to use this Biblical passage to go back – the atmosphere is typical of guilt (one of the women is innocent, the other is guilty) – to what we have called the tragic dimension. It is a dimension that clichés, which are by their very nature reductive and hostile to nuance, tend to conceal.

One of the two mothers wants the death of the child, in line with a totally egocentric logic: either mine or nobody's. What is certain is that this expression alone would justify a psychiatrist or a psychoanalyst describing the woman as psychotic, with strong murderous instincts. In other words, she is mad. Certainly she has no maternal instinct. But all this does not exclude the possibility that she is the real mother.

To continue to explore this hypothesis freely: the other prostitute could have taken the child because she felt that her companion in misfortune was mad and unreliable. Let us suppose now that the real mother is the one who wants the child to live, as the Bible assures us. By making her proposal to Solomon (give it to her, as long as it doesn't die!) she is choosing the lesser of two evils: the child's life would be saved, but it would be brought up by a psychotic woman with murderous instincts. Both women are "harlots". Solomon cannot avoid the problems which the contested child will have in future because of the difficulty it will have in identifying with two stable parents in a healthy way. Besides, the profession of these two mothers will in all probability lead to the children growing up marginalised, and perhaps even criminals.

The question is – and this is the reason for this excursus on Solomon and his judgement – why has this passage from Kings been interpreted in such an uncritical spirit for thousands of years? The Bible in many other respects is not particularly tender-hearted towards Solomon. He is portrayed as cruel: on the one hand, he was a king who asked God for the wisdom necessary to govern well, but on the other, he was an absolute sovereign, autocratic towards his subjects and under the thumb of his numerous wives and concubines. Perhaps the truth is quite simple: deep in our hearts we all want mothers to love their children instinctively and naturally, we feel that they should want their children to live more than anything else in the world. There have been numerous studies on the subject of infanticide by mothers with the Medea complex which have proved that that is not always the way things are.[22]

Solomon's famous judgement is based on a *coup de théâtre* which perfectly reflects the brilliant superficiality – which can be both benevolent and at times arrogant – of some more or less cynical authoritarian personalities. The theatrical test staged by Solomon could easily have gone wrong. Solomon (at the time an inexperienced judge with no legal background) does not offer the preventive certainty about the means of reaching a judgement, as every good judge should. Preventive certainty – in other words, certainty based on trial rules and regulations – is another aspect of the "publicity" which ought to govern the agora, the public area which we explored in connection with the "uncle-senator" and rules which are taken for granted and not explained.

We can only speculate about what would have happened if both mothers who appeared before Solomon had given the same answer. Or if the two women (whose profession makes them people acquainted with human nature) had thought that Solomon was a mad despot and had agreed to bring up the child together so as not to submit to his verdict. We should not forget that they take the order to cut the child in half seriously.

I have been trying to describe and analyse some of the reasons why dealing therapeutically with senses of guilt is no easy enterprise. I hope I have succeeded in making it clear that the analyst cannot shirk this responsibility if he wants to cure his patient. In the preceding chapters we have often encountered the term "preconscious" and talked about the analyst's difficulty in "containing" emotions, obviously including those that are guilt-provoking.

I am convinced that, if we want to limit the damage caused by guilt and to look for a way out of the logic based on guilt, we must first of all become more sensitive in our theoretical understanding of the preconscious and containment, and must seek to use these concepts in a spirit of great simplicity. The remaining chapters will look at these two topics in more depth; as in the previous chapters, we shall approach the question from a wide range of different points of view.

Chapter 10

The preconscious and consciousness

Solo recuerdo la emoción de las cosas, y se me olvida todo lo demás.
Muchas son las lagunas de mi memoria.
[I remember only the emotion of things and I forget all the rest. There are many gaps in my memory.]
(Antonio Machado)

When I use the term "preconscious" I mean the mind of the poet.[1] The term Proust used, when describing the structure of *La Recherche*, was instinct, and many still use it today. If we assume that by *intelligence* he meant a faculty of the conscious mind, then his observation in *La Recherche* – "for instinct dictates our duty, and intelligence furnishes us with the pretext to evade it" – takes on some relevance to our discussion. In part this may simply be a witticism, an offhand remark, but it is at least a stimulating witticism. I propose to deal with the subject of the preconscious in some detail because I want to lay the groundwork for an examination of the strategies which can be used to deal with the sense of guilt. And admittedly my angle of vision on this subject is not very easy to describe.

If someone is naturally gifted with a "good", i.e. "well-functioning", preconscious, or has trained himself to acquire one, he is able to "see", or to apprehend, various levels of reality and the points at which they meet. A "good" preconscious works spontaneously on several levels, while a mediocre preconscious, or one which is overloaded, gets bogged down in the stereotypes and clichés of prejudices and acquired mental habits. It tends to rely on theoretical models that have been learnt rationally. It depends on the opinions of others and thus is only capable of limited freedom. Proust seems to be pointing out the "ethical" implications of this state of affairs (and this links it to guilt).

The impression is that principles become genuinely operative – one is tempted to say spontaneously operative – when they are based on the sum of personal experience (something like the sum of knowledge acquired by a craftsman; see below) and when we feel that they are effective independent of reason and the pressures of the Super-Ego. This does not guarantee that these principles will not be ephemeral or considered by others as mad. It only means that they operate out of the preconscious because they have become part of our own flesh and blood.

In the case of psychoanalysts it should be up to the patient who is making progress or who is feeling better (or suffering less, in the most serious cases) to determine whether these principles are ephemeral or illusory. But this does not always happen.[2]

There are various deities in the Greek pantheon that bear the name of psychological functions, emotions or mental activities. The Greeks have among their gods of passion and feeling, Eros, the god of *love* (a complex personality) and Phobos, the personification of *fear* (a male demon who does not feature in any particular legend). Among the lesser known gods we find Pisti, *trust*; Ate, a minor god who personifies *error*; Lyssa, *rage* which leads to madness, fury and the strong desire of the Bacchantes described by Euripides. In this chapter we are particularly interested in the two female figures beloved and impregnated by Zeus, father of the gods: the titanide Mnemosyne, *Memory*, and the titaness Metis, the mother of Athena. Let us turn immediately to this last pair, mother and daughter.

According to some authors who base their work on nineteenth-century research, *tecnica*, just like the whole field of technique, took on certain very specific characteristics in Greece between the seventh and the fifth centuries BC. *Técne* was applied to the craft of the metallurgist, carpenter and some typically feminine sorts of work, such as weaving, which require experience and dexterity acquired over time. But at the same time, *técne* also referred to magic, such as the magic of Epheses, the god of fire. *Tecnica* lost both its magical and religious components when craftsmen started to find a role for themselves in cities.

The intelligence which is an integral part of the mastery of the craftsman (and of magical recipes) is *metis*. *Metis* is based on the peripheral intelligence of touch, hearing and smell. At the end of the nineteenth century, Epinas put forward the view that the turning point which marked the transition from "unselfconscious" technology to technology as we understand it today took place about the beginning of the fifth century. The very idea – *a technology which was still unconscious of itself*!

The figure of the archaic demiurge, *mecanopoiós*, is the figure of someone who asserts himself by virtue of his ability to organise his work. He is also akin to the magician and the shaman, surrounded as he is by the glamour of the exceptional powers conferred upon him by his *metis*. This turning point transformed him into an engineer grappling with nature, who used his skilful tricks to penetrate nature and to force it to produce miracles. The fifth century was the period of Socrates, and it was also the century of Hippocratic medicine – which lacked any technique of dissection. On the one hand, this explains why at the time anatomical and physiological knowledge was poor (it was limited mostly to bone fractures), but on the other hand it shows – as I hope to demonstrate – the continuity of a *metis* which had not yet incorporated the investigating reason that uses the knife to discover the secrets of living beings.

The use of technology in the Greek world was directly connected to guilt: as we know, Zeus condemned Prometheus because he had stolen fire from the gods. Craft *tecné* was not considered true knowledge.[3] The craftsman is not conscious of his method; he does not "understand" what he is doing. "For a long time *homo faber* was a mechanic who knew nothing about mechanics", wrote D. Essertier.[4] In this respect he was like a poet and an artist. Fathers and mothers still transmit knowledge to their sons and daughters (or friends' children) through a secret kind of apprenticeship. This learning process is completely different from the process of theoretical teaching.[5] We could say that the handicraft of *metis* is a *preconscious* skill that exploits abilities not usually taken into consideration.[6]

The fact that in Plato *metis* is no longer a craft faculty is probably no accident. The Greek thinkers, as they started their long odyssey from an understanding based on myth to philosophy, had to give up a feminine, non-penetrative way of thinking. Plato's *metis* was subordinated to the need to work out philosophical theories. Consequently, the *cosmos*, and thus all living beings, become *intelligible*; they can be intellectually apprehended and analysed. Not only is a unifying order discovered beneath the chaos of perceptions, but man also becomes capable of understanding this order rationally in terms of cause and effect.[7] In this respect the Ionian philosophers were revolutionary: they were the first to try to make a clear distinction between subject and object, mind and body. This marks the birth of what we can call masculine or "strong" thought; and it is probably also the point of origin of the risks and costs connected to technology which only in the past few decades have started to give rise to concern.

The myth of Metis and her daughter Athena describes this transition. The name of the titaness Metis means "wisdom", "prudence", "good counsel", but also "machination", "perfidy", "deviousness". It is perhaps the amalgam of such contrasting elements that made the French think that *metis* was *l'intelligence rusée*, intelligence which can come up with expedients, stratagems and clever solutions.[8]

The preconscious is the seat of empathetic intuition, or "instinctive" intuition as Proust would have put it; the point at which various facets of reality converge. It is unfamiliar with the principle of non-contradiction.[9] It accepts what Bion called reversals of perspective. The mythology that embodies this is replete with contradictions. Zeus is the god of light and of the clear sky, but he also sets off the rain and unleashes thunderbolts and flashes of lightning. Among the second generation of the Olympians, Apollo is another god connected to both light and shade, joy and despair. We shall try to explain more clearly the light and the dark side of Metis. To use the terminology of eastern philosophy, we could also add that myths embody the constant (dialectical) exchange between *yin* and *yang*. Drawing on the vocabulary we have used in previous chapters, we could conclude that a "good" preconscious (as the myths demonstrate) is unacquainted with orthodoxy and does not close itself off in Manichaean truth. Thus, preconscious vision can help us to attain what we have called the tragic dimension.

Generally speaking, it is only with difficulty and after much training or education that the conscious mind, the conscious Ego, is able to conceive that other causes may exist on separate levels: psychological and biological, ethological and sociological, religious and legal, and yet others. Only then is it able to understand in full, not so much the concept as the dynamics of complex situations, such as feedback in systems theory, which is a necessary instrument for understanding interrelationships. For the same reasons, if the conscious mind wants to focus on the main points of a problem, it has to use statistical methods such as factor analysis, ways of processing the relationship between data not simply on two levels but across many dimensions.

Let us go back to the words of the poet and to the veil we mentioned at the beginning of the book. There's a remark by Lucien Arréat – "The source of all poetry is the deep feeling of that which is inexpressible" – which points effectively to the difficulty I am talking about.[10] The physicist Jorge Wagensberg once wrote: "I consider art as a form of knowledge based on the principle of the communicability of complexities that are not necessarily intelligible".[11] The conscious mind is incapable of expressing or apprehending the multiple and variegated meanings of the poetic word; it cannot fully grasp the condensed meaning embodied in the poet's lines. There is a sense of depth and disorientation in poetry, a sense of rapture and things beyond one's grasp, and these feelings have their origin in the preconscious and in their preconscious acceptance by those who have a feeling for the poetic word. Also the two sides of the poetic *metis* decree life or death: for Goethe poetry was either excellent or it did not exist.[12]

Again this is a complex subject and one which would take us a long way if we were to examine it fully. Before leaving it behind completely I would like to repeat a brief point that I have made elsewhere.

Some concepts which deal with the complexity of phenomena and the difficulty of understanding them in one single theory have over the centuries been subject to a kind of corruption or pejoration of meaning which we could call symptomatic. The term *eclecticism*, in its original meaning (Greco-Roman as in Philone, for example, or in Galen), referred to the ability to seek and find common denominators which would make it possible to reconcile different doctrines, theories and perspectives. Eclecticism emphasised convergence and compatibility; it thought in terms of dialectics and possible syntheses. Underlying it was the conviction that all theories are limited and that what is important is not so much the validity of individual theories as the discovery of new aspects of the truth.[13]

Syncretism, on the other hand, is the arbitrary reconciliation of doctrines and theories which are in fact mutually incompatible. It tries to put together things that do not belong together. An example would be the attempt to harmonise the conditioned Ego, which is the cardinal concept of Freud's theory of the unconscious, with a philosophy that postulates an Ego divinely endowed with free will from birth.

Those who have a deep (usually unconscious) need to safeguard ortho-dox thinking, as well as those who feel obliged to be moralistic or who have idealised a theory, tend without realising it to confuse "eclecticism" and "syncretism" and are thus forced to ignore or denigrate the efforts of those who are eclectic. They also tend to disparage the use of the preconscious, favouring instead the rationality of consciousness. The confusion between these two terms has grown over the past few centuries.[14]

If the (female) preconscious resembles Metis, then we can explain why, on the one hand, it can grasp subtly and precisely, without uncertainty or doubt, the crux of a problem, the solution to an enigma that has preoccu-pied the conscious mind for a long time, and on the other hand, why it can fail and produce facile, acritical credulity or even delusion.[15] "Eclecticism" and "syncretism" are the two sides of Metis.

Normally the "good" preconscious of someone who has not been specially trained to exercise it at the expense of the conscious mind (there are various techniques for freeing up the abilities of the preconscious) tends to come into operation at moments of transition from waking to sleep, and more often from sleep to waking. At such twilight moments, we can come up with solutions to complex problems that had been plaguing us for ages. At these moments the conscious mind, although already awake, has not yet completely invaded the territory of the preconscious. Arguably, when consciousness is still silent, the preconscious expresses itself through the personal myths of dreams; however, when the conscious mind is awake but not yet dominant, the preconscious helps to bring to the surface solutions that one had only guessed at before. This is probably why we talk about "sleeping on" a problem.[16]

There is a broad range of studies of the preconscious: they touch on primary and secondary thought, the mystery of intuition, the creation of dreams and *rêveries*, mathematical thinking, musical and theatrical inter-pretation, and creativity in general. But they also focus on the problem of direct and conscious, as opposed to "indirect", communication; that is, not only verbal and para-verbal communication, but also coded or displaced discourse. The patient, in the transference, when talking of objects far from his relationship with the analyst, is in fact also (or even primarily) speaking about his relationship with the analyst. This phenomenon, which psychoanalysis has emphasised so greatly but which is not exclusive to the analytical relationship, concerns all relationships and all human communication, since the transference is ubiquitous.[17]

Many ideas have been suggested about women's thinking, which is often confused with "female thinking". Most of these ideas, however, turn out to be clichés: it is said that it is not logical thinking (it does not respect the laws of logic, it does not classify, it does not create hierarchies, etc.) and that it is "uterine". This term is meant as a pejorative or at best humorous synonym of terms such as "irrational" and "emotional", and amounts to saying that female thinking depends on sexual longings rather than the reality of things. But the word *uterine* may also have much more disquieting implications.

If it is true that it is the intuitive ability of the mother to adequately meet the elementary needs of her child that determines its development, if it is the precision with which this ability recognises needs and dangers that decides the future life or death, joy or suffering, of each one of us, then the reference to the "uterus" and its magical ability to give birth to children – who can either be beautiful and lively or monsters and freaks – becomes understandable.

The uterus could also be considered as the first symbol of mortal danger – during birth each human being runs this risk for the first time – both actively and passively. If the *metis*, the preconscious, of the mother functions correctly, then hope and life are guaranteed; if it doesn't, then the result is despair or even death. We could say that *metis* is the source of female thinking that is tied mainly to the preconscious and to the right hemisphere of the brain. Female thinking needs male thinking and vice versa. The interaction has to take place on an equal basis because there is a need not only for a dialectic but also for a relationship of reciprocity. The preconscious ought not to be idealised. All types of thinking – male, female or a combination of the two – have an unconscious, a preconscious and a conscious component. Integrated thinking should be able to move easily between conscious and preconscious, and should be able, when necessary, to decipher messages coming from the unconscious without being subjected to its worst conditioning. For this reason integrated thinking ought to be everyone's goal. It is a goal that is probably unattainable, at least in its perfect form. However, as an ideal, to indicate the path to be taken, it is still very helpful.

Greek culture, with its single-minded dedication to logic and reason, started to attack and sought to destroy mythical thinking, beginning at the same time a process which led us to vitiate and limit the importance of the preconscious, the highly intuitive and "poetic" mind which myths create and sustain. Everything we have said so far may sound abstract and difficult to grasp. Let us see whether the description becomes any clearer if we take a look at myth and etymology.

Metis was the first spouse, or lover, of Zeus. While she was pregnant with Athena, Gaia and Uranas told Zeus that if he received a son after giving birth to a daughter, the son would then usurp him as he had done his own father, Chronos. Zeus, after using sweet words to persuade Metis to lie down beside him, all of a sudden opens his mouth and swallows her. No further mention is made of Metis, although – in the tradition of the priests of Athena – at times she offers Zeus valuable advice from the depths of his belly where she ended up.[18]

When the time comes, Zeus has labour pains which take the form of a terrible headache. On the banks of Lake Titone, Zeus orders Ephesus (or, according to other sources, Prometheus) to split open his head with an axe. Out comes Athena fully armed: she has a helmet, a lance and, in common with her father Zeus, an aegis. The aegis is a pectoral, a kind of light shield made of goat hide, typically worn by young Libyan girls, but it is also his shield. Shield and lance are meant for self-defence, to keep people at a distance; the lance is also for penetrating, for wounding. As if that were not enough, Athena added to the shield the snake-filled head of the Medusa, and as if even that were not enough, beneath it there is always the second hide of the pectoral to ward off contact.

Those who like to find in myths and symbols what Freud called the return of the repressed might note that Athena (who thus puts anyone who might want to touch her at a safe distance) chooses a shield and a pectoral made of hide, and what's more, goats' hide, an animal which in the collective imagination is usually associated with making milk.

Is this the source (we could also ask whether it is "under this aegis") of the scientist's isolation, his ability to detach himself emotionally from the object he is observing? This is the mythical antecedent which embodies the separation between the capacity to contain and interpretation (which we shall look at presently), or which separates theory from emotional involvement. This is the origin of the world of the Platonic Socrates, the world of *Phedone*, where Xanthippe, the only person who seems to have any knowledge about the consequences of death, is banished with sarcasm.[19]

Virgin goddess and warrior, Athena is the protectress of Ulysses the investigator, Ulysses the incarnation of *intelligence rusée*. Athena does not give milk, takes no-one inside her; she never holds a sobbing baby in her arms. She never receives within her an erect penis; she will never have children, or procreate. Since she has not experienced childhood and adolescence herself, she will not be able to understand them. Throughout the whole Greek world, and especially in her city, she will shine as the goddess of Reason. She will be the spokeswoman for Zeus, and today represents for us women's adaptation to power and male paradigms. Born by Caesarian section from a head that appropriated the creative power of woman, the daughter of Zeus and Metis will wield the hand that rocks the cradle of western civilisation.

Containment

> The spontaneity I am talking about also comes from knowledge, but after knowledge has been forgotten. Interpretation is the perennial childhood of music, if childhood is the place where everything happens for the first time.
>
> (Gidon Kremer)

Containment is a psycho-physical faculty that is very important to an understanding of the sense of guilt: it can transform its content and relieve it of its tension. Despite the occasional voices since the 1960s who have argued that the "main task" of the psychoanalyst, in his attempt to bring about change, is to "*contain* the infantile aspects of the mind", most analysts would still maintain that interpretation is the sole and also the "most important and dominant" tool in Freudian technique.[20]

The idea of exploiting the capacity of the mind as a therapeutic factor and insisting that the word is primary might smack of that separation between mind and body we have just referred to. Athena gave prime importance to the head (highlighted with a tall helmet) – this was after all the part of the body from which she had been born and it must have seemed to her the source of all things.

I believe that *containment and interpretation form a single system*. The immediate consequence of this is that if one of the two factors is deficient then the whole system breaks down.[21] At times the analyst has in his care seriously fragmented patients who make the analytic atmosphere inauthentic because they have no hope or confidence that they will meet people capable of containing them.

For obvious reasons the concept of containment in psychoanalysis is often confused with the concept of the *setting*. Besides the concept of the external setting, "which includes the best known formal aspects" within which the analysis takes place, emphasis has also been placed on the "internal setting, which is closer to the analytical attitude, the 'style' of the therapist".[22] The internal setting is a major focus for Bion, who makes it into the scene of his *rêverie*.[23] This concept was to mark the beginning of a flowering of interest in containment, a phenomenon which had previously been largely neglected.

Let us take a brief look at this writer. Bion was born in Muttra in India of a Huguenot family, and much of his thinking has its roots in oriental thought. Joseph Needham was the first person in the west to describe the type of knowledge characteristic of Confucianism as "virile and positive" and Taoism as "feminine and receptive". Although he tended to cite the mystic Meister Eckhart, and Indian texts such as the *Bhagavad-Gita*, Bion was also interested in Chinese thought.[24] His most disturbing and paradoxical statements contained not only Buddhist but also Taoist elements and attitudes. Bion shared the typical sense of humour and self-irony of these teachings; they underlie his taste for the reversal of the point of view from which a phenomenon can be observed.

Bion gave a famous example of reversal of point of view when talking about stammerers. The words of the stammerer – which are meant to *contain* emotions – are overcome by the emotions themselves and are transformed into a sound that no longer expresses meaning. The word becomes a container that is "damaged and broken" by what it ought to contain.

In his short "Notes on memory and desire" (a title that echoed the first lines of Eliot's *The Waste Land*) he issued a ban on the use of memory and desire which among some psychoanalysts has taken on almost mythical (and consequently also disturbing) importance.[25]

> Memory is always misleading as a record of fact since it is distorted by the influence of unconscious forces. Desires interfere, by absence of mind when observation is essential, with the operation of judgement . . . do not remember past sessions . . . the psychoanalyst can start by avoiding any desires for the approaching end of the session (or week, or term). Desires for results, "cure" or even understanding must not be allowed to proliferate.

He also argues that the psychoanalyst must aim at attaining a mental state whereby at every session "he will believe that he has never seen the patient before. If he thinks he has already seen him, then he is treating the wrong patient." Bion's approach is provocative. It is not possible to do away with memory and desire simply in order to comply with a rule, however drastically expressed. A long process of maturation is required as well as a strong commitment. But the Zen master does not say this to his pupils. Paradox, illogic, the use of contradiction, are recurrent expedients in oriental teaching.

There is a risk that the communication becomes confusing as a result of the unconscious double bind. The paradox runs along the razor's edge, especially if it is used as a way of "treating" a patient. But after putting ourselves on our guard against this danger, we then need to recognise that the most obvious purpose of this provocation is to help break down the habitual circuits of the mind and, perhaps, to find a less regressive form of dependence.

This would seem to be the purpose Bion identified. In fact, however, Bion does not say that he wants to force us into paradox. On the subject of memory and desire he explains himself more clearly elsewhere: in opposition to "memory", understood as a deposit of ideas and memories, he sets, in the positive sense, "remembering", which we can call preconscious. "Memory" implies a rational way of speaking (the patient comes to the session with something he has decided to tell his analyst); "remembering", on the other hand, communicates something genuine and spontaneous. One recalls Bion's famous opening remark to one of his lectures: "I am curious to hear what I am going to tell you today". In his *Notes* Bion did not quote Freud, but Freud had suggested similar ideas in his 1912 "Recommendations to physicians practising psycho-analysis", albeit in a less drastic form. Freud formulated a "single prescription" for future analysts: they should avoid dangerous concentration or deliberate attention in favour of evenly suspended attention. This is again probably one of Freud's most brilliant insights, and, as I shall seek to explain later, it was part of a non-moralistic vision of guilt. This prescription was to prove very difficult to put into practice and was therefore abandoned. We shall see how in a way Melanie Klein laid the basis for disregarding it.[26]

Freud was conscious of the importance of his remark, and he underlined it by saying that this was the ultimate goal upon which "the various rules converge". For the analyst this would correspond to the "fundamental psychoanalytic rule" for the patient; namely, to free-associate. Even this task proved to be more difficult and complex than Freud had imagined.[27] To achieve this goal, he made some suggestions which remain extra-ordinarily relevant even today (although constantly neglected). He advises the analyst not to take notes, not to gather material for later publication in scientific journals and not to cultivate therapeutic desires. Here Freud is clearly being self-critical.

Bion was attracted by paradox and often played with the distinction between conscious and unconscious (or preconscious) memory. For his part, Freud simply urged the analyst to free himself from all mental preoccupation and not to worry about retaining ideas and information at all costs out of fear that something could escape him. Taking notes is a sign that the analyst is afraid that he has not assimilated and therefore not appropriated something which remains in some way extraneous or external, something he fears will be lost. Freud favours a more relaxed approach (so as to avoid "the effort of paying attention", he explains) and an attitude of trust in the analyst's non-evident ability to contain information that might prove useful.[28] He advised against effort and tension.

The analyst must "proceed without any intention, allowing himself to be surprised every time, facing what comes gradually with a clear and unpre-judiced mind" (Freud, 1912). Today one might find this idea somewhat ingenuous. Freud preached well, but then when reading his books one gets the impression that he expected his patients to confirm his theories – which is very understandable and human. What is less human and less under-standable is his ability to describe this required state of expectation with such originality and accuracy. Those who manage – after going through an appropriate apprenticeship – to enter into perfect, receptive harmony with the patient discover that they are *surprised each time*. Those who write or talk primarily on the basis of their preconscious find themselves being surprised by what they write or say. This insight of Freud alone ought to make us think again about the many criticisms that have been made of his supposedly "primitive" performance as an analyst.

If the preconscious is like that of the poet or the craftsman and has assimilated *in a non-intellectual way* what needs to be interpreted and understood, at the right moment and spontaneously, it will make its contribution by passing on to consciousness the key to interpretation. It is not a question of being without memory, but of waiting confidently for non-evident memory – Proust's involuntary memory, Bion's remembering – to enter the scene prompted by some unexpected stimulus.

In giving recommendations about the correct behaviour to adopt in analysis, Freud uses three metaphors that have since become famous: the surgeon, the telephone and, lastly, the mirror (or screen).[29] These metaphors are the product of the preconscious of Freud-the-writer and consequently go far beyond the obvious meanings which have been attributed to them and which Freud would probably have found in them. The preconscious of the artist expresses things which his consciousness cannot even imagine.

The first metaphor is intrusive in nature (Freud, 1912):

> I cannot advise my colleagues too urgently to model themselves during psycho-analytic treatment on the surgeon, who puts aside all his feelings, even his human sympathy, and concentrates his mental forces on the single aim of performing the operation as skilfully as possible.[30]

In some cases this approach can be useful. At the point when the patient has recognised that there is a major conflict, a certain firmness without "human piety" may stop him from running away out of pure fear of suffering. But often this technique is much less useful than one might think. The important fact is that the surgeon uses a scalpel; he enters the patient. He is guided by the peripheral mediating intelligence of his hands and his sense of touch (a kind of "tact" which fits in well with the gifts of sensibility, skill and prudence that every therapist should possess).[31] The unconscious imagination which underlies this active and masculine image is at the basis of certain concepts and psychoanalytic definitions (and is even present in our ordinary way of thinking), whereby identification amounts to entering the other and taking his place. Here we are in the area of projective identification. There are various current expressions which reflect this way of thinking: we talk about knowing how to "put oneself in the place of the other", about "the ability to penetrate into the deepest recesses" of a person's mind, and so on. "Intuition" comes from the Latin *intueri* which means "looking" (*tueri*) "inside" (*in*); the German word *ein-sehen*, which in turn recalls the English *in-sight*, points in the same direction. Latin also offers learned words such as *indagare* and *investigar*. Empathy, the capacity to put yourself in the position of the other person, is an attempt to render the German *Ein-fühlung*: "feeling that goes into", which also indicates becoming one with the other.

The Freudian (1912) metaphor of the telephone, however, points in the opposite direction:

> the doctor must put himself in a position to make use of everything he is told for the purposes of interpretation and of recognizing the concealed conscious material . . . He must adjust himself to the patient as a telephone receiver is adjusted to the transmitting microphone. Just as the receiver converts back into sound waves the electric oscillations in the telephone line which were set up by sound waves, so the doctor's unconscious is able, from the derivatives of the unconscious which are communicated to him, to reconstruct that unconscious, which has determined the patient's free associations.

We have now entered the area of introjective or receptive identification; in other words, the idea of accepting that another person can enter your house, come inside you and talk to you. Some years previously Ferenczi had introduced the term "introjection".[32] We are close to Bion's *rêverie*: this time it is a procedure based on containment. The Latin terms *comprehendere*, *capere*, *concipere* all express aspects of the same idea. But with this metaphor Freud-the-writer is not only saying that the analyst must train the receptive organ of his own unconscious on the unconscious of the "transmitting" patient; he is also describing the way in which containment and interpretation, to go back to our starting point, make up a single system: *the receiver converts back into sound waves the electric oscillations in the telephone line which were set up by sound waves*.

According to the last metaphor, the mirror, the analyst is supposed to reflect what the patient brings to him, without contributing anything of his own, and this is by far the most intriguing metaphor (Freud, 1912):

> The doctor should be opaque to his patients and, like a mirror, should show them nothing but what is shown to him.

For a start, what is called *fallacia speculi* (the deception of the mirror) sends back a "specular" image! Since the time of Plato and Lucretius, the mirror has become the symbol of *falsity*, of deception and error.[33] Freud-the-writer, unknown to Freud-the-theorist, seems to condense into this image all his ambiguous concerns about the real possibility that the analyst may respond in a distorting, delusory manner, rather than with an appropriate and therapeutic interpretation. We are now back at the dark face of Metis.

The openly pedagogical tone which Freud adopts in these *Recommenda-tions*, echoed closely by Bion half a century later, could also be considered as a reflection of certain persecutory anxieties and a kind of dejected hardening on his part. He knew very well how difficult it was to keep to his own rules. Sometimes – for example, when he advises his patient not to repeat important dreams but then tells them to narrate dreams "so as to fix them in the mind" – he does not even notice that he is breaking the very rules he himself has set up.[34]

The containing mind

> *Facesti voce quivi, e quindi uscissi*
> *per il suo becco in forma di parole,*
> *quali aspettava il core ov'io le scrissi.*
> (There it became a voice, and issued thence
> From out its beak in such a form of words
> As the heart waited for wherein I wrote them.)
> (Dante, *Paradiso*, XX, 28–30)

What terminology does psychoanalysis use to talk about how the analyst contains the projective identification, and in general the even violent emotions which the patient expresses through that communication? We can choose between various symbols and metaphors: the "psyche", the "soul" (in Freud's own language, *die Seele*), the "interior world", or the more ambiguous term "mind" – the term probably approved by Freud himself. This internal "mental space", where understanding and thinking take place, is located in various parts of the body, depending on the culture in which one has grown up. A normally educated European, asked point-blank, "Whereabouts in your body is your mind?", will almost certainly point to his forehead. A Japanese or a Chinese, on the other hand, will point to his heart.

H.H. Oshima brings us back to the origins of Taoism in China:

> "*Mind*", which is apparently equivalent to *hsin*, is a term used indiscriminately to illustrate the concept of *hsin*, at the cost of not being faithful to its original meaning . . . "heart" is the more precise translation.[35]

The origin of its ideogram was based on the image of this bodily organ.[36] Oshima continues:

> The heart is a barometer of the passions; it beats rapidly in times of fear and excitement, and is tranquil and unnoticed in periods of calm.

[In Taoist thought] the important differences between the ordinary man and the wise man are said to lie in the *hsin*.[37]

Chuang Tzu urges his disciples to "sit down and forget", to practise *hsin fast*. Oshima explains: "By forgetting he means emptying the *hsin*, in the same way as one empties one's stomach by fasting". This idea of "forgetting" is essential and repeated several times: "You forget your feet when your shoes are comfortable, you forget your waist when your belt sits comfortably". Oshima concludes: "In modern terms this suggests that 'forgetting' corresponds to a certain satisfaction or feeling at ease which results from a lack of conscious worry". What is registered by preconscious memory is – in the sense we have just been using the term – "forgotten". It does not disturb, it does not create the worry of forgetting, so it doesn't generate guilt.

To go back to the subject of Freud's mirror: in the same book we find this passage from Chuang Tzu: "The Perfect Man uses his *hsin* as a mirror, not following anything, not noticing anything, replying without retaining." In ancient China the mirror was an object of great importance and as a term can be considered interchangeable with mind–heart–*hsin*. It is worth remembering that the mirror has the "warmth of the scorching fire", and that it remains unchanged in itself and has the "cold of solid ice".

Such considerations and precepts form part of *wu wei* – one of the central concepts expounded by Lao-tzu, the great master of Taoism. Translators have often failed to do it justice by translating it as "not doing"; this poor translation has cast a negative light on Lao-tzu's thinking, exposing it to the accusation of fatalistic passivity.

A.C. Graham, one of the fathers of modern Sinology, points out:

Wu wei is refraining from trying to force spontaneous trends by deliberate action.[38]

This, in my view, is a key idea. All analysts who have grasped the importance of this rule will be able to build necessary precautions into their strategies of intervention.

It is superfluous to emphasise how closely all of these descriptions match the ideal analyst as described by Freud and Bion and, of course, anticipate their words. A more interesting point, however, is that the two different approaches – the oriental approach of the Taoists and the western approach of Freud – describe how to achieve an "uncluttered mind without preconceptions" (Freud, 1912). For Freud the *via regia* which is able to calm the *hsin* is personal analysis; for others it is correct breathing.[39] One could also mention other oriental traditions, such as the practice of meditation under the guidance of a mentor.

As regards comprehension, both the psychoanalytical and the oriental approach take the emotions into account. But oriental traditions such as Taoism believe that consciousness is achieved through cheerfulness. A broader-ranging comparison of the two approaches would require much more space.

Holding

One could add that Freud seems to go back to pre-Aristotelian concepts. Indeed, in their oldest meanings the two Greek terms that correspond to the Latin *mens*, namely *noos* and *phren*, show some continuity with oriental thought. *Noos*, which is translated as "(conscious) mind", "spirit", refers explicitly to the ability to contain mentally. The English expression *to forget* maintains this meaning. *Webster's Collegiate Dictionary* defines it as "putting out of mind". Then there is also the expression "to go out of one's mind", meaning to go mad. But the verb which corresponds to this noun is *noeo* which means "see", "understand" and thus recalls Bion's *rêverie* which, as we know, means literally "daydreaming". As for *phren*, which takes the idea of movement from Sanskrit, still in Homer's *Iliad* it meant "diaphragm".[40] Finally, *psiche* means breath, or "vital force" and is connected to *psycho*, to "breathing". So the living body is confirmed as the origin of psychic symbolism.[41]

In analysis, the therapist needs *confessions* from the patient to be able to help him; so it is important that, progressively and as far as possible, he should manage to restore the patient's expressive freedom. But these confessions will be all the freer and deeper the more the analyst knows how to contain them and not to pass judgement on them; in other words, *the more the analyst has resolved his compulsion to judge and to expel*. While this is, of course, not the only condition, it is an essential one.

The patient will then learn from the analyst that *comprehension* depends on his capacity to contain and not to reject the emotions aroused in him by others. Containment of anguish and other strong emotions is only possible if we have been able to introject someone who has been able to understand us. This introjection may constitute the genesis of "mental stability". Today, analysts who identify with the position of Hanna Segal and who take the same view as Bion on the ability to enter into a state of *rêverie* are agreed in viewing the problem in these terms: when a child experiences an anxiety he cannot contain he projects it onto the mother. The mother's reaction is to accept this anguish and to do everything necessary to reduce the suffering of the child. The child's perception is that it has projected something intolerable onto its object, but that the object has been capable of containing it and dealing with it. Then it re-introjects not only its original anxiety but also, and most importantly, an anxiety which is no longer the same because it has been contained. Winnicott has reminded us that the mother sometimes fails in this. Only in this way is it possible to break down the barriers to interpersonal communication (and communication between the various parts of the Self).

Successful containment depends on the therapist abandoning a perspective that is deeply rooted in our culture, the prejudice that bodily signals are necessarily signs of "illness" (an idea that we could compare to Freud's and Klein's first reactions to counter-transference). On the other hand, this does contradict the fact that, when we are really ill, our ability to contain suffering, fear, pain, diminishes; we are less able to tolerate accusations and the sense of guilt. This confirms that containment is psycho-physical containment; only this type of containment will provide the basis for a healthy and facilitating relationship, a response which takes into account those qualities of refractoriness and closure which are signs of ambivalence. At the beginning of the 1960s, W. Baranger wrote that the analyst "responds with his own body to the unconscious communications of the analysand".[42]

It is not easy to reach a better understanding of the minute and unconscious reactions of bodily counter-transference, but this is an area that is beginning to interest a growing number of therapists and analysts. If the therapist is familiar with his own body he is less likely to stiffen, thus raising the threshold of his sensitivity. If the analyst enters this new dimension resolutely, when he is exposed to the patient's hate or love, he will realise that he feels them more *concretely* above all in the various parts of his body: variations or disorders in breathing, for example, tension in the lower limbs, the back, the neck, tired eyes, erotic arousal in unexpected places and many other reactions. Everyday expressions such as "that saying struck me", "to rub salt into the wound", a "heart-rending cry", reflect the fact that emotions touch us first in our bodies.

Psychotics differ from neurotics because they take the real need to emotionalise the analyst to extremes. All patients, to varying degrees, especially when they are dealing with their most serious conflicts, test the analyst as a container of those emotions (those parts of the Self) which they are terrified they will not be able to contain themselves; this can raise some disquieting questions.

After years of analysis, a seriously ill patient of mine had reached the point of wanting, with my help, to face up to the parts of his Self that he most feared. He was concerned that I might not be able to contain the murderous and intrusive violence of these parts (parts that were at the same time, as we shall discover, also capable of extreme tenderness). During one session he said: "I feel threatened, invaded by something that constantly escapes me, like mercury. I can't grasp what it is." After a long pause he added, with a certain hesitation: "During our sessions you don't smoke your pipe, but out on the street I once saw you smoking. Why do you need to do it? I find it difficult to reconcile this weakness of yours with your solidity."

Perhaps now the statement that I made at the beginning of the book will be comprehensible, namely that only if the analyst has a low psychological and physical centre of gravity (and this in general is associated with the ability to breathe deeply), only if his psycho-somatic Self has achieved sufficient cohesion and "hold" on his emotions, will he feel well enough equipped to accept within himself, and therefore during his sessions with patients, the violent emotions that otherwise they will unleash against him or split off and live out elsewhere, far from the analysis.[43]

The therapist must be able to *detoxify himself* of everything destructive that the patient has placed inside him. In my view this is best achieved through the correct use of breathing, something we usually know how to do spontaneously as children but an ability we lose as adults and which needs to be re-learnt. If the analyst, despite knowing about the projective identification of the patient, fails to notice that he is being contaminated and fails to see the sedimentation that this has left in him, he runs a serious risk: these residues can mix with his unresolved personal conflicts and provoke destructive reactions, depression and loss of hope.

Earlier we talked about Freud's view that the counter-transference ought to be mastered – not used and worked through – and also how he himself felt that he did not know about it in detail.[44] Ferenczi was extremely disturbed when Freud said: "patients are riff-raff . . . they serve to give us a living and offer us material to study and in any case we cannot help them", and when he expressed his rejection of psychotics and antipathy for perverts. Ferenczi thought this was therapeutic nihilism.[45] Even though I cannot exclude a priori either cynical traits in Freud's personality or moments of despondency, I would tend rather to emphasise his uncertainty about his ability to contain the severe pathologies of his patients.

This lack of an appropriate hold prompts us to consider two phenomena which are crucial to the success or failure of therapy. On the one hand, clinical experience seems to suggest that prolonged and repeated explosions of aggressiveness towards the analyst during analysis are more probably the product of an insufficient ability to contain than the result of mistaken interpretations. Especially in supervision, where the phenomenon is clearer, it emerges that patients excuse the analyst's misreading of the nature of their anxieties much more easily than they can shake off the sense of precariousness that inadequate containment provokes or heightens. When failure to contain becomes a serious problem, the patient seems to want to spare his therapist and consequently splits off and acts out his negative transference in another relationship, outside the analysis.

Alternatively he or she might abandon the analysis. H.H. realised that his analyst, on the various occasions when he had managed to present him with all his anxiety, had concluded the session several minutes early. During the next session the therapist was obviously embarrassed and had apologised. As a result of these experiences H.H. started to think about discontinuing his analysis. Two points emerge here: one is that the analyst fails to contain the patient's anxiety beyond a certain level, the other is that his embarrassed apologies show that he is unable to work through his own sense of guilt and discomfort.

It is easy to see that someone who has not resolved the problems that result from an inability to contain, who has not resolved his conflict with his unconscious traces and the wounds which arise from lack of affection in childhood, can also have difficulty in conceiving what it means in concrete terms to be able to contain. Usually this arises out of traumas resulting from a deficient relationship with the mother in the feeding period, a mother who did not provide a sufficiently good holding environment. The analyst who finds himself in this conflictual situation will tend to neglect the problem of containment, possibly even dodging the problem completely by arguing that analytic interpretation is what constitutes authentic containment. Interpretation clarifies the content and the defences (the unconscious fantasies); containment has an influence on the way in which it is interpreted, the choice of the right moment and the length of the interpretation.

The analyst whose method of treatment is to focus essentially on interpretation *enters*, so to speak, into the patient and reveals to him what is wrong. The analyst who – without neglecting interpretation – allows the patient to become as active as possible (the limits are often those of his conflictuality) and collaborates in the quest for the truth, uses a receptive model such as that suggested by the metaphor of the telephone, a model that starts from the idea of containment.

Winnicott talked not only about *holding*, but also about the *use of the object*. These are two models that both go in the direction we are taking; in fact, to a certain extent, they anticipate the approach I am outlining. When he talks about *holding*, Winnicott is referring to a form of containment which starts from the physical capacity to accept and to support which the mother offers to the child with her arms and body: "It is a form of love. It is probably the only way that a mother has to show her love for the small child." Holding meets physiological needs as well. A second characteristic of *holding* – here understood not only as what the mother does but also as the facilitating environment – is the quality of being trustworthy which allows her to help the child to mature and to discover itself. This should not be mechanical trustworthiness: holding becomes trustworthy when "it brings with it the empathy of the mother".[46]

Some mothers are able to hold their children, others are not; those who cannot soon produce in the child a sense of insecurity and provoke desperate tears.[47] Likewise there are analysts capable of containment and others who lack this ability.

Y.Y., a forty-year-old woman, after finishing her therapy with her analyst, had sexual relations with him. In the recurrent nightmare that led her to turn to another analyst for advice when her neurosis resurfaced, she appeared as a very young child constantly falling out of her cot in a panic because the bars were down.

There is one paper which takes the concept of holding as its starting point and which probably more than any other sums up Winnicott's thinking at the moment when he split from Klein. In "The use of an object" he explains what he means by the capacity to use an object. He read this work to a group of psychoanalysts in New York in 1968, at the height of the student revolt.[48] He argued that our capacity to use an object implies something more sophisticated than being in relation to it (although being in a relation to it must come first); it presupposes that we take into consideration the very nature of the person who lives in the external world and interact with that person. Winnicott emphasised that, in order to be able to use another person constructively, that person must not let himself be destroyed by our aggressiveness. Only if he has passed this test can he be an object of love, can he escape from our omnipotent control. And from that moment we can say: "you are of value to me because you survived my destructive attack", as Winnicott sums up. There seems to be a change in perspective: *it is no longer the reparation coming from the patient who is trying to recover that saves the relationship, but the ability on the part of the person receiving the attacks to contain them.*

The second point worth recalling is a question of the technique used to intervene: "Only in recent years," confesses Winnicott, "have I become capable of waiting even a long time for the natural development of transference to arise out of the trust in the technique and the psychoanalytical setting that the patient gains progressively". He goes on to say that there is something else that he is pleased to have acquired over time: the capacity "to avoid interrupting this natural process by making interpretations". This remark bears remarkable similarity to the definition of *wu wei* given by Graham.

Chapter 11

Projective identification and containment

I would like to open this last chapter by touching upon the most disquieting phenomenon we have come across in our discussion of the various aspects of guilt and the sense of guilt: *projective identification*. It is a topic which, as will soon become clear, would require much more space to analyse in full.

> I am one of those who are most sensible of the power of imagination: every one is jostled by it, but some are overthrown by it. It has a very piercing impression upon me . . . Simon Thomas was a great physician of his time: I remember, that happening one day at Toulouse to meet him at a rich old fellow's house, who was troubled with weak lungs, and discoursing with his patient about the method of his cure, he told him, that one thing which would be very conducive to it, was to give me such occasion to be pleased with his company, that I might come often to see him, by which means, and by fixing his eye upon the freshness of my complexion, and his imagination upon the sprightliness and vigour that glowed in my youth, and possessing all his senses with the flourishing age wherein I then was, his habit to body might, peradventure, be amended; but he forgot to say that mine, at the same time, might be made worse.[1]

This passage from Montaigne's *Essais* would seem to offer a description *avant la lettre* of several of the characteristics of projective identification, although, of course, some qualities are missing. There is also none of the attentiveness and ability to transform one's observations into something clinically useful that we find in writers such as Herbert Rosenfeld, León Grinberg or Thomas Ogden. Nevertheless, Montaigne seems, with his amiable irony, to have gasped the possible movements of what is called "projective identification as imagination" with great clarity.[2]

Projective identification is clearly a complex phenomenon: it has to do with the pressure that an individual exerts on another individual, a pressure which comes from his unconscious fantasy life. At one point, Ogden, who describes the details of the phenomenon with great care, introduces the

concept of actualisation to talk about its central aspect.[3] Projective identification implies an effort to change the other person, not just the image that
we have formed of the other person (this would be projection *tout court*).
An individual can unconsciously manoeuvre another, meaning that he can
direct him, control him, fill him with a sense of guilt; and he can do this by
putting his split-off parts into the other. Also the thoughts and emotions of
these split-off parts are evacuated and come to occupy the other. But this
is not the end of the process, as Hanna Segal points out. Projection is
followed by incorporation: the person who has been made the object of
projective identification can be re-internalised by the other, together with
what was previously injected, but also with something more (the ability or
the inability to contain, for example).

We are coming closer to the core of a process which is one of the most
important discoveries of psychoanalysis and of modern dynamic psychiatry.
But it is a process that is not easy to understand and is often diagnosed
erroneously as if it were a *passe-partout*.

We said that in projective identification a person receives a part of the
Self that the other expels and then re-appropriates. But this is not always
possible: death, for example, can prevent it. The violence of projective
identification can, in some extreme and fortunately rare cases, induce the
victim to use the murderer to commit suicide. In forensic psychiatry this
phenomenon is known as "victimisation". However, a subtle and profound
interpretation of the dynamics set in motion between the victim and the
tormentor is only possible from a point of view that considers projective
identification: the strong self-destructive impulse, probably combined with
other components, is placed inside the other, together with the "order" to
kill.

We are in the presence of a harrowing phenomenon, one that "over-
throws" us, to use Montaigne's expression, a phenomenon which has also
provoked drastic reactions and at times unexpected resistance in the scientific field. And not only from outside psychoanalysis.[4]

I recall an episode that goes back some twenty years, which may give a
concrete idea of the upset and the inadequate responses that can occur even
in a well-trained therapist. A middle-aged psychoanalyst (who on a rational
level was perfectly aware of these phenomena and accepted them), stood up
at a meeting and, highly agitated and tense, interrupted a colleague who
was in the middle of talking, diagnosed the latter as suffering from
depression and told him in an exasperated (and in some ways also protective) tone to go back and undergo analysis. This colleague was explaining
the reasons why he thought that a schizophrenic patient of his had placed
inside him both thoughts and memories, together with their corresponding
emotions; the analyst was expected to accept and live through this set of
experiences as a unified whole (this is precisely what most split people
cannot allow themselves to do).

Martin Wangh called this type of phenomenon the "evocation of proxy".[5] The other analyst's reaction was so violent because his colleague was describing how he had twice started crying in sessions with the patient. Clearly, the idea that an analyst could cry like that can cause a violent disturbance and galvanise someone into action (the colleague jumped to his feet, possibly as a first step to leaving the room), and most importantly it can destroy a fragile containing capacity. Incidentally, after these sessions (which made him feel very grateful towards his analyst), the patient found himself able to be moved by the memory of a fundamental experience, something which previously he had not allowed himself to do.

I am reminded of a phrase I found somewhere in Goethe: "however much the world tries to poison that moment, when a man is moved, he has a profound sense of wonder". But the sense of wonder can often prove to be uncontainable.

From a phenomenological point of view, we could add that various analysts who have to contain situations like the one we have just described very often go through a similar experience: their "observing Ego" remains calm and watches itself cry and be moved, in some cases with a feeling of joy and gratification "for something that had to be done". Obviously the ability to contain presupposes experience; but it also presupposes that particular relationship with one's body I have been trying to describe: this is what produces the healthy ability to abandon oneself in the certainty that one will not go to pieces and not destroy anything.

The strength necessary for the ability to contain comes in part from the ability to let oneself go at the service of the Self, to use an outmoded psychoanalytical expression. If a person can afford to abandon himself in his relationship with others, this shows that there is a limit to his rigidity and his fear.

The difference in the responses of these two analysts suggests another hypothesis which seems to me to be important and worthy of closer examination. Depending on the ability of the analyst (or the receiver) to contain effectively projective identifications loaded with emotional tension, projective identification can be perceived – and thus interpreted – as an attack (and thus to some extent blamed), or as an extreme attempt to communicate a need for responsive containment.[6] During the case I am describing, the projective identification of the patient, together with the response it provoked, was experienced by both the analyst and the schizo-phrenic patient as an extraordinary opportunity, as a turning point, but by the analyst who interrupted it was felt to be something intolerable.

I mentioned earlier the idea of joy: an analyst who is not hypersensitive to aggressive attacks from patients (as long as they are not too intense, of course) can experience satisfaction at being attacked. This is not because he is a moral masochist, but because the direct expression of aggression can signify progress: in many cases the patient who manages to attack shows that he is less afraid of his anger, and – the paradox is only apparent – proves that he sees his analyst as less persecutory, less vindictive. It is no surprise then that this progress can convey a sense of pleasure to the therapist. This type of reaction is also a sign that the analyst is observing and experiencing the behaviour of the patient on more than one level, as is typical of the point of view that transcends the logic of guilt.

On the other hand, if the analyst has only partially resolved his own conflicts, he will provide a defective model of containment. As is often the case, appropriate techniques make it possible to improve a particular function, and containment is no exception. But the likelihood is that it is the analyst's general maturity and not mere technique which makes for a supple and resistant ability to contain, one which is ready for surprises and even violence.

Attention and guilt

> *To strip down, to purify, to breathe again,*
> *to remove the scum and the gilding.*
> (Bruce Chatwin)

Containment is connected to breathing and this also depends on posture, that is to say, the habitual bodily attitude that results from the contraction (or the slack state) of muscles. Breathing with the diaphragm is certainly not the only form, as every good doctor learns during his studies; all types of breathing have a vital function. This point is still very important and the well-known instruction typical of a certain military tradition – namely, "stomach in, chest out!" – sacrifices this, paradoxically creating weakness rather than strength. And yet our society, despite substantial changes, still believes in the model which sees the flat stomach as the ideal form of the human body.

One need only observe young children or primitive peoples to realise that the walls of the abdomen expand naturally at every breath. If we want to avoid this expansion we need, consciously or unconsciously, to keep our chest out and the abdominal muscles inwardly tense. In this way thoracic breathing is also to some extent sacrificed.

Why does this posture create weakness? The answer to this question is complicated. The main point is that it is a static position which expresses a reaction to fear, or the need to strike fear into another person. "Stomach in, chest out" – which we shall take as our extreme model – also leads to overburdened shoulders, pronation and flexing of the arms, pushing the head forward and prognathism of the lower jaw. We know that this expresses challenge and an attitude of strong will. It is the posture of the primate who mimes the aggressiveness and threat of the gorilla. But it is a communicative posture, not an active one; it is a posture that is designed to be short-lived. When the gorilla has to prepare to fight, his bodily attitude changes totally: he makes himself mobile, as indeed do human beings.

The static posture is meant to frighten the adversary; it is not really meant as a way of attacking. It is a posture adopted by the macho male. Eibl-Eibesfeldt shows how men have reproduced this position in costumes and various military uniforms (one need only think of the epaulettes which artificially emphasise the raising of the shoulders).[7] If we are right in this, we can conclude that, when we hold our breath, because the diaphragm and the chest are less free, we are also less able to contain our emotions.

The mother's ability to contain is something lasting and – perhaps this will not appear to be a paradox – is attained more easily in people capable of using aggressiveness (capable of defending their little ones) than in those whose aggressiveness is held in check. Psychoanalysis sees in the martial posture a need to identify with the phallus to defend oneself against profound anxiety and insecurity. Although it has dealt with the aspect we could call dynamic and symbolic (purely psychological aspects), it could have gone further in its investigation by looking more closely at the psychosomatic consequences we have just been talking about. This particular posture, one might add, blocks the lungs, and thus the source of oxygen, presses on the spleen and consequently prevents the regulation of the quantity of red globules circulating in the body, acts negatively on the intestines, and so on.

Anyone with any experience of body psychotherapy will have recognised how important it is to make sure that the patient gradually realises that an improved ability to contain lessens the need to project feelings, emotions and parts of the Self. As we said, what helps in this task is deep, modulated breathing; this presupposes an outlet for certain bodily contractions. The bodily approach has identified a series of problem areas which limit and – in some extreme cases – prevent containment. We said that a man or a woman who has only a limited ability to contain bad objects, and even good objects, will resort to projective identification on a large scale. To take a simple example: the mobility of the pelvis (in all directions: backwards and forwards, in making circular motions, clockwise and anticlockwise) is directly proportional to the ability to contain.

If it is true that only when we are able to contain the presences in our internal world will we be able to think about them, we could also say that pelvic rigidity corresponds to a difficulty in working through conflicts. However, I do not believe that the opposite is true: that a lack of rigidity makes it easier to work through conflicts. I have found that the need in some patients to project internal objects and parts of self (whether good or bad) is closely connected to the inability to work through them.

The process of working through is set in motion or comes to a halt when the objects and parts of the self come out of the unconscious into which they have been repressed, "frozen" or "buried" (in the dreams or free associations of depressed patients, or those suffering from latent depression, this is often the way that the persecutory objects relegated to the unconscious are symbolised). When they take the form of people in prison or trapped in some way (to take other common examples), this means that they have come back to life, even though they are not free to move. But in order to come back to life and to feel the need to manifest themselves they need space, and internal psychic space seems to be connected to the space that is filled by correct, deep breathing. In other words, it is fairly improbable that an anorexic would be able to work through her persecutory objects if she continued with her shallow breathing.

But this does not exclude the possibility that introjective and containment skills can be acquired with the help of a good analysis (in this case greater psychic well-being has a positive effect on somatic tensions). With the help of bodily techniques, these results can be achieved earlier, more easily and probably to greater advantage. The focus on breathing is something we have taken from the Orient.

The interpretative function of the analyst depends on his ability to recognise within himself the emotions, even violent emotions, which the patient provokes in him or places in him; and it presupposes the capacity to let these emotions settle. Not until the analyst has acquired a certain calm can he decipher, drawing on his experience and his models, and thus provide interpretations which are not intellectualised.[8] Without this settling process, his interpretations will be largely inauthentic, defensive, rationalised; at worst they will be dictated by revenge, by the fear of not understanding in time, and so on. We know very well how these responses can come to all of us, analysts and non-analysts alike, and how these responses tend to take the concrete form of accusations.

So only if none of these phases is skipped will the analyst succeed in fully developing the equally suspended attention which allows him, by using the preconscious, to put the non-verbal communications transmitted by the body on a par with the word: not only the most obvious expressive gestures, but also pauses, intensity, tonality, the timbre of the voice, the rhythm of speaking. Changes in tone and rhythm, for example, or a sudden hardening of the face, or the deepening of a wrinkle, can reveal that a process of rationalisation (in defence of something) has been set in motion.[9] Stepping outside psychoanalysis one need only recall the extraordinary chapter on "The rhythm of the Proustian sentence" in his 1928 book Leo Spitzer wrote: "The rhythm of the Proustian sentence . . . is that which most clearly reveals his vision of the world: these complicated and intricate sentences, which the reader has to untangle and 'construe' as if they were ancient Greek or Latin, are the very image of the complex and intricate world that Proust contemplates. Nothing in Proust's world or in Proust's style is simple."

Many experiences seem to confirm the idea that refining the receptive faculty and attention enlarges the range of perceived stimuli, and consequently makes for more relevant, modulated and convincing interpretations. I should like to recall a brief episode which involved an analyst's sense of guilt.

E.E. suffered from a serious form of hysteria which made her life extremely difficult, complicating all her relationships in a sado-masochistic way. The colleague who had been treating her for years with apparently very little success approached me for my opinion and told me that he thought that he had got over a moment of impasse by placing himself in a particular position of listening which had produced a kind of *rêverie* and by thinking about what he called an "interpretation of character".

One day, lying comfortably on the couch, with her hands linked behind her head, E.E., in the tone of someone who was having a friendly chat, had started talking about "what was going through her head": an episode from her working life, then a change of subject, an exclamation such as "the distant stars in the sky . . .", a story about her relationship with her younger daughter, another switch, a comment about the carpet in the analyst's studio, another "cut" and so on. This technique, which she had used very frequently, disoriented my colleague and prevented him from thinking. Every previous attempt to draw the patient's attention to this behaviour had been unsuccessful. She had been using it constantly for some months. One day at the end of a session the analyst exploited his ability to produce a *rêverie* and "hallucinated" a cat which was lying comfortably on the floor and tormenting a mouse by making it run in all directions and then blocking its path all the time. The analyst had seen this as an accurate dramatic portrayal of the situation and if the session had not been over he would have used it as a metaphor and offered it as an interpretation to the patient who was behaving precisely like a cat with a mouse.

As we discussed this idea we looked at various points: the cannibalistic atmosphere of the counter-transference fantasy (the mouse is food for the cat); then the limited amount of time that my colleague had to formulate his hypothesis. This appeared to us as the sign of a state of relative, unresolved tension. Lastly, in the relaxed atmosphere we had created, he became gradually aware of a painful twinge of a *sense of guilt*. After we had worked through these elements, particularly the last, my colleague, almost without my intervention, realised that he had not understood the complex dynamic of the situation and that he had formulated his interpretation inside himself in a state of exasperation, driven by an impulse of revenge: this is where his sense of guilt, *which he had not noticed during the session*, had come from. He hadn't noticed it because his threshold of sensitivity had risen as a result of the stress.

In my presence this colleague had been able to relax and in this state he had started thinking in a more acute and subtle way. But in this new light the first interpretative hypothesis, which had had the conscious aim of drawing the patient's attention to her sadism towards the analyst, ultimately appeared to him inappropriate. He realised that if he had given this interpretation to the patient, he would have reinforced her sense of guilt without showing her a way out: just like the cat in his *rêverie*.

A more effective containment allowed him to acknowledge his sense of guilt, and this led him to intervene in a different way. To sum up briefly, he told the patient that the behaviour pattern she was using with him had given rise to a *rêverie*, which he then went on to describe. He asked her if these images suggested anything to her. The patient smiled, then said that she agreed. Especially the bit about "lying comfortably": she felt good during the session and added: "Probably if I say things that are true, then the analysis will finish". If we were to follow the movements of the cat and the mouse suggested by my colleague's counter-transference, it would take us too far. What I do want to emphasise, however, is that through his intervention (we may or may not agree with it, but it was certainly not meant to inculcate blame), the therapist managed once again to get the patient to speak in an authentic and collaborative way.

The empathetic ability to enter into *rêverie*, to expose oneself without defensive filters to the stimuli produced by the patient; the emergence of guilt as a signal that – once it has been correctly understood – warns the analyst that something is wrong; retaliation as an index not only of a vengeful response but also of a lack of containment (the emotions provoked by the patient had not been allowed to "settle" properly) – these are some of the themes which we have been looking at and which reappeared in this brief "slice" of analysis.

Perhaps if we look at another case, focusing on my counter-transference and on what I can conclude from my understanding of it, these ideas will become clearer. A.A., a man of about thirty years of age, has been in analysis for almost a year when I begin to realise vaguely that something has changed in our relationship. In the past I had noticed that he closed himself off by intellectualising when he came close to moments of separation: towards the end of each session and towards the end of the week. Now the sessions had become uniform and this was making me feel somewhat uneasy.

I manage to put myself in an attitude of "equal suspension" as I await a *rêverie*. My patient's words fade into the background; I no longer follow what he is saying and this enables me to perceive that the volume, the intensity of the sound of his voice is standing out against the background. I realise that the volume is excessive and that A.A. does not really need to speak to me in such a loud voice. The *rêverie* that starts up in me depicts him as if he were detached from the couch, as if he were levitating. When I start to decipher the *rêverie* as if it were a dream, my associations lead me to see the distance of A.A.'s body from the couch as equal to the excess in intensity of his voice. I then formulate the hypothesis that, in the transference, the couch represents for the patient my maternal, receptive side, a mother's body. The excessive volume seemed then to indicate a conflict in our relationship (perhaps brought about by me in some way, perhaps only a re-creation from his past). All this made me think that my patient had no confidence in me and in particular did not trust my ability to contain him. Consequently he controlled the persecution that emanated from me, kept himself at a distance using the volume of his voice, as sometimes happens when we want to tell someone we see as dangerous or disturbing to keep away from us, or when we ask for help.

This last case should make clearer what I meant earlier by integrated thought: the *rêverie* that I engage in is the product of my preconscious, but the interpretation with which I try to explain myself is produced in collaboration with my conscious mind.

The patient must be enabled to internalise, day after day, an analyst who above all is not omniscient, who is not afraid of recognising his mistakes, an analyst who is not fixed in his thinking and who usually needs time, relative tranquillity, what Bion called "patience" and assurance. All these are elements that are signs of effective containment at work trying to reach an interpretation.

Only by recognising the importance of these needs of the analyst will the patient, helped by sensitive interpretations, come into contact with the part of himself that he needs to change if he is to live better and more freely. He will then realise that in order to become aware – to stop repressing, projecting and denying – he needs to become capable of observing and understanding. He must also learn to appreciate and describe what is happening inside him. In other words, he will discover that it is important to learn how to "see", to think through, his own suffering and difficulties before trying to resolve them. I would underline that if this does not happen, we will find ourselves in the presence of acting out, in both behaviour and thinking (intellectualisation, rationalisation). But every patient should come to understand that the more violent his emotions, the more tolerant he has to be towards his limitations. We are not always successful at doing this, at least not at the first attempt.

When the path to a greater inner freedom does open up – which is after all what we are trying to achieve – we usually forget that the continuation of the path from the insight to its practical application is often very long. It implies a journey made up of attempts – which can be more or less successful – both to focus on the problem and to engage in effective action. Through this slow and complex process of change, the patient will, if the analysis is successful, ultimately discover spontaneity – the quality which for adults is probably the most important and at the same time the most difficult to achieve. A *spontaneous* response is the exact opposite of what we normally call a mechanical response. It can have the directness of a mechanical response, but differs from it in that it involves the whole person, body and soul.[10]

If I have been successful in my attempt to show the interaction between mind and body in containment which can lead to interpretation, the question asked by Nietzsche's Zarathustra should be clearer: "There is more reason in your body than in your best wisdom. And who knows what is the purpose for your body of your best wisdom."[11]

Guilt and atmosphere

The points we have just been making could also shed new light on the importance of the empathetic use of the preconscious. This use implies the right dose of "concerned distance" that makes it possible to contain everything the patient brings to the analyst in order to find (with the patient's help, when possible) the point which is most likely to facilitate his maturation.[12] This subject leads us to the only prescription that Freud lays down in the context of "equally suspended attention" and to Bion's warning against weighing down our memory. We said earlier that Freud's prescription can be easily ignored; we could now add that it can in fact be systematically ignored.

Melanie Klein had been analysing Ruth for a little over four years. She was a young patient with a serious infantile neurosis, "who had suffered hunger for a considerable period of time because her mother did not have enough milk". As we can see – if we want to come back to the quarrel with Winnicott – Klein is here pointing out the defects of the mother.[13] Not only did she suffer "from a great deal of undisguised anxiety which often led to anxiety-attacks and from various other neurotic symptoms, but also from apprehensiveness in general".[14] Klein's intention was to establish a healthy transference relationship with the child so as to be able to work alone with her. Generally she would stay in the analysis room only if her elder sister was present.

> but all my efforts, such as playing with her, encouraging her to talk, etc. were in vain. She played with her toys but only with her sister (although the sister was also quite solitary); she ignored me completely. Her sister told me that my efforts were pointless . . . So I was forced to adopt other measures – measures which once again offered surprising proof of the effectiveness of interpretation in reducing the patient's and her negative transference.

Klein goes on to explain how one day the child – who as usual focused all her attention on the sister – drew a round glass with some balls inside it and a kind of lid on top. On the basis of previous material, which the child had expressed through games, Klein ventured to give the child an interpretation based on her desire to keep the children enclosed within the mother's tummy "so as not to have other brothers and sisters". In this analysis, she explained, "the child's desire to rob the mother's body and her consequent senses of anxiety and guilt, dominated the picture from the beginning. The neurosis broke out . . . after the mother's pregnancy and the birth of the younger sister" (ibid.).[15] Yet the effect of the interpretation "was surprising". For the first time Ruth turned her attention to her and started to play in a different, more natural, way.

This episode reveals all the creativity that distinguishes Klein; the feeling of "being forced" from inside (perhaps a preconscious suggestion, her daemon) to choose a certain path; there is surprise, not so much because of the novelty of the instrument used as for the further confirmation it provides.

Following this type of experience, the patient's negative transference took on crucial importance for her. From the very beginning the most characteristic aspect of her technique had been, according to Money-Kyrle, the way she privileged the interpretation of the "unconscious anxiety, based on an unconscious phantasy, every time she could see it – *even when the initial results were an increase in anxiety*".[16]

Whether she wanted it or not, this insight of Melanie Klein's led many analysts to give up equally suspended attention in favour of what Freud called deliberate "dangerous" attention – attention *to the search for the point of highest anxiety*.[17] The risk lay not in the fact that this meant abandoning the will of the founding father of psychoanalysis; Klein in her technical approach had already introduced many other innovations. The risk was that a code became established between the patient and the analyst, a kind of grammar and syntax, and that this was what would then be responsible for the atmosphere. To use a musical metaphor, we could say that the risk lay in the fact that all sounds belonged to one *tonality*; in other words, that all emotions had to sound one *keynote*, a preferred emotion around which and towards which the other emotions and affects had to gravitate.

We can come back to Riviere and to her warning against the excessive insistence on the analysis of aggressive impulses (the main source of anxiety and guilt, according to Kleinian theory),[18] a warning based on the opinion that nothing leads to a standstill or failure of therapy more than that type of blindness whereby the analyst sees only aggressiveness.[19] The principle that inspired Riviere is so appropriate that it deserves general application.

It goes without saying that a sensitive analyst will be affected by the suffering of his patients, by their pain and their anxiety. We must also take it for granted that often at the centre of the communication that a patient makes in a session – at the centre of the fantasy underlying it – lies the point of greatest anxiety, just like every cyclone has its eye. This is especially true in situations in which the anxiety is strong, as we saw in the case of little Ruth. I don't want to be misunderstood on this point: the main task of the analyst is to help his patients to live better lives and consequently to free themselves progressively from anxiety and guilt. What I want to come back to is the strategy, the timing, the choice of atmosphere that enables us to reach this objective.

The strategy question is complicated. Right from the beginning of an analysis, Klein aimed to reach the deepest level of unconscious fantasies with her interpretations, at the risk of arousing even stronger anxieties.[20] Only the analyst can intuit that deep level. If the analyst makes a mistake, he can be responsible for creating a negative atmosphere.

But first we need to say something about correct timing. In the same book, Klein adds that it is "*absolutely necessary* to give interpretations as soon as the anxiety and the resistance becomes manifest or in cases where the analysis begins with a negative transference".[21] The interpretation must be prompt.

It is also probable that this rather drastic didactic approach – similar to what we see in Freud and thirty-five years later in Bion – is in part because she felt the need to warn analysts and therapists against wasting time when dealing with their patients' suffering. But these words might also indicate a certain insensitivity on the part of Melanie Klein due to the constant state of anxiety which she, without knowing it, betrayed in the work where she describes her psychoanalytical "observation" of her own son Eric.[22] Thirty-five years later she said that she saw in that case the beginning of her technique of play in psychoanalysis and so we must think that, from this point of view, she had not changed her mind.

We shall also find this "hurry" in one of her great disciples, Herbert Rosenfeld. In an article I wrote upon the publication of his posthumous *Impasse and Interpretation*, I expressed my debt of gratitude towards this analyst who – as I have recalled on several occasions – at an old age was brave enough to assume just and courageous positions. But at the same time I expressed some reservations. I mention them now because I think they illustrate an extremely important point.

In a chapter about the various therapeutic and non-therapeutic factors that affect the way the analyst functions, Rosenfeld says that the analyst's capacity to function is reflected in the path his understanding takes to reach an interpretation, more than by the choice of material to interpret. He then adds: "one may say that the patient's feeling of being accepted and cared for depends to a large extent on the interpretative function of the analyst". Like several others, I have found that patients respond to interpretations not only as to instruments which make them aware of the meaning of unconscious and conscious processes, but also as reflections of the state of mind of the analyst, "particularly in his role of maintaining calm and peace and focusing on the central aspects of the conscious and unconscious worries and anxieties of the patient".[23] One should incidentally note how in Rosenfeld's words "the point of maximum anxiety" has been watered down. By virtue of his relative calm – re-found if necessary – the analyst obtains the right "involved distance" which, as we have seen, is essential.

Talking of a patient of his called Adam, he writes: "He was intensely restless on the couch. This panic was very impressive and I felt in my counter-transference that something very overwhelming was happening. I realised that I had to understand something fundamental and quickly, because the situation seemed to be getting out of hand and he was becoming deluded. I therefore interpreted then that Adam believed that he had really devoured and killed his girl-friend through his greedy, sexually overpowering approach and as a result he believed she was concretely dead inside him."

Rosenfeld does not describe this intervention as one of those inter-pretations which every analyst occasionally makes out of a feeling of being ill at ease: he offers it as an example and this authorises us to discuss it. The interpretation seemed, according to Rosenfeld, to have a positive effect, but in the long term the case was not resolved. The haste which the patient creates in the analyst is not understood and hence not worked through.[24] Rosenfeld says that he was forced to come up with an interpretation *quickly*.

We have insufficient information to go into the case of Adam in any more detail. The fact remains, however, that in this interpretation we can see evidence of the logic of guilt (Adam is described as "overpowering" and "greedy") and there is a suspicion that haste and the logic of guilt go hand in hand.[25] It is difficult to avoid the impression that in the long run these elements create an atmosphere that tends to emphasise anxiety and guilt.

I remember once many years ago watching a fight between four small boys in a park. As it started their mothers were all sitting on a bench reading. When three of the mothers realised what was going on, they got up in a state, ran to separate their children and then took them back to their benches, where they told them off. The boys cried and were annoyed. The fourth mother didn't move; her son – who had punched and been hit as much as the others – got up, blew his nose and walked slowly back to his mother. They started talking as if nothing had happened. When I think of atmosphere (which I cannot help but associate with Winnicott's mother-environment), this episode often comes to mind.

In order to understand correctly, the analyst must move at his own speed. If he manages with his interventions to make sure that everything necessary for paying attention in the right manner (not only timing, but also relative peace, absence of interruptions) is not disturbed, this analyst will make sure that the patient progressively realises that he is not dealing with someone omniscient. He will also communicate in many ways which, if the core of the problems is to be reached, will need the collaboration of the patient. In my experience even seriously ill patients feel the benefit of this different pace, this different atmosphere. Clearly, this atmosphere is, to a certain extent, constantly disturbed but the analyst ought to give his patients the idea that it needs to be restored.

Anyone who is able to maintain an equal level of suspended attention is unlikely to be driven by urgency. He will notice, unwittingly, that at a certain point his attention will *spontaneously* focus on something, as if drawn by a particular detail (the volume of A.A.'s voice, for example). Obviously this attraction towards that detail should not be an escape, should not result from a defence on the part of the therapist; he should not lean too far in one direction and take his eyes off another. In the case of A.A. I am sure that my attention was attracted by the point of greatest anxiety.

I would like to describe another case I supervised, the case of R.R., where things did not go exactly like this. It goes without saying that if one makes an effort, using one's intelligence and forcing things a little, everything can be brought back to the point of greatest anxiety, but this would be rigging the cards.

R.R. was young man of about thirty years of age who suffered intense anxieties about being abandoned which resulted from a serious maternal deficit in his early childhood (his mother had died when giving birth to him and he was brought up by his maternal grandmother who was an alcoholic), but he was also very intelligent and determined to break out of his extreme suffering. For years, he would spend the weekend (when he was "abandoned" by his analyst) and his analyst's holidays in a state of marked maniacal excitement which led him to commit potentially self-destructive acts apparently without any sense of guilt.

During a long initial period he acted out his despair by racing around on a motorbike. He used to overtake cars going round corners at high speed "crossing the double white lines". During his sessions he reported fantasies of head-on fatal crashes with other motorbikes. His accounts must have been true because on a couple of occasions the police took his licence from him, even though he hadn't actually had an accident. In the second phase he moved on from his "wild" motorbike races to free climbing – the sport where people climb rockfaces without any equipment, using only the strength of their feet and their hands (strength obtained by exhausting, rigorous training). Finally, after some two years he gave up this form of "giving vent" to his emotions and started going to loud discos to be "stunned" by the music, at the same time as keeping up his sporting activities in "less extreme forms".[26]

From the beginning, the colleague who told me about this case registered a counter-transference that reflected her disturbed feelings: she fantasised about offering the patient seven sessions a week and giving up her holidays; she felt incapable and even played with the idea of giving up the profession. All this was decoded in a progressively more accurate way. My point, however, is that this analyst – who registered this mainly because of the growing anxiety she felt in counter-transference – always, at every separation, interpreted the point of greatest anxiety as being connected to the patient's anxiety about being abandoned and his desire to blame the analyst for leaving him alone. He did this with slight variations during all three of the periods referred to above. There came a point where the analyst – invited to pay marginal attention to this repetition of similar (if not identical) interpretations – realised that she felt driven by an "internal rule of safety" as a way of putting a stop to her patient's high-risk activities.

After working meticulously on her patient's ability to cheer up and so to improve his containment, my colleague began to appreciate two hypotheses which previously had escaped her. On the one hand, she was attracted by the almost imperceptibly dramatic tones – theatrically "studied" and play-acted – with which the patient created anxiety in her with his suicide threats; on the other – and this is what attracted my attention more than anything else – she began to see that there were significant differences between the three activities which the patient had come up with to get through the periods when they were separated.

By focusing on the "theatricality" with which the patient elicited extreme anxiety in her, the question arose as to whether his intention was "studied", sadistic, destructive or relatively "free" of anxiety and guilt. Or was it a way of testing the containing ability of the analyst? Was he using violence to try out her holding capacity? The three ways of spending the time when they were separated showed different qualities: in crossing the double white line, his suicidal and homicidal impulses were apparently given totally free rein. During free climbing the risk of falling was counterbalanced by the obsessive (but still real) effort directed at controlling his suicidal impulses and the phobic terror of being swallowed up by the abyss. These were partially contained (the effort to "cling on", "not to let go" was an index of the distance he had come since his days of racing madly round bends in the road on his motorbike).[27] The risks involved in going to loud discotheques to "be stunned" (he was a health fanatic and didn't take drugs) were considerably smaller (at the most he might damage his hearing; certainly nothing compared to the previous risks he had run).

What I was trying to suggest is that the analyst was able to recognise this positive movement only by tuning in to aspects which were not part of the moment of greatest anxiety.[28]

The case of Z.Z. could be seen as part of what early psychoanalysis, in the words of Theodor Reik, called the *compulsion to confess*.[29] We could use it to trace once again our interpretative line. Z.Z. was a highly respected and esteemed young industrial manager who had been in analysis for some years. One day he came to the session in a state of extreme anxiety because the evening before he had read that there had been a fall of 5.9 points in Volkswagen shares as a result of the flaring up of the legal controversy which saw Opel, part of the General Motors group, accuse Volkswagen of stealing industrial secrets by head-hunting its ex-managing director José Ignacio Lopez de Arriortura.

Reading this news had triggered a memory which had shaken him and filled him with anxiety. Some years before, in his first job, he had happened upon a top-secret industrial study. His interest aroused, he had photocopied it "without the slightest hesitation" and calmly taken it home. He had kept it in a drawer for years until he finally gave it to a childhood friend who had set up his own small factory. His friend, explained Z.Z., had used the study in a way which was "infinitely marginal, of little importance. The relationship between the data contained in the study and the use made of it by my friend was of similar proportions to a NASA secret being used to construct a carpenter's lathe or something like that."

Z.Z.'s anxiety mounted. He discovered more reasons for "being in a state of panic": there was a very high risk that he might be caught; if he had been found out, his career would have been ignominiously ruined before it had really begun. And the fact that he had jeopardised it for something of little importance revealed that he was, above all, "irresponsible". The fact that he had completely forgotten the episode proved that he had "a split personality", he concluded. As is easy to imagine, his reconstruction didn't stop there. Eventually I asked him what had happened in him recently that had made him stronger. I reminded him that the case of Lopez de Arriortura had come out some time earlier, that the papers had talked about it in some detail, and had even reported that the German government had intervened to limit the damage. I added that, given the nature of his job, he must have heard about the publicity given to the case. "Why only now that the news has been repeated does it provoke such a reaction? I think that for some reason you feel stronger now than you were then, more capable of accepting inside yourself that part of you that terrorises you so much."

If the analyst – for the good of his patient – thinks that he must always look for the point of greatest anxiety (in the case I have just cited there was an *embarras du choix*), if he thinks that this point provides the basis for his most useful interpretation, in my opinion another danger arises. Deliberately and continuously placing the stress on anxiety can create a network of unconscious subterranean trails of communication. This is what I meant earlier by "code". And these trails can weave a kind of "culture of suffering" between the analyst and the patient: only if I show him my anxiety will the analyst talk, deal with me; one has to suffer and cause to suffer to be loved! This type of belief can be found in many neurotic people from an early age, and an analysis can reinforce it.

But this culture of suffering might also summon up in the analytical relationship – independently of the tone used by the analyst – the anxious mother, too concerned to help (or tell off) the child in difficulty. The problem also concerns the fathers. It is very probable that this type of behaviour will not facilitate what we may call the progressive development of the capacity to contain and to deal with everything that causes suffering in the lives of each one of us.

Conclusions

There are many aspects that show the will of the gods,
which lead through unexpected means to men's affairs.
(Euripides)

A theme which we have touched upon several times without ever addressing it directly is the relationship between psychoanalysis and free will. This is a question which is not secondary to the construction I have tried to give to this book. The debate about free will and determinism has taken various forms; these have been a central concern of theology, philosophy and jurisprudence for centuries, and of psychology since the end of the Second World War.[30] Freud seemed unwilling to commit himself too deeply on this subject. And yet many positions expressed in the discussions which preceded him brought out deep motives of disquiet in his writings.

Freud belonged to a generation that became increasingly conscious of the tragic dimension of human life *in new terms*: we could say that he contributed to the imposition of the modern vision of tragedy. But he was clear-headed enough to say that he was dealing with only a small part of mankind. His insights into what he called the Super-Ego, the unconscious sense of guilt that can precede a crime, and into the compulsive role of drives, have been subjects of discussion ever since.

Every age has probably had just one or two approaches to the great intellectual debates on the subject of human liberty. There don't seem to be that many possible approaches: materialist, religious, determinist, non-determinist, with some other positions in between. In the distant past of ancient Greece – as recalled in the lines from Euripides' *Elena* quoted above – human beings are mostly at the mercy of the gods, who use odd, *unexpected means*; just as the rules that underlie and sustain the subtle balances of the savannah are odd to the members of West African tribes. When they break these rules they are not aware of doing so. Nonetheless, they have to give an account of the disruption of these balances to the community.[31]

The old Israelite who lived around the year 1000 BC not only lost his sense of identity in the tribe, "he was not even conscious that his thoughts and ideas were his. Everything came from God."[32] When talking about the sectarian subjects of his time, the first-century historian Joseph Flavius mentions belief in fate and identifies three points of view. The Sadducees, who took a radical position in favour of free will, denied "Fate and said that there was no such thing". The diametrically opposed position was held by the Essenes, who maintained that everything was determined and that man is not granted even the slightest possibility of choice. Between these two extreme doctrines was that of the Pharisees, who argued that "some acts, although not all, were the result of the work of Fate, and with regard to some of them we have the chance to decide whether they should occur or not".[33]

In the more recent past, the period which saw the start of the controversies about free will that were to last for centuries – from the fourth century (Jerome, Augustine of Hippo) up to at least the sixteenth century (Luther, Calvin) – the problem became one of the relationship with God, whether or not divine grace depended on good works, whether there was such a thing as "predestination" (which was a total negation of all manoeuvres to avoid damnation). Pelagius, who at the beginning of the fifth century had said that man was the sole arbiter of his own destiny and had no need of divine help when choosing between good and evil, was contested by Augustine and condemned by the Church. In the sixteenth century Luther responded with his *De servo arbitrio* to Erasmus' *De libero arbitrio*.

Freud encouraged us to examine these views, allowing us to see in radical positions such as that held by Pelagius a kind of obsession which denies our need to depend on others, or to count on their help. Likewise we can see that there is a rigidly persecutory core to the position held by Luther, who outlines the figure of an omnipotent parent whose control it is impossible to escape. If one resists the reductive temptation implicit in all cross-sections – here the danger is that we reduce the whole question to a problem of the pathology of the psyche – this new key may be sufficiently "detached" to provide some stimuli for reflection.

In the modern era, although the religious tradition continued, a lay, earthly vision of the problem began to take root. We can see in this change a process which, with the help of monotheism, moves slowly and inexorably across the centuries and changes from being *projective* to being *introjective*. Many will see this change as positive. The problem of our limitations thus becomes the problem of the conditioning we experience – biological, relational and environmental, all closely interrelated. Unlike other philosophers whose diffusion has been limited (the sole exception is possibly Marx) but who have had notable influence in the history of ideas, Freud has been helped by the expansion of mass culture. He has spread the idea that there is an unconscious which limits our will and our knowledge, and this, he added, represents a deep wound to our narcissism.

The questions remain more or less the same; it is only the key to their interpretation that changes. The idea of predestination, freed from Luther's religious ideology, can take on a more everyday form: we all know people who have either been "tainted" by their heredity or marginalised by their conditioning and who are clearly "never going to make it", even though they do not belong to the multitudes of the *damnés de la terre*.

In the past few decades, the advent of television has exposed incalculable numbers of people to the reality of droughts, wars and ethnic massacres. These phenomena are visible to everybody, as is their incapacity to intervene. Likewise the mass media make it clear to us that we have absolutely no way of controlling world-wide economic processes: financial capital moves rapidly from one point on the globe to another and the power of governments, even when they are united, is very limited in the face of movements that follow laws (also psychological laws) which are difficult to decipher or understand.

Today's climate is radically different from that which mobilised "the forces of good" during the Second World War, when the sense of total disorientation provoked by man's capacity for organised destruction became mixed up with the strong desire to re-establish freedom and, in the post-war period, the drive towards reconstruction. Those who experienced this period first-hand recall the strong will to "repair" what had gone wrong in those years. It is perhaps no accident that the Kleinian term "reparation" – which, as we have seen, appears inadequate to some – came into currency precisely during that period.

Psychoanalysis, by explaining the mechanisms of our self-deception, allows us to see the ambiguity that lurks behind every drastic position that people take up. Even being totally determinist or totally on the side of free will is after all a deception. Some partisans of determinism defend it with such radical conviction that they would seem to be not so much totally conditioned beings as people quite capable of making their own choices and judgements who therefore must be endowed with a high degree of freedom.[34]

At first sight, it might seem that psychoanalysis has sided with determinism. The very concept of the unconscious (a place where a "will" that has escaped consciousness operates), the idea that the behaviour and psychic life of an adult depend on childhood conditioning, whether biological or intersubjective or both ("psychic determinism") are enough to suggest that it has taken sides. Freud insisted that we were guided by irrational forces, forces that we can at most only rationalise defensively; he even described the ways in which we are led to narcissistically overestimate our functions and our psychic abilities, so that we can continue to entertain a deceptive sense of liberty – a sense of liberty that makes us feel we possess those superior mental faculties we are so fond of. (Although we may feel guilty about it, I might add.)

Again, at first sight, psychoanalysis also seems to have been born out of a deeply-rooted confidence in man's ability to throw off ties. People have seen the unconscious as a source of emancipatory forces and even thinking faculties. Otherwise what is the point of therapy? Psychoanalysis derives its original *raison d'être* from its capacity to transform and liberate.

Kohut summed up what he called the Freudian ambiguity. The contradiction inherent in Freud's position, he said, lay in the fact that although Freud, between the lines and when expressing personal opinions, always subscribed to the opinion that there was an area of freedom in the human psyche, an area where choices and decisions were possible, he was for a long time extremely reluctant to incorporate this conviction into the theoretical framework of his science. "It is characteristic of this indecisiveness that he put in a footnote his famous . . . remark about the purpose of psycho-analysis as psychotherapy".[35]

The statement that Kohut was referring to is in *Ego and Id*, and empha-sises that psychoanalysis aims at "creating for the sick ego the *freedom* to choose one solution or another". The italics are Freud's.[36] Freud's early theory, according to Kohut, tended in the direction of absolute deter-minism; there was little room in his initial theoretical system for an Ego capable of making real choices.[37] Only later did he concede some form of freedom or independence.[38]

To Kohut, the leading exponent of the psychology of Self, should go the credit – considerable credit within the context we are discussing – of having been the first in psychoanalysis to make a distinction between *the guilty man* and *the tragic man*, whereby the latter term refers to the man who finds himself acting within a chain of events: "Man is an incompletely trained animal, reluctant to give up his desire to live according to the pleasure principle, incapable of giving up his innate destructiveness" (Kohut, 1959). In line with the *Zeitgeist*, the spirit of the times, psychoanalysis has made this hunted animal a "guilty man" rather than a "tragic man". In an echo of the dispute between Winnicott and Klein that has been the focus of so much of our attention, Kohut points out that the wrongs committed by Oedipus and Orestes are the faults of men who have been tragically aban-doned or sent into exile.[39]

So, for Kohut, Freud was irresolute and contradictory on these subjects. He did not consider one possibility, however, which although it cannot be fully demonstrated can also not be easily dismissed. We could ask our-selves, in other words, whether Freud, with his acute vision of human affairs, was not simply "detached" from the problem of liberty: detached like the Voltaire of *Dictionnaire Philosophique*, who at the entry *liberté* reports an ironic, banal dialogue between two elementary characters, A and B. Freud was detached because he was profoundly convinced that he was one of the great liberators of mankind and, as a lover of Cervantes, he saw himself as belonging to the dimension of tragic responsibility. Did he not say, referring to Jung's speculations, if I remember rightly, that he preferred to leave to others the investigation of the upper floors, electing to focus his attention on the foundations? And did he not always prefer the term "analysis", avoiding use of the more weighty term "synthesis"?

The tragic dimension, just like the phenomenon of simultaneous coexist-ence within the two dimensions of the schizophrenic paradox (both inside and outside the logic of guilt), should perhaps be seen as part of a process which in some (predestined) people allows wide margins of awareness and liberty, while denying such margins in others (also predestined). For those who do not believe in the law of karma, this fact alone should be enough to describe the tragic point of view. This point of view does not imply surrender, in my view, but only scepticism. It is not a question of withdrawing into Voltaire's garden. Those who remember the figure of Dr Bernard Rieux in Camus' *La peste* will perhaps better be able to understand what I am trying to say. When the city of Oran is closed and cut off from the world because of the plague, some inhabitants adapt to the new situation, others insist on denying the reality of the epidemic; few understand. The task is hard: the doctor Rieux, with his friend Tarrou, Grand, and a few others, continue the battle. Many people die before the plague recedes.

The psychoanalyst who has learnt that, however good he is at his work, he will never manage to help everyone to become more free, should know that some people are given the opportunity to attain a greater degree of freedom through increased awareness. Awareness does not necessarily mean a greater freedom to choose. The cases that I have talked about in this book have perhaps given an idea of these greater degrees of freedom.

In the light of these reflections we come to discover that while the sense of guilt can be responsible for serious suffering, real delusion, and can even lead to suicide or murder, at the same time it can also lead to reparation, to the useful sublimation of drives, the structuring of a mature personality, as well as helping the individual to enter into human relationships.

Of the many questions that remain unanswered here, I am spontaneously drawn to look once again at the question of "responsibility". Let us ask, by way of conclusion: what is responsibility in psychological terms, in relation to guilt, in relation to the sense of guilt, beyond the rhetorical spirals which we have been trying to escape from? The partial answer that comes to me – more in an attempt to sum up my ideas than to fill some void – could be this: responsibility is that inner motion, similar to Socrates' demon, which presents itself as unavoidable and which we become aware of at some point during our maturing process. For example, we feel it spontaneously when we are faced with a project that we know is risky (and therefore involves actually taking on specific risks), or when we are faced with negative or positive results which we have caused, whether we wanted them consciously or unconsciously.[40]

The implication is that we make "subjective" (or internalise) what the law calls "objective responsibility". But on a deeper level it could mean a feeling of love (the word may be out of place but it expresses the idea) for one's "guilty" parts, for those parts which fail to understand in time, which have not been contained, understood or sustained in time. Which have not been chosen by God.

But then, when I think about it again, Winnicott's idea that responsibility can be exemplified by parents who make love and accept the child that could be born as a result of their action – an idea that I earlier considered somewhat ingenuous – is perhaps the example that can be best understood.

Appendix: a note on terms

So full of artless jealousy is guilt,
It spills itself in fearing to be spilt.
(Shakespeare, *Hamlet*, IV, v, 19–20)

Guilt and "sense of guilt" are, as we have seen, two terms forced to negotiate a busy crossroads teeming with words like "malice", "error", "crime" "wrong", "responsibility", "sin" and many more from the fields of the law, religion and psychology; and often corresponding foreign terms come along to intensify the traffic. At first I thought of expanding the terms of this book to include shame, which stands in a variety of relations to guilt, but I decided to leave this subject aside. This will perhaps mean slightly less traffic at the intersection.

In Chapter 1 we found "guilt" defined in a dictionary of philosophy and psychology as the "state of someone who has committed a crime". And yet even in such contexts it has to be asked whether this definition is correct, because *guilt* is understood here as an objective state or situation (similarly to the entries I have found in Italian dictionaries under *colpa*),[1] or whether the definition is wrong because it appears in a dictionary of psychology – mention should be made of, or indeed the first definition should be about, subjective experience or state of mind, which is why some would argue that it is more correct to talk of "sense of guilt". But the dictionary fails even to refer to this aspect.

We seem to be observing the crossroads during the rush hour. This serves at least two purposes: it helps us to understand better the intricate tangle and at the same time to observe more closely the variety and the osmosis of meanings of the numerous terms which relate to guilt in both the specialised and ordinary usage of the main European languages.

So, in addition to the definition of "guilt" which talks about an objective condition (one is "guilty" of committing a crime) independently of the emotions that are aroused in the guilty person, there is a definition of "sense of guilt" ("feeling of guilt", or more rarely "guilt complex") which refers to the emotional experience of the person who believes – rightly or wrongly – that he or she is guilty.

We also know that there is a reflective guilt, feeling the guilt of others, which comes into play when we interact with a person who has committed an objective wrong, with his sense of guilt or with his need to accuse.

In both British and American English, and not only in the vocabulary of psychoanalysis and psychiatry, a special use of the word "guilt" has established itself. This use is reflected in the 1971 edition of the *Oxford English Dictionary*, where *guilt* is defined as follows: "(d) misused for 'sense of guilt'". The American *Random House Dictionary*, on the other hand, does not view this use as incorrect, and in its 1966 edition has as its third definition of guilt: "a feeling of responsibility or remorse for some offence, crime, wrong, etc. whether real or imagined".[2]

One could argue that the use of "guilt" to talk about subjective experience was legitimised centuries earlier by Shakespeare: there can hardly be any doubt that his use of "guilt" in the words of Hamlet's mother (see the quotation at the beginning of this appendix) refers to sense of guilt, and possibly even alludes to what the psychoanalyst Theodore Reik has called the impulse to confess. Poets work with the imagination, and in our imagination the sense of guilt often takes the form of crimes, infringements, offences; in other words, objective wrongs.

In France the situation seems to be different. "Guilt" is expressed as *faute* (which corresponds to English "fault" and Italian *fallo*), and this is the term used in ordinary language; in the theological sense the word used is *coulpe*. *Culpabilité* is a rather rare technical term, as is *colpabilità* in Italian, which is a legal and psychiatric term. The legal term corresponds to the use in Italian of *colpa*; the psychiatric term indicates a pathological feeling of *culpabilité* (as can be found in Larousse), accompanied by disquiet and anxiety, which leads the ill person to self-punishment. The latter term is used by psychoanalysts, as well as *sentiment de culpabilité*, with the same meaning (see, for example, Goldberg (1985) and Laplanche and Pontalis (1967)). At any rate, *culpabilité* is felt by French speakers to be a technical, professional word, and is usually not connected to *faute*.[3]

Italian (and indeed Spanish) psychoanalysts have a tradition similar to that of the English and use "guilt" in the objective sense, but also instead of sense of guilt, and find support for this choice in the *Enciclopedia Einaudi* and *UTET's Grande Dizionario Enciclopedico*.

This English and Italian "misuse" does not seem to exist in German. There are numerous terms which – depending on the context – could be translated with "guilt". These include *Fehler*, which means "mistake", *Vorsatz* (or the archaic *Dolus*), for a certain type of voluntary, punishable wrong ("with malice aforethought"), and finally *Schuld*, the term that interests us most because it is the term used by Freud as the first element in the compound noun *Schuldgefühl*, or, in other words, sense of guilt. Sense of guilt which, in his most famous hypothesis, Freud – as we have seen – related to actual objective guilt, the killing of the father.[4] One of the prime meanings of *Schuld* is "debt".[5] The Spanish word *culpa* includes one meaning which is very close to this.[6]

When talking of the sense of guilt, Freud adopted a psychological category: the sense of guilt is by definition a subjective feeling the study of which belongs to psychiatry and can be present even in someone who has not committed any misdeed at all. In various works, but especially in *Civilization and Its Discontents* (1929), Freud makes a distinction between *sense of guilt* and *remorse*: "When one has a sense of guilt after having committed a misdeed, and because of it, the feeling should more properly be called *remorse*". He adds that "if the human sense of guilt goes back to the killing of the primal father, that was after all a case of 'remorse'". In his view, psychoanalysis is thus justified in excluding from the discussion the case of a sense of guilt due to remorse, "however frequently such cases occur and however great their practical importance". We also know that for Freud a misdeed can be the result of an unconscious sense of guilt (Freud, 1929, pp. 131–132). Throughout this book I have criticised this distinction of Freud's and so I have used *sense of guilt* and *remorse* as synonyms.

Let us move on briefly to some of the really knotty points, more as a way of demonstrating the way things fit together in a system than to repeat what I have already expounded in this book. It is clear to anyone that a person can easily incur guilt without feeling a sense of guilt. If a Muslim who has grown up in a polygamous culture were to marry two women in the west, from the point of view of western law he would be "guilty", but he would not feel himself to be guilty; if anything he might feel persecuted. Ethically we will see him as guilty or innocent according to our vision of the world. A non-religious feminist, respectful of cultural differences, although she may fight for other models of the family (where the woman is not used as an object by the man, where polygamy would not be allowed), might not feel the Muslim in question to be guilty and might study the reasons why he feels persecuted. A western man who has grown up in a Christian culture might even feel an unconscious sense of envy for the bigamous Muslim, and as a reaction, condemn him moralistically.

Even today in India there are ways of reacting to Aids which are based on magic. In relation to sexually-transmitted diseases, there is sometimes a refusal to believe in the illness itself, or a miraculous cure is sought through recourse to ancient myths: "People in India have believed since ancient times that if one has a sexually-transmitted disease it can be cured by having sexual intercourse with a virgin", reports Dr Sunita Soloman.[7] What would happen if an Indian who had grown up believing this were arrested for having sex with a virgin? It is reasonable to imagine that he too would see himself as the victim of persecution. What would be our reaction, given that that act corresponds to extreme moral violence and to a possible delayed-action murder? Would we react in the same way as to the bigamous Muslim? What can we deduce from the fact that a virgin was chosen as the source of a magical cure? What hypotheses would be put forward by anthropologists and psychoanalysts, considering that in the Europe of the seventeenth century it was still believed that an infected man could be healed in the same way? What becomes clear is the idea that sexual relations with an impure woman (venereal disease, a disease of Venus) who has caused the illness can be undone by intercourse with a virgin, the pure woman *par excellence*. Does this explanation exonerate the Indian? I have tried to show that psychoanalysis has some things to say about this absence of sense of guilt and about this relationship between man and woman.

A similar point can be made about sin, which as we know is a type of guilt involving a breach of divine law. Anyone who marries only in a registry office is, according to the Catholic church, objectively living in sin, whether they feel they are sinners or not.

To come back to psychoanalysis: in this book I have put forward the hypothesis that what I have just suggested in the case of the Muslim and the Indian can in some way also happen to the patient lying on the psychoanalyst's couch. We have seen that he can be accused by the psychoanalyst, usually by an analyst unaware of what he is doing, when he – the patient – does not feel guilty. But he could equally be convinced that he is. Freud used the term "sense of guilt" for the first time in 1906 in *Psychoanalysis and the Establishment of Facts in Legal Proceedings*, where, talking about the methods used to determine the guilt of the accused, he wrote: "In your investigation you could be led astray by the neurotic, who reacts as if he were guilty, although he is innocent, because a sense of guilt which already existed and lay hidden in him takes over the specific accusation made against him".

When the sense of guilt seems to be "absent" because a person belongs to a certain culture (or religion or ideology), psychoanalysis continues to think that there is an internal world which corresponds to the external world and that senses of guilt can be at work in both, even in ways which are not transparent.

I have tried to explain why, although there are good reasons for distinguishing between them, guilt and sense of guilt in actual fact, more than being two sides of the same coin, are interwoven and share the same logic.

The patient who feels guilty because he has done harm to his analyst (by spreading false rumours about him, to take a rare example but one that can happen), is, one could say, objectively guilty. The same is true of the analyst who, whether he is conscious of it or not, has damaged his patient with mistaken or perverse interventions. On the other hand, we have defined the sense of guilt as an experience that might not – although it can – correspond to reality.

The psychoanalyst must not focus attention only on the sense of guilt and ignore the fact that a crime, a misdeed has been committed or only fantasised. This is true not so much because a punishment must be meted out as because a personality that only fantasises and one that also acts present different problems. Again, this is also true about the analyst: one thing is a counter-transference from which fantasies and aggressive desires towards the patient emerge; another is a counter-transference which leads to perverse or harmful behaviour for the patient. In this latter case, effectively a "crime" will have been committed.

To describe more clearly the possible circular motion which involves guilt and sense of guilt, perhaps it would be useful to take another example. Driven by an unconscious sense of guilt, a patient accuses his analyst of having done something that damaged him; he accuses him of an objective misdeed. This misdeed could be real and the accusation well-founded (although in theory it would not be so and one can only hope that usually this is not the case), and this misdeed (due, as I suggested, to a mistaken or perverse intervention) can in turn be the cause, or one of the causes, of the patient's initial unconscious sense of guilt.

When I warned that things can get tangled, I was referring to situations like this. There is one point I would like to make absolutely clear in conclusion: I believe that in cases like this, if the analyst only interprets experience (the *sense of guilt* of the patient) he will not be taking the right path. But if this is the way things are, it will not be so easy to share the opinion of those who think that psychoanalysis should not deal with the facts of guilt but with only the experience of guilt (Rycroft (1968) is quite drastic on this point).

Freud thought that the factors that produce conscious senses of guilt can also operate beyond the conscious mind. He thus talks about unconscious "sense of guilt", with a play on words that he himself notes (*unbewusstes Schuldgefühl*: unconscious sense of guilt). He is aware that there can be philosophical and semantic objections to the idea that emotions and feelings are described as unconscious: the expression "unconscious sense of guilt" "would be psychologically incorrect". For this reason he suggests replacing it with "need for punishment, which respects the observable facts with equal precision" (Freud, 1924 (p. 166), but also earlier (1922b)). He concentrated on this particular aspect of guilt, even though he focused on the internal psychic relationship between the Super-Ego and the Ego, which is responsible for all senses of guilt.

I would like to try to clarify this point in line with my model by replacing the word "guilt" with the term "cause" and explaining in more detail why "guilt" and "sense of guilt" are two phenomena that are not – in the final analysis – tried at two different courts. *Schuld* is, on the other hand, immersed within *Schuldgefühl* (sense of guilt) and *Schuldbewusstsein* (consciousness of guilt), both terms used by Freud. This immersion seems to represent, symbolically more than semantically, the identification which in my view justifies the use of "guilt" also for "sense of guilt".

Postscript

The more I examine my soul, the more I want to admit what the examination proves, namely, that I cannot find one single misdeed that I have witnessed in recent times about which I have not understood both sides. I don't mean excused, not that, but understood. Human beings and their blindness. This compulsion to understand seems to me to be a vice I cannot shake off and which isolates me from the others.

(Christa Wolf, *Medea. Stimmen*)

Notes

Chapter 1

1 Goldberg (1985), p. 11.
2 In 1895 in the *Draft K to Fliess* (p. 52ff.), which forms part of Freud's first attempts at a theory of defence neuroses and childhood sexual trauma, *thus with a real persecutor*.
3 Freud (1915–1917).
4 Freud (1907), in *Obsessive Actions and Religious Practices*, p. 346 and note.
5 L. Grinberg chooses this Freudian expression as the epigraph to his work *Guilt and Depression*, the most profound study of the subject of guilt.
6 Freud (1912–1913). My italics.
7 Jones (1957).
8 This point is also made by Goldberg (op. cit., p. 13).
9 Freud (1915), p. 103.
10 Freud (1930), p. 196. Freud put forward three different explanations of the genesis of the Super-Ego: the internalisation of the threat of castration as the Oedipus complex begins to wane; a remote structure connected to early vicissitudes in object relations; or the Super-Ego as an agency opposite to the libido, which is a pure concentrate of the death instinct.
11 Freud (1934–1938), p. 446.
12 Freud (1937), p. 552.
13 In his 1948 book on guilt J. Rickman wrote: "Religion has not yet recovered from its initial, and possibly inborn, mistake of separating God from the devil. In this way the problem of the ambivalent relationship with the great Father creator is left unresolved and unsolvable on the basis of the premises it uses. Religion and law offer ways of avoiding solutions – *they institutionalise psychic defences*" (p. 125). My italics.
14 *Totem and Taboo*, pp. 157ff. and again *Moses*, cit. p. 408.
15 The quotations are taken from Grinberg (1963–1971), p. 25.
16 Reik was writing twenty years after Melanie Klein's *Love, Guilt and Reparation*.
17 Among the suggestions as to what his father had done wrong, a secret his son never in fact revealed, one is that his father had an affair, while his wife was still alive, with the woman he later married.
18 Written under the meaningful pseudonym of Johannes de Silentio.
19 Commenting on Bach's *Passions*, Paolo Russo (1995, p. 47) observed that the insistence on the figure of the sacrificial lamb is characteristic of the pietistic tradition, which "often played with the image of Jesus as a scarificial lamb." *O Lamm Gottes, unschuldig* . . . O innocent lamb of God, slaughtered on the cross: this is the invocation that opens the St Matthew Passion, which inspired the Pasolini film *The Gospel According to St Matthew* (to which we shall return later).

20 J.S. Bach, *Matthäus-Passion*, BWV 244: Chorale 46 in the 1989 Archive edition, given as 55 by others. Quoted from Piero Leone, *La Passione secondo Matteo* by Johann Sebastian Bach, *pro manu scripto*.

21 Here, as elsewhere in this book, "to deny" is used to mean "to subject to denial" (*Verleugnung*).

22 With regard to masochistic pleasure, see Anna Freud (1965). She speaks about it, for example, in "Therapeutic Perspectives", the last chapter of *Normality and Pathology in the Developing Age*, p. 922, vol. III.

23 Milton, *Paradise Lost*, II, 105.

24 "Revenge" in *Essays*, 1597.

25 From *Gedanken und Einfälle*.

26 The passages quoted from Reik (1945–1959) come from pp. 355ff.

27 Euripedes, *Medea and other plays*. Translated with an Introduction by Philip Vellacott, p. 59, Penguin Books, Harmondsworth, 1963.

Chapter 2

1 The terms "preconscious" and "unconscious" will be examined in Chapter 10.

2 Denial, which Freud originally called "Scotomisierung" (a blind spot in one's field of vision), is one of the first notions in psychoanalysis and is defined as a manic defensive process whereby part of that which is perceived is erased. Denial can be denial of the reality of some aspect of the mind, of some distressing experiences, and also denial of psychic reality.

3 Grinberg (1963–1971), pp. 74–75.

4 W. Mitchell (1993).

5 Freud (1916).

6 This case was suggested to me by Dino Vallino.

7 I have tried to explain this mechanism in Charles Bovary, Emma Bovary's husband, in Speziale-Bagliacca (1992a).

8 Klein (1928), p. 188. For a historical reconstruction of the differences between Freud and Klein in the subject of aggressiveness and sadism, and for an account of the evolution of Klein's thinking on this point, see Hinshelwood (1989).

9 M. Klein (1945), pp. 415ff.

10 M. Klein (1927), (1933) *passim*.

11 M. Klein (1932) p. 128. On this point it has been argued that Klein moved away from the meaning that Freud gave to the *Todestrieb* (e.g. Rycroft, 1968, p. 91). In fact, Freud (1922a) argued that this drive "manifested itself in the form of destructive or aggressive impulses".

12 Strictly speaking, it is not true that Klein hypothesised only two positions. Initially she used the term "position" more freely and described a paranoid position, a manic position and an obsessive position. Later she only referred to the two positions here discussed and abandoned the others, considering them to be defensive structures of anxiety. We will see that she also refers to a third possibility.

13 Klein gives a definition of "projection" in *Weaning* (1936), but this is not the only one. In psychoanalysis the term is used to refer to diverse phenomena, and Melanie Klein uses it in all its meanings (as a perceptual phenomenon, as projection and expulsion, which Freud links to paranoia, as the externalisation of a conflict, as a problem of identity and as part of the complex phenomenon which is projective identification). Cf., among others, Grotstein (1981), Speziale-Bagliacca (1983) and Hinshelwood (1989).

14 One of the earliest critical discussions of this concept of Klein's is to be found in Elizabeth R. Zetzel (1953).

15 Cf. Klein (1935), pp. 287–289. This famous work (1935) showed that, in manic-depressive disturbances, guilt plays a leading role during the self-accusatory depressive phase (as was evident). However, it also demonstrated that, on close examination, there is an active denial of the sense of guilt in the manic phase, *and at the same time a denial of the values that belong to the imaginary internal world.*

16 Cf., for example, outside the field of psychoanalysis proper, the longitudinal studies by Zahn-Waxler *et al.* (1982, 1992). Cole *et al.* have recorded reparation attempts on videotape.

17 Klein uses various terms with similar meanings: *Wiederherstellung* (English *restoration*, Italian *restauro*), *Wiedergutmachung* (English *restitution* or *reparation*, Italian *restitutizione* or *riparazione*). In the end "reparation" was the term she preferred.

18 Rycroft (1968), p. 157. Cf., in particular Klein (1937), pp. 306–343.

19 Klein (1920–1921), p. 38 note. Personally I think that this observation by Klein and the comments she makes about her child (which I disagree with) point to an issue that deserves very careful and rigorous analysis.

20 M. Klein (1957), p. 194. In a book that came out in 1960, the year of her death, she describes a form of primitive guilt and depression, which is typical of schizophrenia. It is to be noted that Klein does not consider the case of the guilt-provoking object being a real persecutor. We shall come back to this point later.

21 Grinberg (1963–1971), p. 368. The responsibility for any additions and comments is, however, mine.

22 On the interaction between the two positions referred to in numerous passages, see, for example, Klein (1946), pp. 14–16. In Klein (1935), p. 274. See also Segal (1979).

23 Goldberg (1985), pp. 50–51.

24 Rickman (1948), pp. 119–126.

25 Goldberg's observation on this point is undoubtedly correct. But he is doing nothing more than expressing in other words the idea developed by Grinberg: Grinberg enriches the phenomenolgy of the two guilts with a minute description of the modalities of dealing with them. In effect, this description is simply an analysis of the defences in operation, which differ fundamentally in the two types of guilt.

26 Letter from Winnicott to Melanie Klein, dated 7 March 1957, in Winnicott (1987).

27 Cf. Whitehead (1926).

28 On the other hand, at least from a certain point of view, it is possible that Goldberg is right when he insists on guilt being "essentially persecutory". However, one does not necessarily have to agree with him when he adds that it is essentially persecutory "at its origin". I do not think Fairbairn would agree, but Goldberg does not cite him. So we do not know if he shares his view.

29 Grinberg (op. cit.) describes this process with precision, referring to Jones (1916) and Isaacs (1929), who, decades before, had described the process that leads from deprivation to guilt.

30 Melanie Klein (1955), pp. 141ff.

31 See Klein (1935).

32 Vegetti (1989).

33 There are numerous interpretations on this point, but in my view they do not exclude this. Cf. Vegetti (1989).

34 Lerminier (1812), p. 138.

35 Speziale-Bagliacca (1998). To continue with this example from Shakespeare: Lear is only partially successful at achieving this turnaround in his relations with Cordelia; he doesn't manage to escape from his depression. What I see as the need to overcome what Melanie Klein calls the depressive position will be dealt with later in the book.

36 Here we enter the sphere of the double bind, which we shall look at more closely later on.

37 *Statua del*

Commendatore:	Pèntiti, cangia vita:/E' l'ultimo momento!
Don Giovanni:	No, no, ch'io non mi pento:/Vanne lontan da me!
Commendatore:	Pèntiti scellerato!
Don Giovanni:	No, vecchio infatuato!/ . . .
Commendatore:	Ah! Tempo più non v'è!

(II, XVII). Lorenzo Da Ponte's libretto for Mozart. Almatea Usuelli Kluzer has dedicated to the theme of the rejection of repentance in Don Giovanni or the rejection of guilt in Job a book entitled *Elifaz: Pèntiti scellerato! Giobbe: No, veccio infatuato!* (to be published).

38 Klein (1940).

39 These are "prevalent" modalities of guilt because, as I have already pointed out, the two types of guilt are intertwined.

40 Various authors have expressed their disagreement with the tendency to push back the origin of human phenomena to increasingly early stages of life, including Winnicott (in the works we shall be looking at), Kernberg (1976, p. 33 and *passim*) and Stern (1985, *passim*).

41 Leaving aside Fairbairn, whom we shall come to presently, and apart from Freud (1929), we must include Ferenczi (1913), Jean Riviere (1936), Melanie Klein (1946), Winnicott (1953), Grunberger (1971 and 1989), Kernberg (1975) and Mancia (1990).

42 J.-B. Bossuet (1679).

43 ¡Ay misero de mi ¡ Y ay infelice!/Apurar, cielos, pretendo/ya que me tratais asi/ que delito cometi/contra vosotros naciendo;/ . . . /(dejando a una parte, cielos, I, ii, 101–108, 115–116). Interestingly, even educated native speakers of Spanish often remember the expression "el delito de nacer" as "the fault of being born".

44 Thinking in terms of causes goes against the idea of attributing events to casuality. The *lapsus* that confuses casual and causal is very common.

45 Freud (1933), p. 164.

46 Wordsworth, "My Heart Leaps Up" (1807).

47 Clearly this is an important qualification. There is a movement away from a view based on linear causality according to the Abraham model (suggested by Freud's famous expression – all this "is nothing but"), summed up in a famous diagram by John Rickman (1957), towards a view based on the multiplicity of causes: this is the first step towards thinking in systemic terms – the model adopted, for example, by Bowlby.

48 Fairbairn (1943).

Chapter 3

1 Kohut, too, uses the adjective "tragic". The context in which I am trying to define this term seems to me very different. It is undeniable that Kohut and I are both in debt to Nietzsche.

2 Speziale-Bagliacca (1999a).

3 Camus (1957), English translation: Knopf, New York, 1961.

4 Genesis 4, 3–5.

5 Szurek (1942), Johnson (1947), Johnson and Szurek (1952) look more carefully at the so-called structural aspects (the lacunae and the very structure of the super-ego) of antisocial personalities than at the psycho-dynamic aspects. Other similar ideas can be found in Rosenfeld (1965) and E. Jacobson (1964), who have influenced many later authors, including Kernberg (1992, Chapter 5).

6 Some ethnologists, such as Robert Lowie, in *Primitive Society* (1947), when talking about primitive societies, refer to the "administration of justice" even in societies where blood feuds continue and where it is impossible to break the endless chain of revenge. The law of retaliation (only an eye for an eye) seems in part to be a limitation of the "ethos" of revenge.

7 Freud, in *Formulations on the Two Principles of Mental Functioning* (1911), explains how, in a psychology founded on psychoanalysis, the reality principle (which would also include abiding by laws) takes over from the more primitive pleasure principle, which is closer to the sphere of drives. For Freud, the formation of realistic thought is the result of an effort – not always bound to succeed – to abandon the modalities and aims of primitive omnipotent thought. In the individual an "impartial *passing of judgement*" takes over, about which Freud never had excessive illusions. These ideas were later examined in *Negation* (1925), where he described the particular way in which the unconscious exercises its influence on the conscious self.

8 Douglas (1992), pp. 21–22.

9 *The Odyssey*, XXII, 462–464.

10 Foucault (1975).

11 This is a kind of imposition of the maternal code. We shall look at more closely at this point when we examine the question of ideology in the sixth chapter.

12 XII, 473–476.

13 It is no accident that in many languages the word "comprehend" also means to justify, excuse, pardon, indulge, and so on. While these meanings remain within the ethos of guilt, they still move in the direction of the ethos that transcends guilt.

14 This is a general rule put forward by E. Jacques (1951) and by English psycho-analysis.

15 See Canevari (1982).

16 By "inevitability" I mean that the individual can avoid it only by deploying psychological defence mechanisms. The sense of tragedy is a state of con-sciousness and thus when I speak of "acceptance" I refer to the abandonment of these defence mechanisms.

17 All great thinkers, whether western or oriental, have insisted on the principle of observing limits. Here, however, we are talking about the moment of the individual's discovery of his own limits and those of men and women in general (which obviously do not coincide). Bion, in his revisitation of the myths of Adam and Eve, Babel, Oedipus (in Bion 1962) and the royal cemetery of Ur (in Bion 1974), makes a connection between "tragedy" and "knowledge".

18 *Aut amat aut odit mulier: nil est tertium.* "Sententiae", A6. Occasionally we find aberrations such as "acquitted due to insufficient evidence".

19 Grinberg (1963–1971). Italics mine.

20 The question arises whether it would be possible to imagine a small child who from the very beginning imagined he had a Self to be repaired. One could hypothesise that the child projects something good onto the object, which it has damaged, or thinks it has damaged, that it then introjects the repaired object and that this introjection has a beneficial effect on the Self. Klein, whose focus is

constantly on the child–mother couple, and who as far as I know does not talk about the reparation of the Self, is probably following this model. Another problem arises for the adult when he or she begins to be interested in the distinction between what are called internal objects (introjected objects) and parts of the Self. Not all analysts distinguish in their theoretical models between internal objects and the parts of the Self that have a place in the internal world, probably because of the hypothesis from which we started. The fact that they can for a long time be confused (which occurs partly because of what we could call "internal" projective identification, or more simply because of a lack of training in self-observation of one's own internal world) does not alter the fact that in the end the individual – in a climate of reconciliation, once a true relationship with the other has been established – is able to reach the point of seeing, let's say, his own internal mother as separate from his Self, sharing some features and characteristics but not others. This is the moment of awareness of identity, when one begins to become aware of similarities. A possible example of projective identification in an internal object is a patient who always recalls a parent as having a certain characteristic, until he realises that the characteristic is really his own (let's say, a certain meanness of spirit, a tendency to be envious) and one which the parent does not in fact possess.

21 When they do not contain the desire to control, triumph or obsess described by Klein (1935, 1940).
22 W. James, *Principles of Psychology* (1890).
23 Speziale-Bagliacca (1999b).
24 M. Klein (1958), p. 245. Grinberg dedicates densely argued pages to this theme. It is his merit to have illustrated in detail how every loss of object implies the loss of aspects of the Self. Grinberg (1963–1971), pp. 169ff.
25 Speziale-Bagliacca (1990a), pp. 1363–1373.
26 Grinberg (1963–1971), p. 158.

Chapter 4

1 Miguel de Unamuno (1913, pp. 261–262), Dover Publications Inc. New York, 1954, original translation MacMillan & Co., 1921.
2 This is one of several observations I owe to Aldo Canevari.
3 The reference is to the idea of "catastrophic change" expressed by Bion. In a certain sense, one could say that there is a caesura between the perspective of guilt and that of tragic responsibility. On this concept, see the comment by E. Tabak de Bianchedi (1992).
4 Freud (1912–1913), p. 158.
5 Unamuno (1913), p. 240.
6 S.R. Nicolas Chamfort, *Massime e pensieri. Caratteri e anedotti*, 1795.
7 I have put the word pathological in inverted commas because in certain circumstances (when there is an unbearable increase in anxiety) the defence mechanisms that are set in motion are adaptive mechanisms; they have the "physiological function of defending us from great evils, such as psychic disintegration".
8 Cf. Kohut (1971 and 1987) and Anna Freud, who had commented perceptively on some of the dynamics of this phenomenon. In *The Concept of the Rejecting Mother*, she explains how "paradoxically the most devoted mother can become . . . the most rejecting mother" (1954, Vol II, pp. 575ff.).
9 Lacan (1966).
10 Klein (1935), p. 264.
11 Klein (1935), p.270.

12 Klein's theoretical discussions and her technique of intervention have been criticised by various authors, for example, by Kernberg (1969, 1976, 1980, 1992). Even Klein's own disciples were to modify quite considerably the ideas they inherited from her (one thinks, in particular, of the collections of essays edited by E. Bott Spillius, 1988).

13 See, for example, Rayner (1990).

14 Grosskurth (1986–1987), pp, 464ff. This work is inaccurate on many points.

15 For example, Melanie Klein (1936), p. 297. Here, Klein thanks Winnicott in a footnote for "many illuminating details". It was not until 1962, the year he went on a lecture tour and talked about the capacity to develop concern, that Winnicott stated his precise theoretical position with regard to Melanie Klein in front of psychoanalyst candidates in Los Angeles. This was later published in *A Personal View of the M. Kleinian Contribution* (Winnicott, 1962b).

16 Winnicott (1951), note p. 286.

17 The first was published in 1956 and was entitled *Psychoanalysis and the Sense of Guilt*. The second, which is much more famous, was published in 1963 and bore the title *The Development of the Capacity for Concern*.

18 Winnicott (1951), p. 464.

19 These transitional areas, which Winnicott recognises as having been described first by Fairbairn, represent a useful bridge in the process of differentiation between Self and the other.

20 Winnicott (1956), pp. 11–12.

21 Winnicott seems to be simplifying when he says that, according to the prevailing psychoanalytical approach at that time, mass and group psychology came to be derived from individual psychology.

22 Legitimate expectations must mean that physiological expectations are innate in human nature. Not all psychoanalytical models seem to accept this, although besides Winnicott, Heinz Hartmann (Hartmann *et al.*, 1964, pp. 44–47) talked of a "generally predictable environment". There is a line of thought which could be reconstructed which goes from Sandor Ferenczi, through John Bowlby, Willy Hoffer, René Spitz, the Balints, Franco Fornari, Paula Heimann and Bion up to the present. I have given my own personal theoretical view of legitimate expectations in my work on *King Lear* (Speziale-Bagliacca, 1998). My impression is that these are fragmentary intuitions, which have not yet been harmonised, and that no overall psychoanalytical theory has yet been elaborated.

23 Freud himself, in one of his last works (*Abriss*, 1938), came to define the relationship between the child and the mother as "unique, incomparable and immutable for the rest of life". According to Bowlby (1969), the fact that in his previous writings Freud had not given due weight to this early relationship has had enormous repercussions on psychoanalytical theory. In the same book Bowlby was responsible for one of the first acute analyses of this complex phenomenon and Winnicott's role.

24 Here we have a concept that is similar to the mother's capacity to engage in *rêverie*, as described by Bion.

25 Later there was to be a broader theoretical integration on the part of various Kleinian analysts. In some cases Winnicott was cited, in others only his influence is felt. See, for example, the anthology edited by Amanuela Quagliata (Alvarez *et al.*, 1994).

26 Winnicott (1962b), pp. 171ff.

27 Ibid., p. 177.

28 Speziale-Bagliacca (1982c), p. 74.

29 The critique that Winnicott develops is: experience based on the analysis of

patients means that one cannot ignore the fact that we meet two mechanisms of vital importance – the terror of retaliatory punishment and the process of splitting objects into "good" and "bad"; "Melanie Klein seemed to think at the end that infants start in this way, but this seems to ignore the fact that, with good enough mothering, the two mechanisms may be relatively unimportant until the ego-organisation has made the baby capable of using projection and introjection mechanisms in gaining control over objects. If there is not good enough mothering, then the result is chaos rather than talion dread and a splitting of the object into 'good' and 'bad'. . . ." Winnicott (1962b), p. 177. Here Winnicott fully embraces Fairbairn's theses. The first to identify one of the theoretical reasons for the disagreement between Klein and Winnicott was probably Bowlby (1967, p. 444), who pointed out that in this case Winnicott did not distinguish between a theory that talks about primary instinctive behaviour and a theory of secondary impulses.

30 The concept of "idealisation" had already been used by Freud, who studied it as part of falling in love and made a point of distinguishing it from "sublimation" (*Introduction to Narcissism*, 1914, and *Mass Psychology and Ego Analysis*, 1921), but it was Klein who understood and described the complex defensive structure of this process. If idealisation is not linked to splitting, which puts all good on one side and all evil on the other, the true nature of its dynamic composition can escape notice. See, for example, Klein (1937), pp. 329–340.

31 Winnicott (1962c), p. 94.

32 Freud (1914), p. 466.

33 Winnicott (1963), p. 223.

34 Winnicott (1962a), p. 89. Appeared in Winnicott (1965), with the date of its first publication, 1963. (My italics, apart from the last two.)

35 The proof of this is that in another passage he writes that he has taken the concept from Klein. In summing up Klein's contributions to modern psychoanalysis, he writes about the "development of a theory of an individual achieving a capacity to experience concern (depressive position)". Winnicott (1962b), p. 178.

36 During the years of my psychoanalytical training, which I started at the beginning of the 1960s, both in London and in Italy the current interpretation was that Winnicott wanted to replace the expression "*depressive position*" with "*phase of concern*".

37 Klein (1940), pp. 348–349. The defences Melanie Klein refers to are those that she had at first called "manic defences" because of their link with psychotic manic-depressive disturbances. These defences include not only *denial* (Freud's *Verleugnung*) of psychic reality and, in cases like the one we are examining, *pining, debasement* (a compromise whereby one does not give up objects recognised as good or useful, but tries to avoid the dangers inherent in dependence by diminishing the importance of the object itself), *sadistic control* (to deny strongly the terror one feels and also so that reparation can be effectively carried out), and finally, *idealisation*, which we have already discussed in some detail. On the use of the term *concern*, equated with *consideration* by Klein, who unlike Winnicott does not theorise it, see, for example, MKW, vol. I, *Love, Guilt and Reparation and Other Works*. 1921–1945, pp. 253, 261ff., 274, 345ff., 437.

38 In *Mourning* (1940), for example. Here the case of Mrs A, "on the death of her son", in reality describes Melanie herself and the death of her son Hans. Another passage is to be found in Klein (1935), p. 287. Another example is J.-M. Petot (1984), vol. II, p. 265, who seems to acknowledge that there is a third phase in Klein's theoretical model.

Chapter 5

1 It is a *sui generis* form of retaliation because the persecutions experienced in the position Melanie Klein calls paranoid-schizoid do not contain that *limitation of reprisal* which is typical of the punishment of *lex talionis* or retaliation: only an eye for an eye, only an arm for an arm. I have emphasised this point at various points in this book.

2 Money-Kyrle (1975), *Introduction* to Vol. I, pp. x–xi.

3 Money-Kyrle, ibid.

4 Winnicott (1962b), pp. 176ff.

5 Winnicott (1962a), p. 73.

6 Melanie Klein (1932), p. 92.

7 Even though the adjective "responsible" is more than five centuries old, the term "responsibility" only entered French and English in the eighteenth century, initially with a legal meaning, although it soon took on an additional moral meaning. German has two different terms, *Haftbarkeit* and *Verantwortlichkeit*. See, among others, Villey (1977). On the difficulty of finding a common terrain to define the term, see also Dworkin's *Law's Empire* (1991).

8 We need to reflect on the many possible definitions of words like "love", "hate" (but also terms like "instinct", "drive", "autoeroticism", "heredity" and so on) and again on expressions like "the search for truth". Basically we need to be very careful about what we could call conceptual habits, in other words, about the fundamentally passive and acritical use of words. A. D'Angelo (1995, pp. 125ff.) talks very perceptively about *rhetoric*. Basically, he writes, on these occasions *one hypostatises a phenomenon to draw from it a whole series of consequences.* "Hypostatise" is used in the figurative sense of transforming a concept or a term into something real and incontrovertible. The movement towards a dialectical approach to these topics is found in Ludwig Wittgenstein's *Philosophical Investigations* (1953) and even earlier in E. Cassirer's *Philosophy of Symbolic Forms* (1923–1929).

9 Winnicott's *Letters* (1987).

10 Melanie Klein (1957), p. 179. The italics are mine.

11 Bion (1985), p. 117.

12 Rodman (1987).

13 (2, 1–10). Job, who is the emblem of innocent pain, has been the subject of energetic discussion both by religious and non-religious scholars. My approach is only one among the many possible, and is also explicitly reductive. For Massimo Cacciari, "Job is the one who breaks the silence . . . Asked to acknowledge his guilt passively, Job cries out . . . '[this is] the inaugural gesture of theology, in other words talking about God' . . ." (in *Questions to Job,* edited by Maurizio Ciampa (1989, p. 65), which contains essays and articles, including some by Gustav Jung, Simone Weil, Karl Barth and Karl Jaspers).

In a personal letter written shortly before he died in September 1997, Abraham Bernstein, in reply to my question about the possibility that the *Book of Job* had opened up the strand of lay Judaic thought, copied out a passage from a letter written by Albert Einstein to the Swiss physician Edgar Meyer in January 1915: "Why do you write that 'God should punish the English'? I have no close contacts with either the one or the other. I see only with deep regret that God punishes many of His Sons because of their numerous foolish acts, for which only He can be held responsible. In my view, his non-existence would be his only excuse."

14 Finkelstein (1938), p. 196.

15 The pact consisting of the Tables of the Law seems to constitute the moment at

which the absolute monarch puts himself forward as a constitutional monarch. In *The Gospel According to Jesus*, the Portuguese Nobel Prize Winner José Saramago opposes the new testament Christ who asks his Father to "forgive them for they know not what they do" with a Christ who shouts to heaven, where God was smiling, "Men forgive him for he knows not what he has done" (1991, p. 347).

16 Freud (1929), p. 619. *Ihr führt ins Leben uns hinen,/Ihr lasst den Armen schuldig werden,/Dann überlasst Ihr ihn der Pein,/Denn jede Schuld rächt sich auf Erden.* "The Harpist's Song" in *Wihelm Meister* by Goethe (ii, p. 13). Freud was so fond of this passage that he also quoted the first two lines in *The Interpretation of Dreams* (1900), SE, Vol. 4, p. 22. Franz Schubert set it to music.

17 Bollas (1992).

18 On the legitimacy of this procedure in the field of literature (psychologising the author through his work), we know about Proust's critique of Sainte-Beuve, who was in favour (*Contre Saint-Bauve*). Proust made a clear distinction between the creator "I" and the earthly "I" of an artist which is valid up to a certain point. One should also add that Proust had an obsessive fear that his parents would find out about his homosexuality. On the other hand, it is one thing to talk about the rules proper to literary criticism and something else to gather various types of information when reviewing a scientific theory.

19 The unfortunate turn of phrase criticised by Winnicott was to the effect that Klein's theory left no "unbridgeable gulfs". Riviere wrote this in her Introduction to *New Developments in Psycho-Analysis* (1952).

20 See also H. Rosenfeld (1987).

21 I recalled this point at the time of the "Masson scandal". Masson argued that Freud gave up the theory of seduction out of a kind of cowardice in the face of the spirit of conformity at that time. Speziale-Bagliacca (1988), pp. 126ff. The idea that unconscious fantasies could exert such a pathogenic role must have been too difficult for Masson to take, probably because, despite his credentials, he was lacking in clinical experience. I finished my review of Masson's work in full polemical flow, citing a rather unkind remark made by E.M. Forster: ". . . true perception began at the point where his intelligence finished". Obviously, the discussion between Winnicott and Klein took place on a very different and more complex level.

22 The reference is to Rene Spitz (1958), to studies by M. Mahler (1968), to Mahler, Pine and Bergman (1975), Lichtenberg (1983), D.N. Stern (1985) and other theoretical models later taken up and illustrated by G. Downing (1995). For several of these authors, following in the path of Mahler and thanks to the insights of Ferenczi, the configuration of a person's world of motor representations is based largely on what actually happened between parent and child. Real events significantly influence the development of the child's affective-motor schemas and this, in its turn, generates the earliest representations of self and of objects. This does not exclude the possibility that fantasy plays a role: the child can have a distorted perception of real events, influenced by various emotions.

23 Rodman (1987), p. 28. Since I have not done so thus far, I feel I ought to mention the fact that in psychoanalysis there are at least two sorts of concept that are translated as "unconscious fantasy" (*fantasy* and *phantasy*). I do not wish to enter into this discussion, but I would draw attention to the remark made by Hinshelwood (1989, pp. 35ff.), which refers to key comments published in King and Steiner (1991).

24 Letter to Madeleine Davis, probably written in 1940, cited by Grosskurth (1988), p. 306.

25 Bowlby (1969). Bowlby's position recalled that of Anna Freud, who for a long time, at various points in her work, insisted on concepts such as trauma, which she analysed from various points of view in relation to unconscious activity.
26 Grosskurth (1988), p. 462. The comments made by Milner in this context (which Grosskurth quotes) are interesting.
27 For this type of interpretation, see. P. Elkman *et al.* (1972).
28 Hilda Abraham (1974), pp. 17–74.
29 An account of what Eric went through – whether one calls it analysis or "observation" – has been published several times by Melanie Klein (1920–1921) and deserves to be studied in depth in view of Klein's disturbing comments and the fact that she never retracted what she wrote.
30 Grosskurth (1986, pp. 116ff.) has reconstructed these events and the salient features of the life of Eric Klein (later, Clyne) in much more detail.
31 M. Klein (1935), pp. 277–278. The italics are Klein's.
32 M. Klein (1935), p. 278 and note.

Chapter 6

1 Little's book put forward the hypothesis that very often, although patients are conscious of the countertransference of their analyst, they do not believe in its reality, unless it is recognised by the analyst himself. Apparently, when Little addressed this subject again some years later, Melanie Klein observed acidly, in the discussion following her paper that it only proved that Little needed to further her analysis (Grosskurth, 1988, p. 479). Is this another personal attack, an *ad personam* argument? Winnicott was chairing the meeting and intervened furiously at that point to say that Mrs Klein had no right to say things like that: "*We all* need to more analysis! None of us can get more than a certain amount, and the same could be said of anybody." This was in 1956, the very same year that Winnicott wrote his letter to Riviere and Klein made her *ad hominem* attack on Winnicott.
   Heimann's work, written in 1949 and published in 1950, was held to be the first to fully describe the use of countertransference. An article written by Racker in 1948 was not published until 1953 and it is probable that Heimann did not know about it. She said in a note that she had not been able to read Leo Berman's 1949 intervention in time. So many authors approaching the same idea at the same time, she commented, "indicate that the time was ripe".
   Among the first writings on countertransference we find Stern in 1924, Ferenczi and Rank in 1925, followed three years later by Glover and then by Fliess in 1942. Freud had discovered countertransference in 1910 and had defined it as "the result of the influence of the patient on the unconscious feelings of the physician".
2 As reported by Hinshelwood (1989, p. 449), who adds that Klein may have been irritated by the fact that she was not mentioned in the work.
3 Grosskurth (1986), pp. 478–479.
4 When Fliess (although we do not know exactly how he formulated the question) asked Freud about this, Freud reacted violently, as can be seen in his letter to Fliess dated 19 September 1901.
5 As it is so difficult to demonstrate, this question was left unexplored in many countries until it affected the interests of the insurance companies that pay for therapy.
6 Heimann (1949/1950), p. 73.
7 Little (1951), pp. 32ff.

8 Heimann (1981).
9 Quoted also by Limentani (1989), p. 18.
10 Freud (1910), p. 200. Freud was not always so convinced that self-analysis was sufficient. He later went on to maintain the need for a training analysis.
11 These ideas recall concepts that have entered the classical psychoanalytical literature under the term *therapeutic alliance*. Among the first to talk about it were Bibring (1937), Stone (1954) and Zetzel (1958), who was the first to give a detailed account of the therapeutic alliance. The final stage in the development of this insight in the Klein camp came with Baranger's theory, which we shall look at presently.
12 Bertin (1982). See also Speziale-Bagliacca (2002), pp. 96ff.
13 Later, various authors would move in this direction, including two Argentinean analysts, M. and W. Baranger. Their article *The Analytical Situation as a Dynamic Field*, published in 1961, starts from some of the insights of the American psychologist Kurt Lewin (who they do not cite directly) and the philosopher Merleau-Ponty (who they do quote), which are then linked to concepts taken from Kleinian theory. The Barangers put forward a very stimulating theory, defining the analytic situation as a *bipersonal* field where only the unconscious imagination of the pair is knowable as it takes shape with the support of the mental activities and the mutual projective identifications that develop between analyst and patient. Fifteen years later, field theory was to be the subject of a book by Langs (1976b), *The Bipersonal Field*.
14 It is difficult to say to what extent Klein's theories were based on the analyses that she underwent (with Ferenczi and with Abraham) or on her self-analysis. Personally, I tend to think that her type of creativity must necessarily draw to a large extent on personal experience. In a letter written in 1926 to Hans Kloetzel, the lover who had a few days previously sent her a letter announcing his final decision to break off their relationship, Melanie mentioned her pain and suffering, which she attributed to their relationship, adding however: "my depression, by the way, also had other causes". Many questions remained unresolved. A year and a half (a very short period) after Klein had started an analysis with him, Abraham fell ill and died. How did Klein work through this major bereavement? Psychoanalysts know from experience that most patients whose analyst dies during analysis suffer from long-lasting pathological reactions, which, unless they are dealt with in a prolonged and in-depth analysis (but it is the patient who must look for help), leave deep, distorting traces.
15 According to Grosskurth (1986, p. 253), the Mrs A whom she refers to in *Mourning* (Klein, 1940, pp. 355ff.) was Klein herself. All the deep-seated acrimony felt by her daughter Melitta towards her mother broke out again on the occasion of this tragedy. Melitta spoke about her brother's suicide. On the following 21 November she presented a brief paper at the British Institute, which contained this comment: "Anxiety and the sense of guilt are not the only emotions responsible for suicide. To mention only one of the other factors: excessive feelings of disgust, provoked, for example, by deep-seated disappointment in loved ones or the collapse of ideals, are often incentives to suicide."
16 My italics. Rosenfeld (1987), p. 43 and *passim* in Chapter II. This also applies to the following quotation.
17 Obviously the patient is rarely able to distinguish between his delusional criticisms and his correct criticisms. One of the hardest tasks facing the analyst is to learn how to separate the patient's constructive criticism from his destructive criticism. Often patients give up therapy because of the therapist's unresponsiveness to criticisms.

Chapter 7

1 Among others, Paul, *Letters*: I. *Thessalonians*, iii, 5; I. *Corinthians*, vii, 5. But even in rabbinical literature the devil personifies the figure responsible for all sins, from the original sin of Adam and Eve to the Golden Calf. In the recently revised Catholic version of the Lord's Prayer the invocation, "lead us not into temptation" addressed to God the Father has been taken out.

2 Freud (1922c), pp. 543–545.

3 Freud expressed his agreement with Otto Rank about the fact that the child's first anxiety arises with the birth. For a re-examination of the various points of view, see Grosskurth (1988), pp. 206ff.

   People with the characteristics of both sexes also fall under what Klein called one of the most terrifying persecutorial *dramatis personae*, the "combined parental figure" (or *imago*), often present in masturbatory fantasies. Klein (1932, *passim*, including pp. 245–246, *The Woman with a Penis*); Klein (1952), p. 52.

4 Here we are touching upon the problem of so-called "retroactivity", what in German is called *Nachträglichkeit*, and in French *après-coup*. See, among others, S. Isaacs (1943, 1948), and Laplanche and Pontalis (1985).

5 Psychoanalysis operates this *reduction* when it includes various sorts of figures in the Super-Ego: demons, devils, spirits. When psychoanalysis goes on to make a more careful phenomenological analysis, then we discover that the super-ego can use seductive techniques, or it can slander and bear false witness; these latter are characteristics of the "devil" (from the Greek *diàbolos*).

6 Guènon (1924).

7 I am referring to Pausanias, the author of *Description of Greece, Periegesi*, a rich source of information about the ancient world in general. See Habicht (1985).

8 Détienne (1978).

9 *Lammia*, or *Lamia*, who corresponds to the Hebrew *Lilith*, is often depicted as a monster with the face of a woman and the body of a serpent who was said to suck the blood of children.

10 Mutilation and laming recall the fear of castration, which is frequently linked in both the collective and the individual imagination with oral anxieties and fears.

11 Fornari (1981, p. 186) came to this important conclusion after analysing the dreams of pregnant women. Though limited to women in that situation, Fornari's idea has the merit of highlighting a certain type of *shift*, which personally I have observed in my clinical work.

12 James Joyce quotes this verse in *A Portrait of the Artist as a Young Man*: "Hell has enlarged its soul and opened its mouth without any limits." The version chosen by Joyce translates the Hebrew *še'ol* with the word "hell", depicted as a voracious and insatiable monster (cf. *Proverbs*, 30, 15–16).

13 "Arselicker" is a common insult. Obviously, orality is not the only determining feature of demonic figures. Mammon (*but'mon*, Armenian for 'wealth') is usually depicted as a golden idol in the form of a demon that casts money around. In psychoanalysis gold and money are anal symbols.

   Reproductions of many of these works can be found in London University Warburg Institute.

14 *Divina Commedia*, xxx, 82–85.

Chapter 8

1 In his warnings against transference reactions, Freud (1915b) used for the first time the word "indifference", which Strachey translated as *neutrality*. Freud believed in the empirical approach.

2 Freud (1932), pp. 262–284.
3 It is to be noted how this last phrase of Freud's hints at a description of those types of persecution (anxiety and persecutory guilt) which are ready to strike those who abandon *orthodoxy*.
4 These are quotations from the Dora case-history. Freud (1901), pp. 65ff. I make a more detailed examination of the way Freud used to analyse his patients towards the end of his life in Chapter 10 of Speziale-Bagliacca (2002).
5 I have written a book about some aspects of ideology in Freud and Lacan in *On the Shoulders of Freud* (1982b); see also another of my books (1980a), in which I mention Rossi-Landi (1967) – an important work, because it helps us not only to understand the wide range of meanings that have been given to this term, but also to understand that the term has a positive as well as a negative meaning. The positive meaning draws on Gramsci and equates ideology with a "general vision" of society, with a capacity for planning. This second aspect interested not only W. Baranger (1956, pp. 103–108) but also R. Money-Kyrle (1961), who some years earlier had looked at political ideologies and the development of moral character (1951).
6 One of the very few analysts to express himself on the subject of ideology, apart from Fornari (whom we shall look at more closely shortly), is Etchegoyen (1973).
7 This point, unlike others that we shall come back to on numerous occasions, deserves an explanation. Baranger writes: "this implicates a normative attitude, because it must place the analysand before his attitude to the world (his behaviour, his values, his involvement in social life, and toward the internal working of his psychism)". The main outline of my own theoretical position on this subject should become clear in this book.
8 Downing (1995), pp. 27ff.
9 *Into* as opposed to *onto* the analyst is when the patient engages in projective identification, a concept I shall come back to in the last chapter.
10 Pert (1998); Biondi and Picardi (1996).
11 This was the case with Sigmund Freud himself. See Speziale-Bagliacca (2002).
12 There seems to be some agreement among analysts that an exception should be made to what I am saying in the case of people (especially minors, children and adolescents) who have been subjected to physical violence by someone of either sex. In such cases a therapist of the other sex would seem to be the right choice.
13 Matte-Blanco (1975b) pointed out that "biologically speaking sex is an attribution of functions which potentially exist in every individual, both from an anatomical and from a chemical–physiological point of view (for example, the chemical similarities between male and female hormones)."

Chapter 9

1 Bateson (1959), pp. 125–148.
2 Watzlawick, Beavin and Jackson (1967), pp. 64ff. Obviously these points only form the framework of the theoretical model. The initial message is axiomatic, it can be taken as understood. For instance, there is no need to say that God is just and good, everybody knows it. The same is true of the mother who "physically" communicates the message: "Trust me. I'm your mother!" Mothers are *by definition* trustworthy!
3 Hoffman, L. (1984), p. 78.
4 In this case we talk of a "tertiary injunction". Here the transmitter, in order to "cover" the double bind, can use a whole range of defence mechanisms, which

psychoanalysis has highlighted: denial, undoing and, especially, splitting and projection.

5 Sluzki and Ransom (eds) (1976, pp. 187ff.), and other comments by these two writers in the same anthology (pp. 222ff., 373ff.). The anthology also includes *The double bind in a retrospective and reflective revision* by J.H. Waekland.

6 I have already looked at some aspects of this case in Speziale-Bagliacca (1995).

7 The reference is to "Semiosi affettiva e psicoanlisi dell'ideologia". Here Fornari (1980) explains in detail the meaning he gives to the term "ideology".

8 It should be recalled that such co-optation is used when selecting both officers and analysts with teaching functions in many psychoanalytical institutions.

9 As rightly pointed out by Juan Petit, when he discussed this case at a seminar, a space of relative non-comment is not necessarily ideological, but justified by the need to learn, for example, technical operating procedures unknown to the newly-elected member. But this does not appear to be the case here and the justification offered by the patronising councillor for his reproach makes no reference to such a problem. It was the chairman of the council, after all, who asked the new member to fill up the time gap created by the late arrival of the other council members, to talk on a subject she apparently knew more about than the others.

10 Bion talks of "thought's need for truth", a subject he looked at throughout his work, in particular in *Learning from Experience* (1962) and, in a more literary form, in *Memory of the Future* (1975).

11 Mead (1950).

12 I think one can legitimately ask at this point whether rituals and taboos did not come into being partly as a way of regulating the anarchic licence caused by the uncontrolled proliferation of double binds.

13 Institutional groups usually act on two levels, shared and legitimised by the majority, in which the *explicit* and the *implicit* go hand in hand. In some institutions the *implicit* is more powerful than the *explicit* "correct" behaviour patterns that one has to comply with. In this case it seems that they must be willingly imitated (even by older people, like our "child council member"). Cf. *Purity and Danger* by Mary Douglas (1995).

14 In my opinion, the definition of the area covered by the concept of *code* used by Fornari is an open question. We need to clarify whether it includes all the elements that belong to the processes of identification with the parent of the same and of the other sex. One can think, for example, of the processes of imitation/introjection of patterns of motor conduction and control and of the physical and mental containment of emotions. Personally, I favour the more restricted meaning of the term.

15 Obviously, as Fornari perceptively noted, it is the context that determines the *private* and the *public*. The discussion of the council we are talking about here is an *agorà* only for the members of the fellowship; for everyone else it is a private area. As Konrad Hoechst suggested, when discussing this case in a seminar, many of the problems that this situation implies are probably connected to the dialectic-conflictual relationship between "public" and "private".

16 Mitscherlich (1966).

17 *Triumph of the Nomads* (1975), pp. 96–98. The subject of the infanticide of malformed babies in nomad populations in Australia has been looked at on several occasions. See, for example, Webb and Thorne (1985).

18 Fornari's model – which keeps to the ego-ideal – helps to clear up any possible confusion between sex and function, as well as many of the issues raised by recent studies on gender. Some terms are understood in their metaphorical rather than in their historical meaning.

It is well known, to take the most obvious example, that the term "*agorà*", even when it is simply applied to the ancient Greek world, had various different connotations depending on the historical period. The *agorà* in Athens was a plenary popular assembly held when someone had to be ostracised. Later, up to the third century BC, the term indicated the place where meetings of particular groups were held, such as the Attic demes, tribes and archons. These were meetings where everyone voiced his opinion in public and took responsibility for it, but in the more general social context they were still private meetings. In the classical period the *agorà* was the central square in the town, surrounded by the most important public buildings. As well as being the political and commercial centre it was also the moral and religious centre. If it is true (as has been argued, with a touch of cynicism) that institutions are the place of the unsaid, the *agorà* then becomes the place of the public and the private, the said and the unsaid. Let us not forget that participation in political debate depended on wealth and the existence of slavery. See Vegetti (1985). When we speak of liberty, we are always speaking of historically determined degrees of liberty.

As an ideal metaphor (I repeat, in the sense of Freud's ideal of the ego, not in the sense of idealistic philosophy), with all its (in my opinion, remarkable) pragmatic hermeneutic charge, the term *agorà* refers to the need for "publicity" on numerous different occasions. These as yet rather cryptic remarks should become clearer later on.

19 This simple statement has become part of so-called "western culture", and is even used by the mass media. One need only think of a series of films that came out towards the end of the 1970s and the beginning of the 1980s, such as Robert Benton's *Kramer versus Kramer*, with Dustin Hoffman and Meryl Streep (1979), or *Ordinary People* by Robert Redford, with Donald Sutherland and Timothy Hutton (1980).

20 *La Bibbia*, Edizione Pontificio Istituto Biblico, Roma, 1979, note p. 484.

21 D'Anna: *Dizionario italiano ragionato*, Firenze, Sintesi, 1988.

22 For example, Emery's editorial on studies into the killing of one's own children (1985, pp. 505–507), Bloch's psychoanalytical investigations (1985, pp. 573–588), the research carried out at the *Centre Hospitalier Pierre-Janet* in Hull (Quebec) into the relationship between killing one's own child and psychosis (Bourget and Labelle, 1992, pp. 661–673), as well as recent studies on the topic more specifically referred to in the Bible, "disguised infanticide" (Butler, 1995, p. 91), and the survey of 17 mothers who killed their own children conducted at the University of Montreal Faculty of Medicine (Marleau *et al.*, 1995, pp. 142–149), which suggests that mothers tend to kill their children by strangling or drowning them rather than using weapons or objects. In Italy two psychoanalysts, Carloni and Nobili (1975), have written about the phenomenological and anthropological aspects of this question.

In the light of Christa Wolf's *Medea* – see the Postscript – perhaps we should stop using the expression "Medea complex".

Chapter 10

1 See also the section on *Manichean Logic and Creativity* in Chapter 3.

2 I am again thinking of the problem of "*negative therapeutic reaction*" (NTR), which was first described by Freud (1922b). It is an "exacerbation of the patient's symptoms in response to interpretation meant to alleviate them" (Rycroft, 1968). The phenomenon has been used to prove the patient's unconscious masochism and the guilt aroused by the prospect of healing *at the*

expense of others. For a clear summary, see Sandler, Dare and Holder (1992), Chapter 8, pp. 121–132. Obviously NTR can be a rationalisation by the analyst whose purpose is – to take only one example – to keep a sense of guilt about his own therapeutic inability at bay.

3 In French "*métier*" may derive from *métis* rather than from *mistérium*. But *mistérium* would also seem to bear out my thesis. The subject of Prometheus's guilt, from Aeschylus's *Prometheus Unbound* on, has fascinated poets and philosophers, including Goethe, Shelley and Heidegger. In common with the disobedience of Adam and Eve in the Bible, Prometheus's act – the acquisition of a tool of emancipation – could be seen as a guilty act according to the authoritarian logic I have referred to: freedom as an act of transgression (Chapter 1, An Ancient Prospective).

4 Quoted by Jean Piaget (1974), p. 7.

5 Cf. Plato, *Protagora*, 328a and 323d; Xenophon, *Economic*, XV, 11.

6 Knowledge, which is the fruit of the preconscious, is to be understood in the meaning (suggested also by Freud), which does not refer to an area of the mind or a quality of thought but to a separate "mind" of the intellect, an *agency* that constructs thoughts autonomously. See the discussion in P. Bria (1981), p. xxvii.

7 Vernant (1965) and, among others, Jaynes (1976).

8 Detienne and Vernant (1974).

9 The preconscious does not acknowledge the principle of (non-)contradiction, which the Greek philosophers considered to be the supreme principle of being and thought, nor the principle of the excluded third, both of which are typical of the conscious mind. But equally it does not seem to exclude them altogether and behaves like the deep unconscious, hypothesised by Freud and explored further by writers such as Ignacio Matte Blanco (1975a) and Stanislav Grof (1985).

   According to the principle of contradiction it is impossible for the same attribute to belong at the same time and in the same way to the same object or person. The principle of the excluded third, another cornerstone of classic logic, says that a meaningful proposition is either true or false; a third possibility does not exist.

10 "*La source de toute poésie, c'est le sentiment profond de ce qui est inexprimible*", L. Arréat, *Réflexions et Maximes*, 12, Paris, 1865.

11 (1984), p. 110.

12 "*Ein Gedicht soll entweder vortrefflich sein oder gar nicht existieren*", *Wilhelm Meisters Lehrjahre*, Vol. II, 2.

13 See John D. Barrow (1991).

14 Numerous dictionaries in many cultures, such as, for example, *The Oxford English Dictionary*, give a pejorative meaning to the term "ecleticism" in the sense of "syncretism".

15 My reason for talking about *female preconscious* should become clear subsequently.

16 According to the model I am embracing here, the preconscious is also to some extent responsible for dreams. In dreams, the presence of the conscious mind does not hinder the formation of symbols and over-determined situations. See also Ferro (1992), p. 65.

   Far be it from me to reduce to this model what is called by many "preconscious" in the technical sense, "*pcs*". The pcs also has the potentially male ability to intuit and to investigate which we shall look at shortly. The model proposed by J. and A.-M. Sandler (1987), which distinguishes a present "unconscious" from a past "unconscious", covers some of the areas which I have tried to look at with my model of the preconscious. These authors talk about a *mode of functioning*, which is different for the two types of unconscious and "two censorships" (p. 337). They write: "*The [unconscious] fantasy is modified within the present unconscious on its path towards the surface, so that the psyche can keep its balance*" (p. 339). See also J. and A.-M. Sandler (1994). The experimental research carried out by O. Pötzl, presented at the Psychoanalytical Society of Vienna in 1917, as well as the pioneering studies by R. Allers and J. Teller, were long forgotten until, thanks to David Rapaport, they were published in *Psychological Issues*, under the title "Preconsciousus Stimulation in Dreams, Associations and Images" (Vol. II, 3, Monograph 7, 1960, New York, IUP). The most exhaustive research into the preconscious has been carried out by Norman Dixon (1981) at the University College of London. For Dixon "the proof of the existence of a preconscious processing, discovered by studies into unconscious perception, is relevant to the theory of selective attention" (p. 259; cf. in particular, the whole of Chapter 11, on "Preconscious processing and attention").

See also Luquet (1983) and Luquet (1988). Between conscious and pcs, depending on which model is used to define them, one can say that there is reciprocal communication, but also "blocks", censure, perhaps repression. There are some pcs accesses to reality that do not pass through the conscious mind (subliminal perceptions, psi phenomena, etc.) and this could explain many events that are normally attributed to other causes, for example, divination. The compartmentalisation of knowledge, typical of our age, appears to me to be a force that clips the wings of the preconscious.

17 I have illustrated this duplicity in my interpretation of Shakespeare's *King Lear* and Flaubert's *Madame Bovary*. I showed how a discourse between two people can have two different – even antithetical – meanings, depending on the contexts in which they are understood. Cf. Speziale-Bagliacca (1998).

18 The myth of Métis and Athena has several variations: in one of these Athena is born of Métis by parthenogenesis. The pre-Hellenic myth of Athena depicts a goddess of multiform character, often wracked by internal conflict. Like her mother, Athena protects the arts and the trades, especially female works. In the *Iliad* (II, IV, XVIII) *Prómacorma* is the goddess who provokes the first fights (who divides people, separates them, set them against each other until they kill each other). But Athena is also *Tritogénia*, a name that seems to place her birth in the waves, in a typically maternal element, rather than from the male brain. Again: if on the one hand it is *Parthénos* and *Pallade*, that is, the Virgin (as we shall argue when we look at the myth that has prevailed over all the others), on the other it is Mother in the region of Elide, and it is *Kourotróphos*, Nurse, both names which point back to the pre-Greek, Minoan phase (in the most important myth she never shows her breast, which is covered with an aegis, and she never feeds). It would seem that this myth is the point of arrival of a progressive process of ridding the goddess of her maternal attributes. And this seems to link up with my main point.

19 Xanthippe is a figure that needs to be rediscovered. From a psychoanalytical point of view one could suggest that Xanthippe is also the product of the projective identification of her husband and his disciples. In the case of Phedone, what else could Socrates and his friends project on to her if not the fear of death and the preparation for farewell, separation? Sloterdijk (1983, pp. 226–228) writes ironically about Xanthippe and Socrates from a kinetic-female point of view, reaching the conclusion that "it is the evil Xanthippe who is the true victim of her presumed victim, Socrates, finally unmasked in his true guise as the real villain".

20 More references are to be found in Speziale-Bagliacca (1990a), as well as in parts

of another of my books (1992b). The first quotation of this paragraph is by Donald Meltzer, the second by Eissler. Again in 1987, in the already-mentioned posthumous work, H. Rosenfeld maintains that ". . . the *main means* with which the analyst achieves his aims is accurate verbal interpretation" (my italics). Rosenfeld dedicated several other chapters in that same book to the analyst's containment, showing how his function was fundamental to prepare for an interpretation. This view of containment coincides only partly with the view I expressed in my 1990 book.

21 Speziale-Bagliacca (1982b, 1988b, 1990a).

22 Grinberg (1981). The following passage is taken from L. and R. Grinberg (1966); my italics.

23 Bion (1962b).

24 He was a *dabbler* in Chinese, according to Grotstein (1981a). Elizabeth Tabak de Bianchedi presents an illuminating picture in a work we have already cited, *Transcending the caesura between East and West through Bion's psychoanalytic ideas*, del 1992.

25 Bion (1967).

26 The expression used by Freud for "deliberate attention" is "*absichtlichen Aufmerken*"; for "evenly suspended" "*gleichschwebende Aufmersamkeit*".

27 Cf. Mahony (1979).

28 Note Freud's agreeement with Proust about the potential of preconscious (or unconscious) memory. Whether they actually met or not, Freud and Proust shared the same "spirit of the age".

29 Freud (1912), pp. 536–537, 539.

30 Freud also uses this metaphor in his *Introduction to Psychoanalysis* (Freud, 1915–1917) p. 607.

31 On mediatory peripheral intelligence, see Sternberg (1985). The surgeon knows that his hands tell him exactly where to cut.

32 Ferenczi (1909), pp. 78ff.

33 Baltrušaitis (1979).

34 I go into a deeper analysis of this subject in Chapter 10 of Speziale-Bagliacca (2002).

35 Oshima (1983).

36 Wieger (1965).

37 There is an interesting Spanish expression relating to the heart and the mind – "*tener una corazonada*" [*corazón* = heart] – which means having a premonition. English, too, has expressions such as "*have a change of heart*" (to talk about "changing one's mind"), or the expression used by Hamlet "*in my heart of hearts*" meaning "in my most intimate thoughts" (*The Random House Dictionary*) and "to know something by heart", (cf. French "*par coeur*").

38 Graham (1981), p. 35, note 85.

39 Sufficiently deep breathing involves different areas of the body, as every medical student knows. But it is especially important that there should be no lowering of marginal attention on breathing, no wavering between the conscious and the unconscious, especially at moments of tension.

40 Jaynes (1976). Vegetti (1985) maintains that the identification with the diaphragm entered medical language later. In Homer the term referred to the "lungs".

41 Fornari (1979).

42 W. and M. Baranger (1961), p. 136.

43 The image of "centre of gravity" comes from Meltzer (1973), who talks about the "centre of gravity" of identity.

44 Freud (1910), p. 200 and note p. 201. See Speziale-Bagliacca (2002), pp. 247ff.
45 Ferenczi (1932), Carloni (1997).
46 Ainsworth's studies are of remarkable interest, and follow in the path of Bowlby (Ainsworth *et al.*, 1978). Ainsworth studied the models of interaction between mother and child. One of the things she points to are data proving that the firmest attachment, with least insecurity, of the small child to the mother, is when the mother shows herself to be more tactile and interested in physical contact.
47 Winnicott (1960), pp. 44ff.
48 It was published a year later. Winnicott (1969), pp. 711–716.

Chapter 11

1 Michel de Montaigne, *On the force of the imagination*, Ch. xxi, *Essays*, 1580.
2 Others have also outlined aspects of this phenomenon; one thinks, for example, of the passage in which Kierkegaard in *Enter-Eller* (*Either/Or*, 1843), writes about Don Juan: "his passion sets in motion the passion of others" (Volume I). The concept in psychoanalysis has been clearly expressed and widely discussed by, among others, Rosenfeld (1987), Grinberg (1976, Chs. 6–12) and Ogden (1991). Not all are in agreement with Klein.
3 Not all are in agreement with Ogden's definition. See Speziale-Bagliacca (1994b, pp. 7–14); I only make partial reference to these remarks here.
4 See Grossman (1981).
5 Wangh (1962).
6 On the distinction between projective identification as an attack and as communication, see Rosenfeld (1987). What I am saying should not suggest that I am denying the clinical observation that leads various authors such as Rosenfeld (1971, 1987) and Kernberg (1992) to talk about "sadistic" or "malign" narcissism, alluding to particular forms of destructive narcissism. I am only trying to urge a certain caution in defining the contours of this figure and in interpreting it (Speziale-Bagliacca, 1977 and 1988). On the subject of caution, I would like to cite the model of interpretation provided by Kernberg (1992, p. 37).
7 Eibl-Eibesfeldt (1970).
8 For a precise summary of the role of the analyst in this situation, see Sandler and Sandler (1986), which suggests a proper strategy of how to intervene in cases of guilt.
9 Freud (1917) evaluated the various tones starting from considerations about the Chinese language. Tone and rhythm (together with other important elements) make it possible to reconstruct meaning. In psychoanalysis David Liberman (1970–1972) has dedicated particular attention to this subject.
10 I would like to point out that the first person in psychoanalysis to appreciate the importance of these questions was probably Marion Milner, writing under the pseudonym of Joanna Field (1934).
11 F. Nietzsche, *Also sprach Zarathustra. Ein Buch für Alle und Keine.*
12 Cf. Gill (1983).
13 Klein (1932), p. 10.
14 Ibid., pp. 26–27.
15 Ibid., note p. 27.
16 Money-Kyrle in the *Introduction* to the first volume of Klein's Collected Works (MKW); my italics.

17 This point of maximum anxiety is also referred to by Hinshelwood (1989, p. 10) in the section on "technique" in the *Dictionary of Kleinian Psychoanalysis*.

18 Although Klein, as we know, preferred to talk about unconscious phantasies, the "mental equivalents of the instincts", in the noted definition by Isaacs (1948).

19 In this book (Riviere, 1936a, pp. 134ff.) she writes: "not all negative reactions to treatment should be seen as attempts of the patient to defeat the analysis", a remark also highlighted by Rosenfeld (1987), p. 99.

20 For example, Klein (1932), pp. 22–25. Susan Isaacs devoted a large amount of space to the "test and to the verification of insights" (1939), pp. 151ff. Fairly surprisingly, Isaacs prefers the term "perception" to "insight", which for her has a "mystic" connotation (p. 150). It is as if this word, apart from having been used by the mystics, had not found its way into much of western philosophy, from Descartes to Locke, from Leibniz to Bergson and contemporary Intuitionism. One wonders what frightened Isaacs; one could investigate but this is probably not the right place to do so.

21 My italics.

22 Klein (1920–1921), pp. 1ff.

23 These observations appeared in the *Rivista di Psiconalisi*. Speziale-Bagliacca (1988b), pp. 515ff. The authors that Rosenfeld mentions in this passage are Segal (1962), Loewald (1970), Langs (1976) and Sandler (1976).

24 Those familiar with the interpretative techniques Rosenfeld normally applies will notice that he is doing something unusual for him: he carries out on the patient what one might call a "reality test" – what you are worried about is a fantasy! What's more, he interprets the transference relationship only later, when it is certainly less effective. If he had tuned into the question of the hurry immediately, he would have been able to bring the situation directly in relation to the transference, showing the patient that he knew how to contain and tone down the threat. I have expounded this criticism in Speziale-Bagliacca (1988b), pp. 541ff.

25 Apart from the case of the "good analyst who nourishes" (where there does not seem to have been any particular hurry, perhaps only an example of automatism), one thinks of the *rêverie* of the cat and the mouse, which initially was also translated into a formula expressing blame.

26 The terms in inverted commas are those used by the patient.

27 The analyst was very good at making sense of the content of this behaviour and this clinical material: it seemed to her very probable that the rock faces that her patient clung onto symbolised the dead mother, just as the "abyss" symbolised the fact that he both feared and wanted to follow his dead mother through suicide. And so on.

28 The area of the interpreted themes would tend rather to fall into what Rosenfeld called "central aspects".

29 Reik (1945–1959).

30 I go into this question in more detail in Speziale-Bagliacca (1999), where I look at Freud, free will and ethics.

31 For a recent picture of ethno-psychoanalysis which will give the reader some guidelines for understanding some aspects of the sense of guilt, see, among others, Nathan (1993) and Nathan and Stengers (1995).

32 Finkelstein (1938), p. 196. This phenomenon – as is known – seems to be common to ancient peoples or at least those who have remained in this sense primitive. It is a modality that one could possibly see as part of animism.

33 Joseph Flavius, *Antiquities*, xviii, 1.3. *The Loeb Classical Library*, London, 1926–1937. Flavius, who erroneously identified fatalism with divine providence,

has been criticised, for example by Louis Finkelstein (1938), pp. 195ff., in "Providence, Determinism and Free Will". For Finkelstein, the position of the Sadducees had been natural for the patricians of Jerusalem since earliest times, and the position of the Pharisees had been typical of uncivil plebeians since the seventh century BC; the teachings of the Essenes was the simple piety of the fellahîn, uncontaminated by metropolitan sophistication.

34 In Scholasticism free will is after all a synonym of *liberum judicium* – the capacity to decide freely on a particular question.

35 Kohut (1959), p. 480.

36 Freud (1922b), p. 512. Interestingly, Freud wrote this remark in a footnote on the subject of guilt.

37 The very concept of "ego drives" (*Ichtriebe*), the idea that the Ego comes out of the Id, or that the reality principle is simply the pleasure principle modified, would, according to Kohut, illustrate this opinion. Kohut (1959), p. 480.

38 The emphasis on the Ego as a psychic structure in *The Ego and the Id*, some remarks in *Analisi terminabile e interminabile* about the independent genesis of the Ego, were later exploited by Hartmann (1939) to theorise areas of the Ego free from conflict.

39 Among the post-Kleinians who have taken up this point of view are Eric Brenman in "Cruelty and Mental Limitation" (1970), pp. 274ff.

40 We have now reached the last – but again probably only apparent – paradox. This subjective responsibility is dictated by a criterion that in many ways resembles ancient Roman law. See Von Jhering as quoted in Chapter 3.

Appendix

1 The *Dizionario italiano ragionato* by G. D'Anna (published by Sintesi in 1988), for example, says: "involuntary breaking of a regulation or law" (unlike a crime, which presupposes voluntary infringement).

2 Also, the *New Shorter Oxford English Dictionary* (1993) includes the definition: ". . . (c) a feeling or sense of being guilty", so the imputation of misuse has disappeared.

3 At the beginning of the twentieth century, Henri Joly dedicated a very successful book to his daughter (*L'Enfance Coupable*, Joly, 1904), which talked about the crimes committed by minors.

4 *Vatermord als psychische Realität* (the killing of the father as a psychic, not factual, reality in neurotics), *Gesammelte Werke*, IX, p. 192. The hero takes on guilt to relieve his brothers (the choir): "he had to bear the burden of what was known as 'tragic guilt'" (*Er hatte die sogenannte "tragische Schuld" auf sich geladen*), p. 187; *Gesammelte Werke*, IX, corr XIII, SE pp. 155ff.

5 See also Nietzsche, "Second dissertation", *On the Genealogy of Morals*, 1887.

6 *Schuld* in legal vocabulary has the same meaning as the Spanish term *culpa* when used in the legal sense: "that which offers a reason for demanding some responsibility" (*responsabilidad* in Spanish, *Haftung* in German). Cf. *Diccionario de la Lengua Española*, Real Academia Española, 1956, where *guilt* also means "cause", "error" and "crime". See also Rudolf von Jhering (1873), and Nietzsche (1887, pp. 45ff.), who came back to the idea of wrong and guilt as "debt" from the point of view of the victim. Interestingly, in the ancient Greek world a distinction was made between guilt in the legal sense (*aitia*), guilt as sin and guilt as error (*amartema*).

7 Soloman is a doctor working in an Aids clinic in Madras, here speaking in an interview on "Aids in India" broadcast by the BBC World Service in its *Outlook* programme on 23 December 1996.

Bibliography

Abraham, H. (1974). Karl Abraham: An unfinished biography. *International Journal of Psycho-Analysis*, **17**, pp. 17ff.

Ainsworth, M., Blehar, M.C., Waters, E. and Wall, S. (1978). *Patterns of Attachment: A study of the strange situation*. Hillsdale, NJ, Erlbaum.

Alvarez, A. *et al.* (1994). *Un buon incontro. La valutazione secondo il modello Tavistock*, ed. E. Quagliata. Rome, Astrolabio.

Baltrušaitis, J. (1979). *Le Miroir. Révélations, Science-Fiction et Fallacies*. Paris, Ed. du Seuil.

Baranger, W. (1957). Interpretación e ideología. (Sobre la regla de abstención ideológica). In *Revista de Psicoanálisis*, **14** (1–2), 1957. Republished in *Problemas del campo analitico*, W. Baranger and M. Baranger, Buenos Aires, Kargieman, 1969, pp. 103–108.

Baranger, W. and Baranger, M. (1961). *Problemas del campo psicoanalitico*. Buenos Aires, Kargieman, 1969.

Barrow, J.D. (1991). *Theories of Everything*. Oxford, Oxford University Press.

Bateson, G. (1959). Cultural problems posed by a study of a schizophrenic process. In *Schizophrenia, an Integrated Approach*, ed. A. Auerbach. New York, Ronald Press.

Bertin, C. (1982). *La dernière Bonaparte*. Paris, Perrin.

Bibring, E. (1937). Contribution to the symposium on the theory of therapeutic results of psycho-analysis. In *International Journal of Psycho-Analysis*, **18**, pp. 511–519.

Bion, W. (1962a). *Learning from Experience*. London, Heinemann.

—— (1962b). A theory of thinking. In *Melanie Klein Today*, ed. E. Bott Spillius, vol. I. London, Routledge, 1988.

—— (1967). Notes on memory and desire. In *Melanie Klein Today*, ed. E. Bott Spillius, vol. II. London, Routledge, 1988.

—— (1975). *A Memoir of the Future. The Dream*. London, Ronald Harris Educational Trust.

—— (1985). *All My Sins Remembered and the Other Side of Genius*. London, Karnac.

Biondi, M. (1995). Beyond the brain – Mind dichotomy and toward a common organizing principle of pharmacological and psychological treatment. *Psychotherapy and Psychosomatics*, **64**, pp. 1–8.

Biondi, M. and Picardi, A. (1996). Clinical and biological aspects of bereavement and loss-induced depression: A reappraisal. In *Psychotherapy and Psychosomatics*, **65**, pp. 229–245.

Blainey, G. (1975). *Triumph of the Nomads*. Melbourne, Macmillan.

Bollas, C. (1993). *Being a Character: Psychoanalysis and Self Experience*. London, Free Association Books.

Bossuet, J.B. (1679). *Discours sur l'histoire universelle*, part I, chapter 1. Paris.

Bott Spillius, E. (1988). *Melanie Klein Today*, vols I and II. London, Routledge.

Bowlby, J. (1969). *Attachment and Loss*, vol. I. London, Hogarth Press.

Brenman, E. (1970). *Cruelty and Narrowmindedness*. In *Melanie Klein Today*, ed. E. Bott Spillius, London, Routledge, 1988.

Camus, A. (1957). *Reflexions sur la guillotine* (*Riflessioni sulla pena di morte*. Milan, SE, 1993).

Canevari, A. (1982). Ideologia, biochimina encefalica e interpretazione del comportamento. In *Controversie in psichiatria*, ed. V. Andreoli. Milan, Masson.

Cassirer, E. (1923–29) *The Philosophy of Symbolic Forms*, 3 vols, New Haven, CT, Yale University Press, 1955.

Chamfort, S.R.N. (1795). *Maximes et Pensies*. Paris, Larousse, 1928.

Detienne, M. and Vernant, J.-P. (1974). *Les ruses de l'intelligence. La métis des Grecs*. Paris, Flammarion.

Dixon, N.F. (1981). *Preconscious Processing*. Chichester, Wiley.

Douglas, M. (1966). *Purezza e pericolo*. Bologna, Il Mulino, 1995.

—— (1992). *Risk and Blame*. London and New York, Routledge.

Downing, G. (1995). *Il corpo e la parola*. Rome, Astrolabio.

Dworkin, R. (1991). *Law's Empire*. London, Fontana Press.

Eibl-Eibsfeldt, I. (1970). *Liebe und Hass. Zur Naturgeschicte elementarer Verhaltensweisen*. Munich, Piper & Co. Verlag.

Ekman, P., Friesen, W.V. and Ellsworth, P.C. (1972). *Emotion in the Human Face*. New York, Pergamon.

Etchegoyen, H. (1973). A note on ideology and psychoanalytic technique. *International Journal of Psycho-Analysis*, **54**, pp. 485–486.

Fairbairn, W.R.D. (1943). The repression and the return of bad objects (with special reference to the "war neuroses"). In *Psychoanalytic Studies of the Personality*, W.R.D. Fairbairn. London and New York, Routledge, 1952.

Ferenczi, S. (1909). Introjection and transference. In *Contributions to Psycho-Analysis*. Boston, R.G. Badger.

—— (1913a). Stages in the development of the sense of reality. In *Contributions to Psycho-Analysis*. Boston, R.G. Badger, p. 213.

—— (1913b). Belief, disbelief and conviction. In *Further Contributions to the Theory and Technique of Psycho-Analysis*. London, Hogarth Press, p. 487.

—— (1932). *Journal clinique*. Paris, Payot.

Ferro, A. (1992). *La tecnica nella psicoanalisi infantile*. Milan, Cortina.

Finkelstein, L. (1938). *The Pharisees. The Sociological Background of their Faith*. Philadelphia, The Jewish Publication Society, 1962.

Fornari, F. (1979). *I fondamenti di una teoria psicoanalitica del linguaggio*. Turin, Boringhieri.

—— (1980). *Semiosi affettiva e psicoanalisi dell'ideologia*. In Formazione e percezione psicoanalitica, ed. R. Speziale-Bagliacca, Milan, Feltrinelli.

Fornari, F. (1981) *Il codice vivente. Femminilità e maternità nei sogni delle madri in gravidanza*. Turin, Boringhieri.

Foucault, M. (1975). *Discipline and Punish: The Birth of the Prison*. Trans. A. Sheridan. Harmondsworth, Penguin, 1977.

Freud A. (1965). *Normality and Pathology in Childhood: Assessments of Development*. New York, International Universities Press.

Freud, S. (1894). *The Neuro-Psychoses of Defence. The Standard Edition of the Complete Psychological Works of Sigmund Freud* (SE), 24 vols, ed. J. Strachey *et al.*, London, The Hogarth Press and the Institute of Psychoanalysis, 1974, Vol. 2.

Freud, S. (1985). *Studies on Hysteria*. SE, vol. 2.

—— (1901). *Fragment of an Analysis of a Case of Hysteria*. SE, vol. 7.

—— (1906). *Psychoanalysis and the Establishment of Facts in Legal Proceedings*. SE, vol. 9.

—— (1907). *Obsessive Actions and Religious Practices*. SE, vol. 9.

—— (1910). *The Future Prospects of Psycho-Analytic Therapy*. SE, vol. 11.

—— (1911). *Formulations on the Two Principles of Mental Functioning*. SE, vol. 12.

—— (1912). Recommendations to physicians practising psycho-analysis. In *Papers on Technique*. SE, vol. 12.

—— (1912–13). *Totem and Taboo*. SE, vol. 13.

—— (1914). *On Narcissism: An Introduction*. SE, vol. 14.

—— (1915a). *Mourning and Melancholia*. SE, vol. 14.

—— (1915b). *Observations on Transference-Love*. SE, vol. 12.

—— (1915–17). *Introductory Lectures on Psychoanalysis*. SE, vol. 15.

—— (1916). *Some Character-Types Met with in Psycho-Analytic Work*. SE, vol. 14.

—— (1920). *Beyond the Pleasure Principle*. SE, vol. 18.

—— (1921). *Group Psychology and the Analysis of the Ego*. SE, vol. 18.

—— (1922a). *Two Encyclopaedia Articles: "Psycho-Analysis" and "The Libido Theory"*. SE, vol. 18.

—— (1922b). *The Ego and the Id*. SE, vol. 19.

—— (1922c). *A Seventeenth-Century Demonological Neurosis*. SE, vol. 19.

—— (1924). *The Economic Problem of Masochism*. SE, vol. 19.

—— (1925). *Negation*. SE, vol. 19.

—— (1929). *Civilization and Its Discontents*. SE, vol. 21.

—— (1932). Lecture XXXV. *The Question of a* Weltanschauung. SE, vol. 22.

—— (1934–38). *Moses and Monotheism: Three Essays*. SE, vol. 23.

—— (1937a). *Constructions in Analysis*. SE, vol. 23.

—— (1937b). *Analysis Terminable and Interminable*. SE, vol. 23.

—— (1938). *An Outline of Psycho-Analysis*. SE, vol. 23.

Gill, M.M. (1983). Il paradigma interpersonale e la misura del coinvolgimento del terapeuta. In *Psicoterapia e Scienze Umane*, **3**, pp. 5–44, 1995.

Goldberg, J. (1985). *La colpa*. Feltrinelli, Milan 1988. (*La Culpabilité Axiome de la Psychanalyse*, Presses Universitaires de France, Paris, 1985.)

Graham, A.C. (1981). *Chuang-tzu. The Inner Chapters*. London: Allen & Unwin.

Grinberg, L. (1963–1971). *Culpa y depresiòn*. Alianza Editorial, Madrid, quoted edn. 1983.

—— (1976). *Teorìa de la identificación*. Buenos Aires, Paidós.

—— (1981). *Psicoanalisis. Aspectos teoricos y clinicos*. Barcelona and Buenos Aires, Paidós.

Grof, S. (1985). *Beyond the Brain*. New York, State University Press.

Grossman, L.P. (1981). Letter to the editor, "Projective identification". *International Journal of Psycho-Analysis*, **8**, p. 458.

Grosskurth, P. (1987). *Melanie Klein: Her World and Her Work*. Cambridge, MA, Harvard University Press, 1987.

Grotstein, J.S. (1981a). *Splitting and Projective Identification*. New York, Aronson.

—— (1981b). Wilfred R. Bion: The man, the psychoanalyst, the mystic. A perspective on his life and work. In *Do I Dare Disturb the Universe?* Beverly Hills, Caesura Press.

—— (1981c). *Do I Dare Disturb the Universe?* Beverly Hills, Caesura Press.

Grunberger, B. (1971) *Le Narcissisme*. Paris, Payot.

Guenon, R. (1924). *Oriente e Occidente*. Turin, Einaudi, 1965.

Habicht, C. (1985). *Pausanias' Guide to Ancient Greece*. Berkeley, Berkeley University Press.

Hartmann, H. (1939). *Ego Psychology and the Problem of Adaptation*. New York, International Universities Press, 1958.

Hartmann, H., Kris E. and Lowenstein, R.M. (1964). *Papers on Psychoanalytic Psychology*. New York, International Universities Press.

Heimann, P. (1949–50). On counter-transference. In *About Children and Children-No-Longer*, P. Heimann. London, Tavistock/Routledge, 1989.

—— (1981). La sfida di Freud al coraggio e alla creatività dell'individuo. In *Neuropsich. Infantile*, **242**.

—— (1989). *About Children and Children-No-Longer*. London, Tavistock/Routledge.

Hinshelwood, R.D. (1989). *A Dictionary of Kleinian Thought*. London, Free Association Books.

Hoffmann, L. (1981). *Foundations of Family Theory*. New York, Basic Books.

Isaacs, S. (1929). Privation and guilt. *International Journal of Psycho-Analysis*, **10**.

—— (1943). The nature and function of phantasy. In *The Freud–Klein Controversies: 1941–45*, Ed. P. King and R. Steiner, London, Tavistock/Routledge, 1991, pp. 264–321. Republished in *International Journal of Psycho-Analsysis*, **29**, pp. 73–97.

Jacobson, E. (1964). *The Self and the Object World*. New York, International Universities Press.

James, W. (1890). *Principles of Psychology*. London, Macmillan.

Jaques, E. (1951). *The Changing Culture of a Factory*. London, Tavistock.

Jaynes, J. (1976). *The Origin of Consciousness in the Breakdown of the Bicameral Mind*. Boston, Houghton Mifflin.

von Jhering, R. (1873). *Der Kampf uns Recht*. (*La lotta per il diritto*. Milan, Giuffré, 1986.)

Johnson, A.M. (1947). Sanctions for superego lacunae. Read at the Chicago Psychoanalytic Society.

Johnson, A.M. and Szurek, S.A. (1952). The genesis of antisocial acting out of children and adults. *Psychoanalytic Quarterly*, **21**, pp. 323–343.

Joly, H. (1904). *L'enface coupable*. Paris, Lecoffre.

Jones, E. (1916). The theory of symbolism. In *Papers on Psycho-Analysis*, London, Hogarth, 1923.

—— (1953–57). *The Life and Work of Sigmund Freud*. London, Hogarth Press.

Kernberg, O.F. (1969). A contribution to the ego-psychological critique of the Kleinian School. *International Journal of Psycho-Analysis*, **50**, pp. 317ff.

—— (1976). *Object Relations Theory and Clinical Psychoanalysis*. New York, Jason Aronson.

—— (1980). *Internal World and External Reality*. New York, Jason Aronson.

—— (1992). *Aggression in Personality Disorders and Perversions*. New Haven, CT and London, Yale University Press.

King, P. and Steiner, R. (1991) *The Freud–Klein Controversies*. 1941–45. London, Tavistock/Routledge, p. 799.

Klein, M. (1920–21). *The Development of a Child. The Writing of Melaine Klein* (WMK), London, Hogarth Press and the Institute of Psychoanalysis. Vol. I, 1. Appeared as 'Aus dem infantile Seelenleben' in *International Zeitschrift für Psychoanalyse*, **VI**, 1920.

—— (1927). *Criminal Tendencies in Normal Children*. WMK, vol. I, 8.

—— (1928). *Early Stages of the Oedipus Conflict*. WMK, vol. I, 9.

—— (1932). *Psycho-Analysis of Children*. WMK, vol. II.

—— (1933). *The Early Development of Conscience in the Child*. WMK, vol. I, 15.

—— (1935). *A Contribution to the Psychogenesis of Manic-Depressive States*. WMK, vol. I, 17.

—— (1936). *Weaning*. WMK, vol. I, 18.

—— (1937). *Love, Guilt and Reparation*. WMK, vol. I, 19.

—— (1940). *Mourning and Its Relation to Manic-Depressive States*. WMK, vol. I, 20.

—— (1945). *The Oedipus Complex in the Light of Early Anxieties*. WMK, vol. I, 21.

—— (1955). *On Identification*. WMK, vol. III, 9.

—— (1957). *Envy and Gratitude*, WMK, vol. III, 10.

—— (1958). *On the Development of Mental Functioning*. WMK, vol. III, 11.

Kohut, H. (1959). Introspection, empathy and psychoanalysis. In *Journal of the American Psychoanalytic Association*, **7**, pp. 459–483.

—— (1971). *The Analysis of the Self*. London, Hogarth Press.

—— (1987). *The Kohut Seminars on Self Psychology and Psychotherapy with Adolescents and Young Adults*. New York and London, W.W. Norton & Company.

Lacan, J. (1957–58). Les formations de l'inconscient. In *Ecrits*. Paris, Editions du Seuil.

Langs, R. (1976a). *The Therapeutic Interaction*. New York, Aronson.

—— (1976b). *The Bipersonal Field*. New York, Aronson.

—— (1980). *Interactions. The Realm of Transference and Countertransference*. New York, Aronson.

Laplanche, J. and Pontalis, J.-B. (1967). *Vocabulaire de la psychanalyse*. Paris, PUF.

—— (1985). *Fantasme originaire, fantasme des origines, origines du fantasme*. Paris, Hachette.

Lerminier, E. (1812). *Dictionnaire des Sciences Médicales*. Paris, Panckouke.

Liberman, D. (1970–72). *Lingüística, interacción comunicativa y proceso psicoanalítico*. Buenos Aires, Galerna.

Lichtenberg, J. (1983). *Psychoanalysis and Infant Research*. Hillsdale, NJ, The Analytic Press.

Limentani, A. (1989). *Between Freud and Klein*. London, Free Association Books. (*Tra Freud e Klein*. Rome, Borla.)

Little, M. (1950). Counter-transference and the patient's response to it. In *Transference Neurosis and Transference Psychoses: Toward Basic Unity*. New York, Jason Aronson, 1981, pp. 33–50.

—— (1990). *Psychotic Anxieties and Containment: A Personal Record of an Analysis with Winnicott*. New York, Jason Aronson.

Loeward, H. (1970). Psychoanalytic theory and the psychoanalytic process. *The Psychoanalitic Study of the Child*, **25**, pp. 45–68.

Lowie, R. (1947). *Primitive Society*. New York, Liveright Publishing Corporation.

Luquet, P. (1983). Tentative de description du functionnement psychique et du "moi" a travers le niveaux de conscience, de pensée et de langage. *Revue Française de Psychanalyse*, **2**, 539–565.

—— (1988). Présentation et résumé "Langage, Pensée et Structure Psychique". *Revue française de Psychanalyse*, **2**, 267–302.

Mahler, M. (1968). *On Human Symbiosis and the Vicissitudes of Individuation: Infantile Psychosis*. New York, International Universities Press.

Mahler, M., Pine, F. and Bergman, A. (1975). *The Psychological Birth of the Human Infant, Symbiosis and Individuation*. New York, Basic Books.

Mahony, P. (1979). The boundaries of free association. *Psychoanalysis and Contemporary Thought*, **2**, pp. 151–198.

Mancia, M. (1990). *Nello sguardo di Narciso*. Bari, Laterza.

Marleau, J.D. *et al.* (1995). L'omicide d'enfant commis par la mere. In *Canadian Journal of Psychiatry*, **40** (3), pp. 142–149.

Matte Blanco, I. (1975a). *The Unconscious as Infinite Sets. An Essay in Bi-Logic*. London, Gerald Duckworth & Company.

—— (1975b). *Female Nature and Bi-logical Structures*. International Symposium on Feminine Sexuality and Maternity. Rome.

Mead, M. (1950). *Sesso e temperamento*. Milan, Mondadori, 1991.

Meltzer, D. (1973). *Sexual States of Mind*. Ballinluig, Perthshire, Clunie Press.

Milner, M. (Joanna Field) (1934). *A Life of One's Own*. London, Virago, 1986.

Mitscherlich, A. (1966). *Krankheit als Konflikt*. Frankfurt, Suhrkamp.

Mitchell, W. (1993). DSM III and the transformation of American psychiatry: a history. In *American Journal of Psychiatry*, **150** (3), pp. 399–410.

Money-Kyrle, R.E. (1951). *Psychoanalysis and Politics. A Contribution to the Psychology of Politics and Morals*. London, Duckworth & Co.

—— (1961). *Man's Picture of His World*. London, Duckworth & Co.

—— (1975). Introduction. In *The Writings of Melanie Klein*, vol. I. London, Hogarth Press and the Institute of Psychoanalysis.

Montaigne, M. (1580). *Essais*, Chapter XXI.

Nathan, T. (1993). *Principi di etnopsicoanalisi*. Turin, Bollati Boringhieri.

Nathan, T. and Stengers, I. (1995). *Medici stregoni*. Turin, Bollati Boringhieri.

Nietzsche, F. (1883–1885). *Also sprach Zarathustra. Ein buch für Alle und Keine*. Leipzig, 1922.

—— (1887). *On the Genealogy of Morals*. Second essay: Guilt, Bad Conscience, and Related Matters. University College, Namaimo, BC.

Ogden, T. (1991). *Projective Identification and Psychotherapeutic Technique*. Northvale, NJ and London, Jason Aronson.

Oshima, H.H. (1983). A methaphorical analysis of the concept of mind in the *Chuang-tzu*. In *Experimental Essays on the* Chuang-tzu, ed. V.H. Mair. Honolulu, University of Hawaii Press.

Pert, C.B. (1998). *Molecules of Emotion*. London and New York, Simon & Schuster.

Petot, J.-M. (1982). *Melanie Klein: Le Moi et le Bon Object 1932–1960*. Paris, Dunod.

Piaget, J.H. (1974). *Preface to Réussir et Comprendre*. (Prefazione a *Riuscire e capire*. Rome, Editori Riuniti, 1976.)

Racker, H. (1969). *Transference and Counter-transference*. London, Hogarth Press.

Rayner, E. (1991). *The Independent Mind in British Psychoanalysis*. London, Free Association Books.

Reik, TH. (1945–59). *L'impulso a confessare*. Milan, Feltrinelli, 1967. (*The Compulsion to Confess. On the Psychoananlysis of Crime and Punishment*.)

Rickman, J. (1948). Guilt and the dynamics of psychological disorders in the individual. In *Proceedings of the International Congress on Mental Health*. Republished in *Selected Contributions to Psycho-Analysis*, J. Rickman, London, Hogarth Press, 1957.

—— (1957). *Selected Contributions to Psycho-Analysis*. London, Hogarth Press.

Riviere, J. (1936a). A contribution to the analysis of the negative therapeutic reaction. In *The Inner World and Joan Riviere. Collected Papers 1920–1958*, ed. A. Hughes. London, 1991, pp. 134ff.

—— (1936b). On the genesis of psychical conflict in earliest infancy. In *The Inner World and Joan Riviere. Collected Papers 1920–1958*, ed. A. Hughes, chapter XV. London, Karnac, 1991.

—— (1952). Introduction. In *Developments in Psycho-Analysis*, M. Klein *et al.* London, Hogarth Press.

—— (1991). *The Inner World and Joan Riviere. Collected Papers 1920–1958*, ed. A. Hughes. London, Karnac.

Rodman, F.R. (1987). Introduction. In *The Spontaneous Gesture, Selected Letters of D.W. Winnicott*, ed. F.R. Rodman. Cambridge, MA, Harvard University Press.

Rosenfeld, H. (1965). *Psychotic States*. London, Hogarth.

—— (1971). A clinical approach to the psycho-analytic theory of the life and death instincts: an investigation into the aggressive aspects of narcissism. *International Journal of Psycho-Analysis*, **50**, pp. 317ff.

—— (1987). *Impasse and Interpretation*. London, Tavistock.

Rossi-Landi, F. (1967). Ideologia come progettazione sociale. *Ideologie*, **1**.

Russell, B. (1957). *Why I Am Not a Christian*. London, Allen & Unwin.

Russo, P. (1995). *Come ascoltare le Passioni di Bach*. Milan, Mursia.

Rycroft, C. (1968). *A Critical Dictionary of Psychoanalysis*. London, Nelson & Sons.

Sandler, J. (1976). Countertransference and the role-responsiveness. In *International Review of Psycho-Analysis*, **3**, pp. 43–47.

Sandler, J. and Sandler, A.-M. (1987). The past unconscious, the present unconscious and the vicissitudes of guilt. *International Journal of Psycho-Analysis*, **68**, pp. 331–341.

Sandler, J., Dare, C.H. and Holder, A. (1973). *The Patient and the Analyst. The Basis of Psychoanalytic Process*. London, Karnac.

Saramago, J. (1991). *Evangelho segundo Jesus Christo*. Lisbon, Editorial Caminho.

Segal, H. (1962). *Introduction to the Work of Melanie Klein*. London, Tavistock.

Segal, H. (1979). *Klein*. London, Fontana.

Schoeck, H. (1966). *Der Neil*. Munich, Freiburg Verl.

Sluzki, C.E. and Ransom, D.C. (eds) (1976). *Double Bind*. New York, Grune & Stratton.

Sloterdijk, P. (1983). *Critica della ragion cinica*. Milan, Garzanti, 1992.

Speziale-Bagliacca, R. (1977) Tecniche dittatoriali esterne e dittatoriali interne. *Rivista di psicoanalisi*, **23** (3), pp. 431–436.

—— (1980a). Resistenza e ideologia nella formazione alla "percezione" psicoanalitica. In *Formazione e percezione psicoanalisi*, ed. R. Speziale-Bagliacca. Milan, Feltrinelli.

—— (ed.) (1980b). *Formazione e percezione psicoanalitica*. Milan, Feltrinelli.

—— (1981). Introduction. In J.S. Grotstein, *Splitting and Projective Identification*. New York, Aronson.

—— (1982a). Lo spazio e il tempo per elaborare. In *L'identità dello psichiatra*, ed. F. Giberti. Rome, Il Pensiero Scientifico.

—— (1982b). *On the Shoulders of Freud*. New Brunswick, NJ and London, Transaction Publishers and Routledge, 1991.

—— (1988). Osservazioni su *Impasse and Interpretation* di H. Rosenfeld. *Rivista Psicoanal*, **34** (3), July–September, pp. 507ff.

—— (1990). La capacité de contenirs: notes sue la façon dont elle opére dans le changement psychique. In *Revue Française de Psychanalyse*, **5**, pp. 1363–1373. (English version in *International Journal of Psychoanalysis*, **72** (I), 1991, pp. 27–33.)

—— (1992a). *The King and the Adulteress. A Psychoanalytic and Literary Reinterpretation of Madame Bovary and King Lear*. Durham, NC and London, Duke University Press, 1998.

—— (1992b). Rete, campo e contenimento 'mentale'. *Biologica*, **6**, pp. 95–112.

—— (1994b). Introduction. In T. Ogden, *Projective Identification and Psychotherapeutic Technique*. Northvale, NJ and London, Jason Aronson, 1991.

—— (1995). La senatrice bambina e altre confusioni. In AA.VV. *Psicoanalisi e identità di genere*. Bari, Laterza.

—— (1999). Etica della psicoanalisi e psicoanalisi della moralità. In *Il secolo della psicoanalisi*, ed. by G. Jervis, Turin, Bollati Boringhieri.

—— (2002). *Freud messo a fuoco. Passando dai padri alle madri*. Turin, Bollati Boringhieri.

Spitz, R.A. (1965). *The First Year of Life: A Psychoanalytic Study of Normal and Deviant Development of Object Relations*. New York, International Universities Press.

Spitzer, L. (1928). Il ritmo della frase proustiana. In *Marcel Proust e altri saggi di letteratura francese moderna*. Turin, Einaudi, 1959.

Stern, D.N. (1985). *The Interpersonal World of the Infant: A View from Psychoanalysis and Developmental Psychology*. New York, Basic Books.

Sternberg, R.J. (1985). *Beyond IQ: A Triarchic Theory of Human Intelligence*. Cambridge, Cambridge University Press.

Stone, L. (1954). The widening scope of indications for psychoanalysis. *Journal of American Psychoanalytic Association*, **2**, pp. 567–594.

Szurek, S.A. (1942). Notes on the genesis of psychopathic personality trends. *Psychiatry*, **5**, pp. 1–6.

Tabak de Bianchedi, E. (1992). *Transcending the Caesura between East and West through Bion's Psychoanalytic Ideas*. Conference held at Japanese Psychoanalytic Association, Tokyo, February.

Unamuno, M. de (1913). *Del sentimiento tragico de la vida en los hombres y en los pueblos*. Madrid, Alianza Editorial, 1991. (*The Tragic Sense of Life in Men and in Peoples*, New York, Dover Publications, 1954; orig. translation Macmillan & Co., 1921.)

Vegetti, M. (1985). Anima e corpo. In *Il Sapere degli Antichi*, ed. M. Vegetti. Turin, Boringhieri.

—— (1989). *L'etica degli antichi*. Bari, Laterza.

Vernant, J.-P. (1965). *Mythe et pensée chez les Grecs. Etudes de psychologie historique*. Paris, Maspero.

Villey, M. (1977). Equisse historique sur le mot "responsable". In *Archives de philosophie du droit*, **22**, pp. 45ff.

Wagensberg J. (1985). *Ideas sobre la complejidad del mundo*. Barcelona, Tusquets.

Wangh, M. (1962). The "evocation of proxy": a psychological maneuver, its use as a defence, its purposes and genesis. *Psychoanalytic Study of the Child*, **17**, pp. 451–472.

Watzlawick, P., Beavin, J.H. and Jackson, D.D. (1967). *Pragmatics of Human Communication*. New York, Norton & Co.

Webb, S.G. and Thorne, A.G. (1985). A congenital meningocoele in prehistoric Australia. *American Journal of Physical Anthropology*, **64** (4), pp. 525–533.

Whitehead, A.N. (1920). *The Concept of Nature*. Cambridge, Cambridge University Press, 1971.

Wieger, L. (1965). *Chinese Characters*. New York, Dover Publications.

Winnicott, D.W. (1953). Transitional objects and transitional phenomena. In *Collected Papers: Through Paediatrics to Psycho-Analysis*. London, Tavistock, 1958.

—— (1956). Psychoanalysis and the sense of guilt. In *Psychoanalysis and Contemporary Thought*, in J.D. Sutherland (ed.). London, Hogarth, 1958.

—— (1960). *The Theory of the Parent–Infant Relationship*. In Winnicott (1965).

—— (1962a). The development of the capacity for concern. In *The Maturational Processes and the Facilitating Environment*, D.W. Winnicott, London, Hogarth Press, 1965, chapter 6.

—— (1962b). A personal view of the Kleinian approach. In *The Maturational Processes and the Facilitating Environment*, D.W. Winnicott, London, Hogarth Press, 1965, chapter 16.

—— (1962c). Morals and education. Published in 1963. In *The Maturational Processes and the Facilitating Environment*, D.W. Winnicott, London, Hogarth Press, 1965, chapter 8.

—— (1963). The mentally ill in your caseload. In *The Maturational Processes and the Facilitating Environment*, D.W. Winnicott, London, Hogarth Press, 1965, chapter 20.

—— (1965). *The Maturational Processes and the Facilitating Environment*. London, Hogarth Press.

—— (1969). The use of an object. In *International Journal of Psycho-Analysis*, **50**, pp. 711–716.

Winnicott, D.W. (1987). *The Spontaneous Gesture. Selected Letters of D.W. Winnicott*, ed. F.R. Rodman. Cambridge, MA, Harvard University Press.

Wittgenstein, L. (1953). *Philosophical Investigations*. Oxford, Blackwell.

Zahn-Waxler *et al.* (1982). Immediate antecedents of caretakers' methods of discipline. In *Child Psychiatry and Human Development*, **12** (3), pp. 179–192.

—— (1992). The development of altruism: Alternative research strategies. In *The Development of Prosocial Behavior*, N. Eisenberg-Berg (ed.). New York, Academic Press.

Zetzel, E. (1953). The depressive position. In *The Capacity for Emotional Growth*. New York, International Universities Press, 1970.

—— (1958). Therapeutic alliance in the analysis of hysteria. In *The Capacity for Emotional Growth*. New York, International Universities Press, 1970, pp. 182–196.

Name index

Subject index

ANIMALS ON MY RAINBOW

by

Gladys O'Rorke

RoseDog Books

PITTSBURGH, PENNSYLVANIA 15222

s,
y
e
k
n

RoseDog Books
701 Smithfield Street
Pittsburgh, PA 15222
Visit our website at *www.rosedogbookstore.com*

ISBN: 978-1-4349-8716-7
eISBN: 978-1-4349-7711-3